CONTENTS

Cover Picture: The Fearrington House, Pittsboro, North Carolina (see page 92).

FOREWORD BY THE EDITOR

This year "Johansens Recommended Hotels and Inns – North America – Bermuda – Caribbean" is larger than before and the diversity of properties we recommend has also grown. Our readers have the opportunity to discover stylish hotels throughout the New World and also to experience the famous American version of bed and breakfast. Many North American inns offer this traditional form of hospitality and the luxurious ambience they enjoy can match those of our English country house hotels.

All our selections are highly recommended and most of them are located in regions where there are lots of things to see and places of interest to visit. North America, which includes of course Canada as well as the United States, and also islands such as Bermuda in the Atlantic, Hawaii in the Pacific and the West Indies in the Caribbean, is a colourful area full of sights and wonders.

Many of the residences we recommend reflect the unique character of their surroundings, providing guests with a whole new collection of original experiences. In this year's guide you will find a wide choice to satisfy the tastes and interests of all Johansens travellers, whether you are in the pursuit of relaxation and pleasure, looking for a stopover, a business meeting venue or all of these.

Summer by the water, winter at the ski-resorts, autumn in the forest, spring in the open spaces or at every season of the year the famous cities...it's all there. Every state is different in its landscape and its culture – our recommendations equally so.

We hope you enjoy planning and going on your travels as much as we have enjoyed finding these destinations for you.

Have a great time!

Rodney Exton, Editor

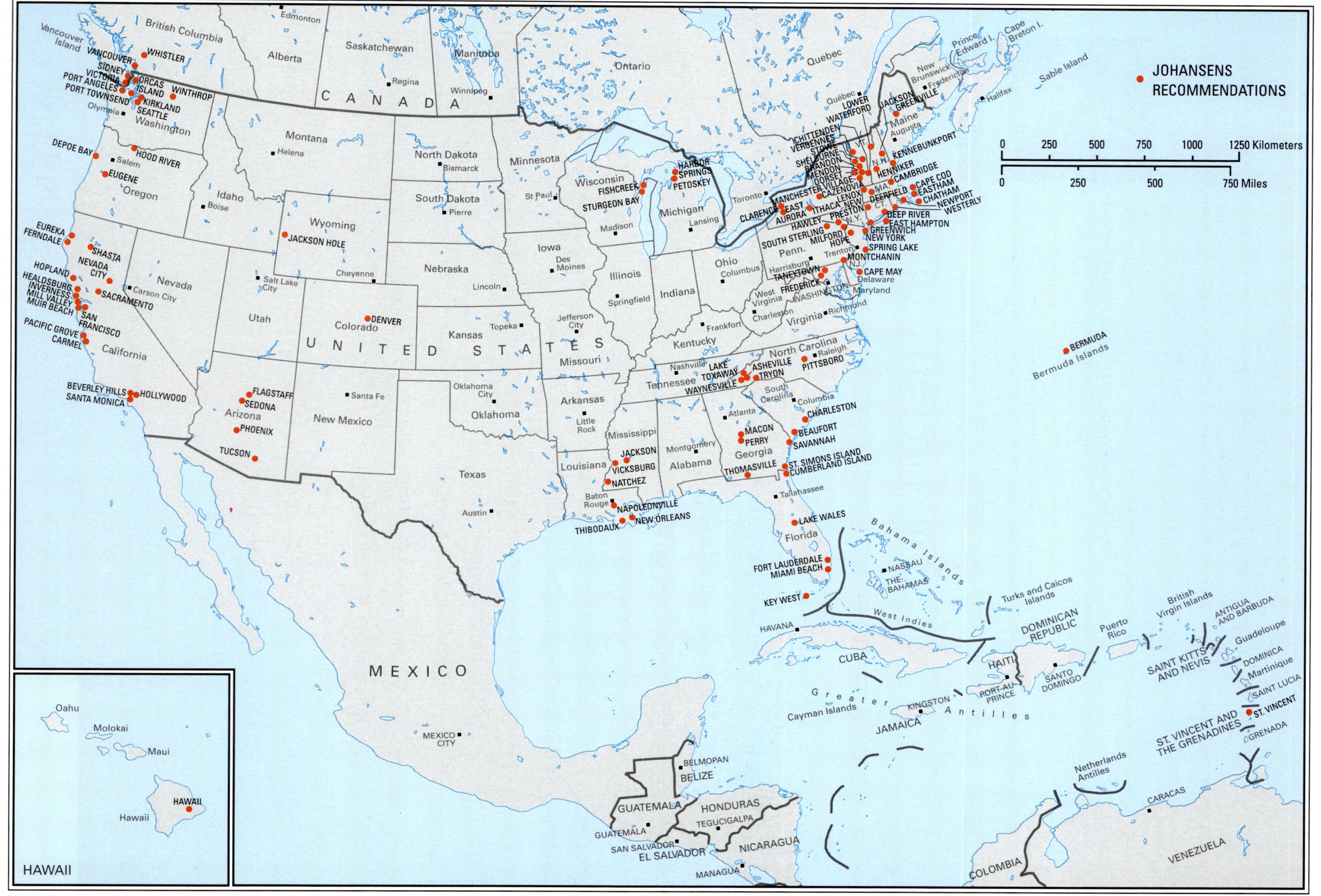

JOHANSENS RECOMMENDATIONS
0 250 500 750 1000 1250 Kilometers
0 250 500 750 Miles
C A N A D A
U N I T E D S T A T E S
M E X I C O
HAWAII
Oahu
Molokai
Maui
Hawaii
HAWAII
Vancouver Island
British Columbia
Alberta
Edmonton
Saskatchewan
Regina
Manitoba
Winnipeg
Ontario
Quebec
Québec
Toronto
New Brunswick
Fredericton
Prince Edward I.
Cape Breton I.
Halifax
Sable Island
VANCOUVER
WHISTLER
SIDNEY
VICTORIA
PORT ANGELES
PORT TOWNSEND
ORCAS ISLAND
KIRKLAND
SEATTLE
WINTHROP
Olympia
Washington
DEPOE BAY
Salem
HOOD RIVER
EUGENE
Oregon
Idaho
Boise
Montana
Helena
Wyoming
JACKSON HOLE
Cheyenne
EUREKA
FERNDALE
SHASTA
NEVADA CITY
HOPLAND
HEALDSBURG
INVERNESS
MILL VALLEY
MUIR BEACH
SAN FRANCISCO
SACRAMENTO
Carson City
Nevada
PACIFIC GROVE
CARMEL
California
BEVERLEY HILLS
SANTA MONICA
HOLLYWOOD
Utah
Salt Lake City
Arizona
FLAGSTAFF
SEDONA
PHOENIX
TUCSON
Colorado
DENVER
New Mexico
Santa Fe
Texas
Austin
Oklahoma
Oklahoma City
Kansas
Topeka
Nebraska
Lincoln
South Dakota
Pierre
North Dakota
Bismarck
Minnesota
St Paul
Iowa
Des Moines
Missouri
Jefferson City
Arkansas
Little Rock
Louisiana
Baton Rouge
THIBODAUX
NAPOLEONVILLE
NEW ORLEANS
NATCHEZ
VICKSBURG
JACKSON
Mississippi
Wisconsin
Madison
FISHCREEK
STURGEON BAY
Illinois
Springfield
Michigan
Lansing
HARBOR SPRINGS
PETOSKEY
Indiana
Ohio
Columbus
Kentucky
Frankfort
Tennessee
Nashville
LAKE TOXAWAY
WAYNESVILLE
ASHEVILLE
TRYON
Alabama
Montgomery
Georgia
Atlanta
MACON
PERRY
THOMASVILLE
Tallahassee
Florida
LAKE WALES
FORT LAUDERDALE
MIAMI BEACH
KEY WEST
ST. SIMONS ISLAND
CUMBERLAND ISLAND
SAVANNAH
BEAUFORT
CHARLESTON
South Carolina
Columbia
North Carolina
Raleigh
PITTSBORO
Virginia
Richmond
West Virginia
Charleston
Maryland
Delaware
CAPE MAY
WASHINGTON
FREDERICK
TANEYTOWN
Harrisburg
Penn.
Trenton
N.J.
MONTCHANIN
SPRING LAKE
NEW YORK
HOPE
MILFORD
SOUTH STERLING
HAWLEY
CLARENCE
EAST AURORA
ITHACA
PRESTON
N.Y.
CT.
GREENWICH
EAST HAMPTON
DEEP RIVER
WESTERLY
NEWPORT
CHATHAM
EASTHAM
CAPE COD
CAMBRIDGE
MA.
HENNIKER
N.H.
KENNEBUNKPORT
DEERFIELD
LENOX
CAZENOVIA
MANCHESTER VILLAGE
DORSET
MENDON
BRANDON
SHELBURNE
STOWE
VERGENNES
CHITTENDEN
VT.
LOWER WATERFORD
JACKSON
GREENVILLE
Maine
Augusta
BERMUDA
Bermuda Islands
MEXICO CITY
BELMOPAN
BELIZE
GUATEMALA
HONDURAS
TEGUCIGALPA
SAN SALVADOR
EL SALVADOR
NICARAGUA
MANAGUA
HAVANA
CUBA
Cayman Islands
JAMAICA
KINGSTON
Greater Antilles
West Indies
NASSAU
THE BAHAMAS
Bahama Islands
Turks and Caicos Islands
HAITI
PORT-AU-PRINCE
DOMINICAN REPUBLIC
SANTO DOMINGO
Puerto Rico
British Virgin Islands
ANTIGUA AND BARBUDA
SAINT KITTS AND NEVIS
Guadeloupe
DOMINICA
Martinique
SAINT LUCIA
ST. VINCENT
ST. VINCENT AND THE GRENADINES
GRENADA
Netherlands Antilles
CARACAS
VENEZUELA
COLOMBIA

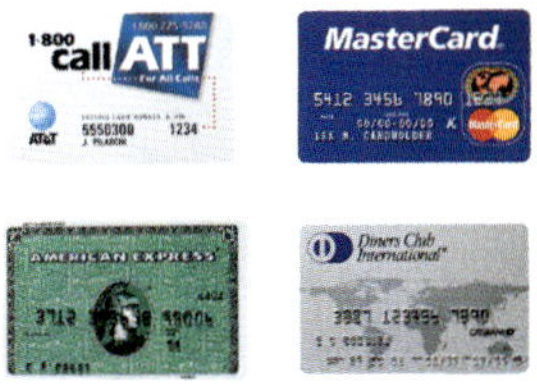

Published by
Johansens Limited, Therese House, Glasshouse Yard, London EC1A 4JN
Tel: +44 171 566 9700 Fax: +44 171 251 6112
Find Johansens on the Internet at: http://www.johansens.com

Publisher: Jane Valentine
Editor: Rodney Exton
Copy Editor: Yasmin Razak
North American Manager: Sarah Berry
Inspectors: Christine Calloway-Holt, Suzanne Flanders, Jonathan Kean, Margeret Sorensen, Paul Stanislas
Production Manager: Daniel Barnett
Production Controller: Kevin Bradbrook
Senior Designer: Michael Tompsett
Designer: Sue Dixon
Map Illustrations: Linda Clark
Copywriters: Norman Flack, Yasmin Razak, Jill Wyatt
Sales and Marketing Manager: Laurent Martinez
Marketing Executive: Emma Woods
Sales Executive: Babita Sareen
Special Projects Editor: Fiona Patrick
P.A. to Managing Director: Angela Willcox
Managing Director: Andrew Warren

Johansens is a member company of Harmsworth Publishing Ltd, a subsidiary of the Daily Mail & General Trust plc

ISBN 1 86017 5864

Printed in England by St Ives plc
Colour origination by Icon Reproduction

Distributed in the UK and Europe by Johnsons International Media Services Ltd, London (direct sales) & Biblios PDS Ltd, West Sussex (bookstores). In North America by general sales agent: ETL Group, New York, NY (direct sales) and Hunter Publishing, New Jersey (bookstores). In Australia and New Zealand by Bookwise International, Findon, South Australia

HOW TO USE THIS GUIDE

The Contents section on page 1 illustrates how this guide is set out.

A small scale map on page 2 indicates where Johansens Recommended Hotels and Inns are situated in North America, Bermuda and The Caribbean. Their actual locations are shown more precisely on the larger scale maps of different regions as they appear in the guide.

If you want to find a hotel whose name you already know, look for it in the Indexes on page 157.

If you want to find a Hotel or Inn in a particular area, first turn to the map on page 2 then to the Contents section on page 1 and select the region in which you wish to stay: Bermuda, Canada, The Caribbean or a named individual state of the U.S.A.. Each Hotel or Inn appears on a regional map with a number that correlates to the page on which its description is published. Because of the geographical grouping of the states they are not arranged in alphabetical order.

Mini Listings pages 158–163. The names, locations and telephone numbers of all Johansens Recommendations in the British Isles and Continental Europe are listed. The Johansens guides in which these recommendations appear are described fully on the outside back cover. Copies of these guides are obtainable direct from Johansens by calling +44 990 269397 or by using the order coupons on page 165–168.

Prices: throughout the guide the majority of prices listed refer to 'room' rate, not 'per person rate'. These prices are correct at the time of going to press, but should always be checked with the establishment when you reserve your accommodation. You may, in addition, wish to note that prices are subject to state tax.

We occasionally receive letters from guests who have been charged for accommodation booked in advance but later cancelled. Readers should be aware that by making a reservation with a hotel, either by telephone or in writing, they are entering into a legal contract. A hotelier under certain circumstances is entitled to make a charge for accommodation when guests fail to arrive, even if notice of the cancellation is given.

WELL... DE GUSTIBUS NON EST DISPUTANDUM
HILDON
AN ENGLISH
NATURAL MINERAL WATER
OF EXCEPTIONAL TASTE
GENTLY CARBONATED
Composition in accordance with the results of the officially recognized analysis 26 March 1992.
Hildon Ltd., Broughton, Hampshire SO20 8DG, ☏ 01794-301 747
750ml e
"FOR BEST BEFORE DATE SEE CAP"
Bottled at source, Broughton, Hampshire
Bottled at source, Broughton, Hampshire
"FOR BEST BEFORE DATE SEE CAP"
HILDON LTD.
Hildon House, Broughton, Hampshire SO20 8DG
☏ 01794-301 747, Fax 01794-301 718

KEY TO SYMBOLS

14 rms	Total number of rooms	Nombre de chambres	Anzahl der Zimmer
MasterCard	MasterCard accepted	MasterCard accepté	MasterCard akzeptiert
VISA	Visa accepted	Visa accepté	Visa akzeptiert
AMERICAN EXPRESS	American Express accepted	American Express accepté	American Express akzeptiert
	Diners Club accepted	Diners Club accepté	Diners Club akzeptiert
other	Other Credit Cards accepted	Autres cartes de crédit acceptées	Anderen Kredit Karten akzeptiert
	Quiet location	Lieu tranquille	Ruhige Lage
	Access for wheelchairs to at least one bedroom and public rooms	Accès handicapé	Zugang für Behinderte

(The 'Access for wheelchairs' symbol ( ) does not necessarily indicate that the property fulfils National Accessible Scheme grading)

	Chef-patron	Chef-patron	Chef-patron
M 20	Meeting/conference facilities with maximum number of delegates	Salle de conférences – capacité maximale	Konferenzraum-Höchstkapazität
8	Children welcome, with minimum age where applicable	Enfants bienvenus	Kinder willkommen
	Dogs accommodated in rooms or kennels	Chiens autorisés	Hunde erlaubt
	At least one room has a four-poster bed	Lit à baldaquin dans au moins une chambre	Himmelbett
	At least one room has a tester/canopy bed	Lit à baldaquin dans au moins une chambre	Himmelbett ohne Decke
	At least one room has a fireplace	Chemineé dans au moins une chambre	Mindestens ein Zimmer mit Kamin
	Cable/satellite TV in all bedrooms	TV câblée/satellite dans les chambres	Satellit-und Kabelfernsehen in allen Zimmern
	Fax available in rooms	Fax dans votre chambre	Fax in Schlafzimmern
	No-smoking rooms (at least one no-smoking bedroom)	Chambres non-fumeur	Zimmer für Nichtraucher
	Elevator available for guests' use	Ascenseur	Fahrstuhl
	Air Conditioning	Climatisation	Klimatisiert
	Indoor swimming pool	Piscine couverte	Hallenbad
	Outdoor swimming pool	Piscine en plein air	Freibad
	Tennis court at hotel	Tennis à l'hôtel	Hoteleigener Tennisplatz
	Croquet lawn at hotel	Croquet à l'hôtel	Krocketrasen
	Fishing can be arranged	Pêche	Angeln
	Golf course on site or nearby, which has an arrangement with hotel allowing guests to play	Golf sur site ou à proximité	Golfplatz
	Shooting can be arranged	Chasse / Tir	Jagd
	Riding can be arranged	Équitation	Reitpferd
	Skiing	Ski	Schilaufen
H	Hotel has a helipad	Helipad	Hubschrauberlandplatz
	Licensed for wedding ceremonies	Cérémonies de mariages	Konzession für Eheschliessungen

WELL . . . DE GUSTIBUS
NON EST DISPUTANDUM

HILDON

AN ENGLISH
NATURAL MINERAL WATER
OF EXCEPTIONAL TASTE

DELIGHTFULLY STILL

Composition in accordance with the results of the officially
recognized analysis 26 March 1992.
Hildon Ltd., Broughton, Hampshire SO20 8DG. ☎ 01794-301 747

750ml ℮

"FOR BEST BEFORE DATE SEE CAP"
Bottled at source, Broughton, Hampshire

Bottled at source, Broughton, Hampshire
"FOR BEST BEFORE DATE SEE CAP"

Arizona and California

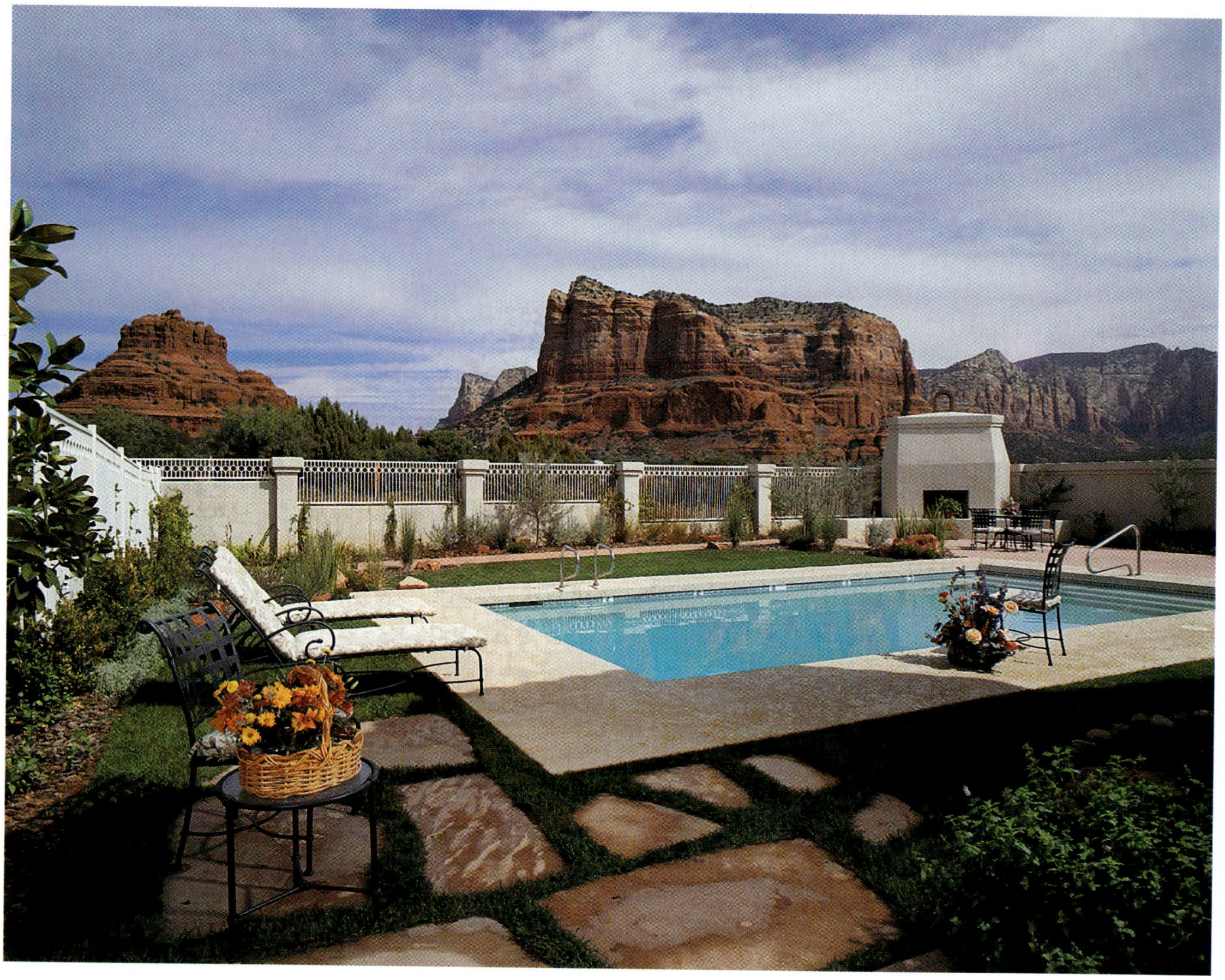

Canyon Villa Inn

125 CANYON CIRCLE DRIVE, SEDONA, ARIZONA 86351
TEL: 1 520 284 1226 FAX: 1 520 284 2114 US TOLL FREE: 1 800 453 1166

In 1992 Chuck and Marion Yadon opened this inspirational Spanish mission style inn at Sedona, gateway to the magnificent Oak Creek Canyon. Set at the foot of Coconino National Forest, against the green trees, red rocks and azure blue skies, this modern hotel maximises on the spectacular countryside. Most of the guest rooms (known as 'view rooms') have balconies or patios. Each has a different theme, with appropriate furnishings including lovely family antiques. All have Jacuzzis, a welcome luxury after clambering over rocks. Marion is responsible for the sumptuous breakfast that is served which includes home-made cinnamon rolls, enjoyed looking across to the mighty Bell Rock and Courthouse Butte. Afternoon hors d'oeuvres are an opportunity to mingle with the other guests. The Villa does not serve alcohol but there is an off-licence round the corner! The Yadons will arrange dinner reservations at recommended restaurants, Jeep tours, hot-air balloons and the Verde River Canyon Train Excursions to explore the area. Grand Canyon is a short two-hour scenic drive. Two golf courses are nearby and Sedona has intriguing galleries and shops. The Villa has a pool, sun terrace and peaceful reading garden. **Directions:** Interstate 17 north for 120 miles, exit 298, left onto Highway 179 for 8 miles then left onto Bell Rock Boulevard to Canyon Circle Drive, turning right. Price guide: Rooms $145–$225.

Inn At 410

410 NORTH LEROUX STREET, FLAGSTAFF, ARIZONA 86001
TEL: 1 520 774 0088 FAX: 1 520 774 6354

Set in the mountain town of Flagstaff, The Inn at 410 offers fine accommodation and a superb location for those travelling to the Grand Canyon. The friendly owners offer advice to their guests on how to avoid crowds and enjoy the best views of this natural wonder. Situated at 7000ft, the Inn retains a delicately cool air throughout the seasons and is popular with sports enthusiasts wishing to tackle the alpine hiking and biking trails. The bedrooms are exquisite, colourful and highly detailed with thoughtful extras and traditional comforts. The true flavour of the West may be experienced in The Southwest with its Santa Fe décor, and the Dakota Suite, reminiscent of the Old West. The intimate setting of a perennial garden, which surrounds the patio and gazebo, is the perfect place to savour a quiet drink in the afternoon. The Inn is two blocks from historic downtown Flagstaff, an easy walk to shops and restaurants. Arizona's dramatic landscape may be admired during the one hour drive through the scenic Oak Creek Canyon to the red rocks of Sedona. Other attractions include the Hopi and Navajo villages and the ancient Indian ruins at Wupatki and Walnut Canon. **Directions:** From I-40, exit 195B north onto Milton. From I-17 continue north onto Milton. Follow Milton under the railroad overpass and curve to the right. Turn left at 1st stoplight onto Humphreys Street. At Dale turn right. Turn left onto N.Leroux. The Inn is on the right. Price guide: Rooms $125–$175.

Inn On Oak Creek

556 HIGHWAY 179, SEDONA, ARIZONA 86336
TEL: 1 520 282 7896 FAX: 1 520 282 0696

This contemporary Southwest style inn affords a glorious vista of the surrounding red rock landscape. The friendly and welcoming atmosphere is evident upon entering the lobby through the large copper-edged glass door. The choice of furnishings, such as denim and floral sofas, creates a sense of casual elegance. Works of art, some on loan from a nearby gallery, adorn the walls throughout the house. Each of the 11 bedrooms is individually decorated and is enhanced by its own gas fireplace and whirlpool tub. The gourmet breakfasts are designed to satisfy the largest appetite, with dishes such as baked cinnamon-raisin blintzes with blueberry sauce or hazelnut orange juice pancakes. Special hors d'oeuvres are served in the gathering room in the late afternoon, or alfresco on the deck. The private park on the banks of the rippling creek, for guests' exclusive use, is ideal for those seeking a truly secluded area. It is easy to travel to many of the Southwest's fine art galleries or set off to peruse the shops and restaurants in Tlaquepaque. For the more adventurous, hiking, horse-riding, jeep tours or hot-air balloon rides can be arranged. **Directions:** Situated off highway 89A, then follow highway 179. The inn is just on the right. Price Guide: Rooms $150–$235.

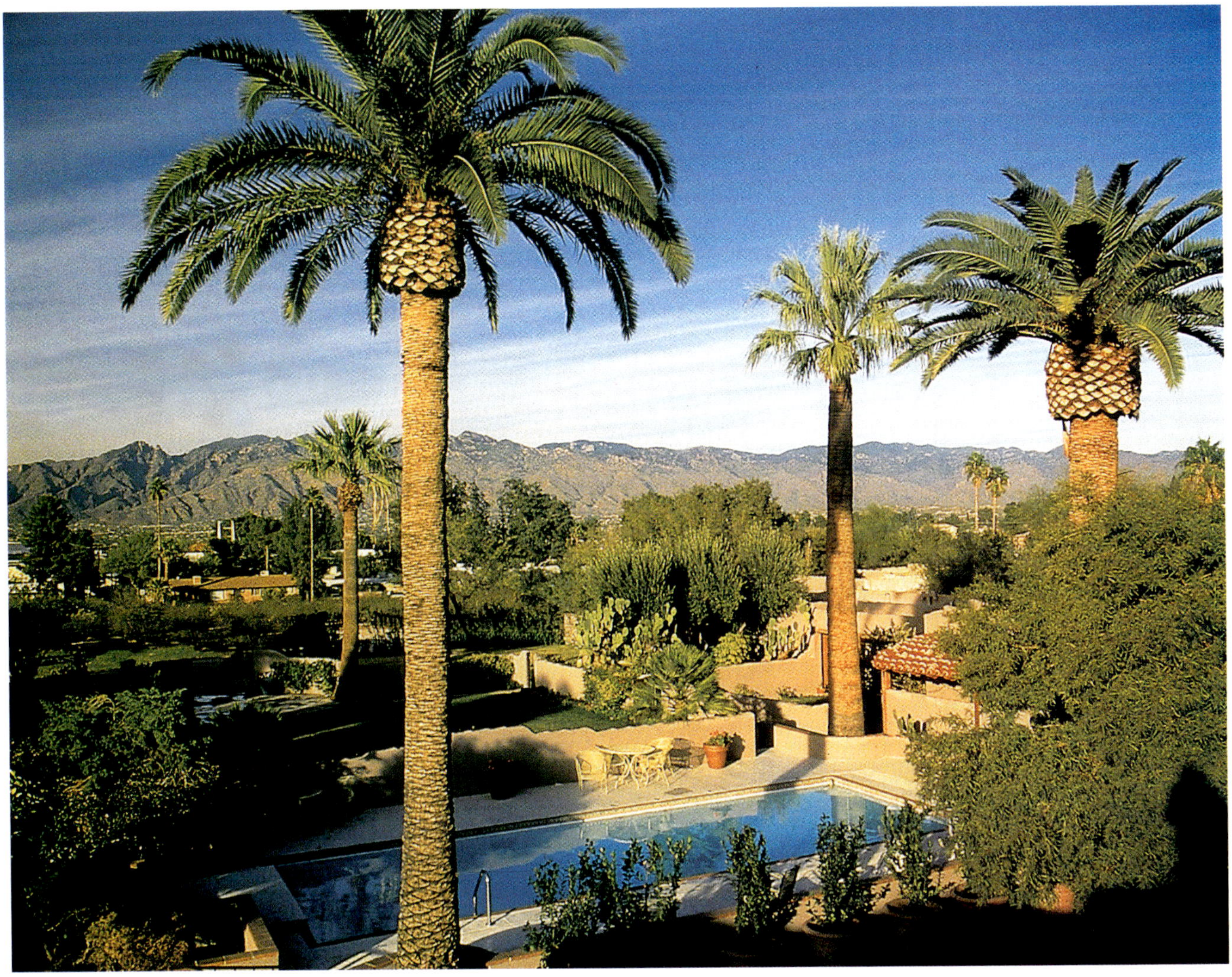

THE LODGE ON THE DESERT

306 NORTH ALVERNON WAY, TUCSON, ARIZONA 85711
TEL: 1 520 325 3366 FAX: 1 520 327 5834

The Lodge on the Desert, an Arizona landmark since its construction in 1936, enjoys a panoramic vista across the magnificent Santa Catalina mountains. Set in the heart of Tucson, the hotel retains its authentic Southwestern atmosphere, extending a warm and hospitable welcome to all its guests. Red tile covered patios and burning fireplaces enhance the interior, which is furnished in traditional hacienda-style. Situated in separate buildings, the 39 bedrooms are decorated with a touch of elegance and offer every modern amenity. The intimate bathrooms contain simple décor and soft towels. Tall palms, native cacti and bright seasonal flowers encompass the lawns, whilst secluded pathways lead the guests to the lodge, casitas and pool. Cielos, the lodge's superb restaurant, is renowned for its versatile atmosphere and imaginative menu. Guests may savour the exquisite dishes in a light and spacious ambience during the morning and afternoon and enjoy the soft lighting and cosy fireplace in the evening. Fitness enthusiasts may use the outdoor swimming pool on site or the challenging golf courses and tennis courts nearby. The Lodge is set in a location suitable for accessing all the major attractions of Tucson and the surrounding area. **Directions:** The Lodge is situated close to the Interstate-10 on Alvernon Way. Price Guide: Rooms $65–$158; suite $175–$225.

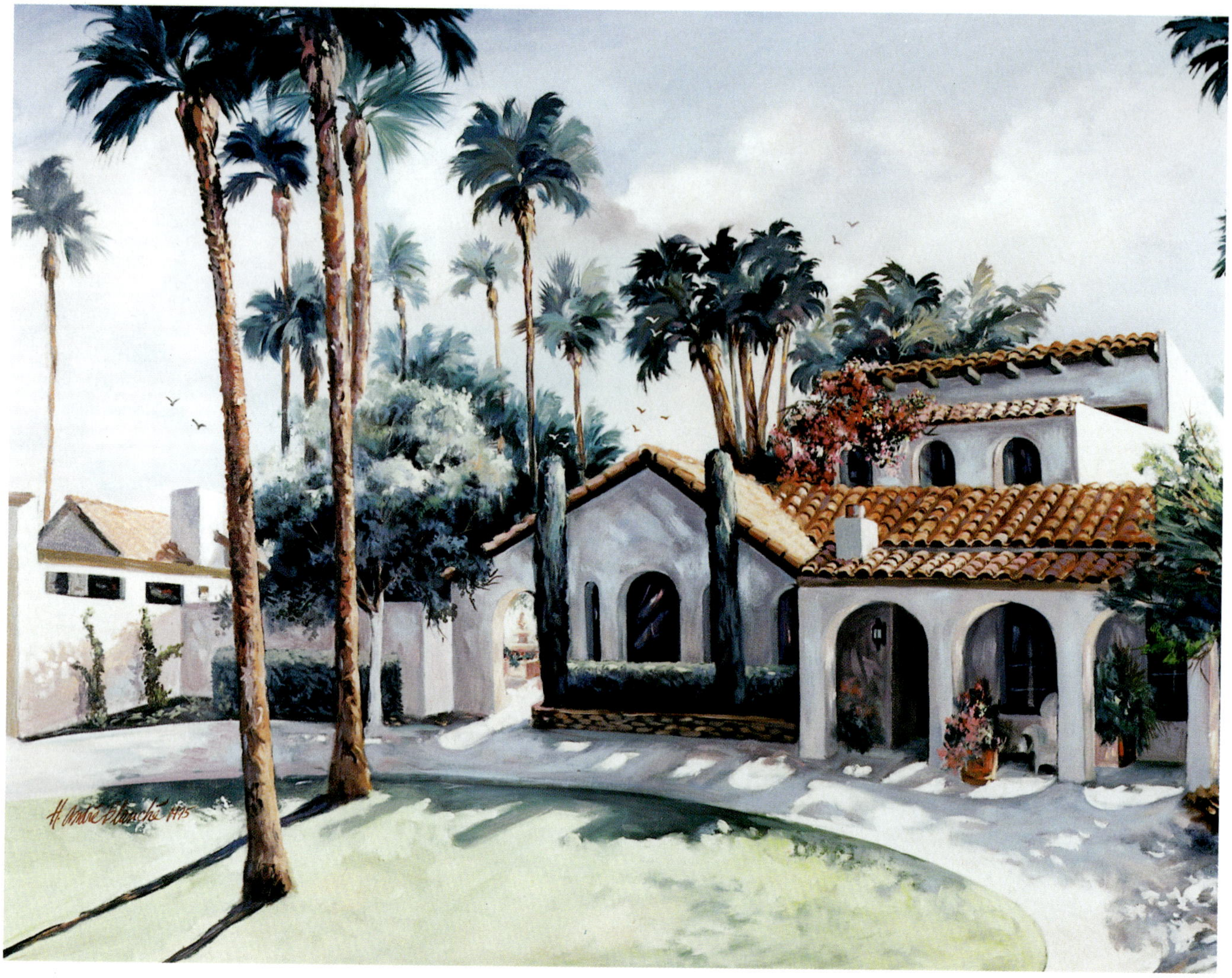

Maricopa Manor

15 WEST PASADENA AVENUE, PHOENIX, ARIZONA 85013-2001
TEL: 1 602 274 6302 FAX: 1 602 266 3904 US TOLL FREE: 800 292 6403

Surrounded by palm trees and flowers, this Spanish-style Manor house, set in the heart of North Central Phoenix, is both intimate and elegant. Built in 1928, Maricopa Manor combines the refined atmosphere of a fine residence with the comforts and conveniences of home. The interior is beautifully furnished with cosy fireplaces and stylish paintings. The 6 suites in the Manor house and adjacent buildings are well-equipped offering every modern amenity. All are individually decorated, creating a sense of warmth and character. The rates include an extensive breakfast menu, featuring home-made breads and fresh fruit, which is served to guests in the comfort of their own suite. The Manor is only 5 miles from the busy centre of downtown Phoenix, which offers a plethora of restaurants and bistros. A variety of outdoor pursuits is available nearby such as hot-air ballooning, golf, horse-riding and tennis. For the less adventurous, museums, theatres, art galleries and boutiques are within minutes of the manor. **Directions:** From Flagstaff, follow I-17 (south to Camelback Road). Turn left on Camelback to Third Avenue. Turn left on Third. Again one block turn right on to Pasedena Avenue and on to 15 West. Price Guide: Rooms $99(summer)–$229(winter).

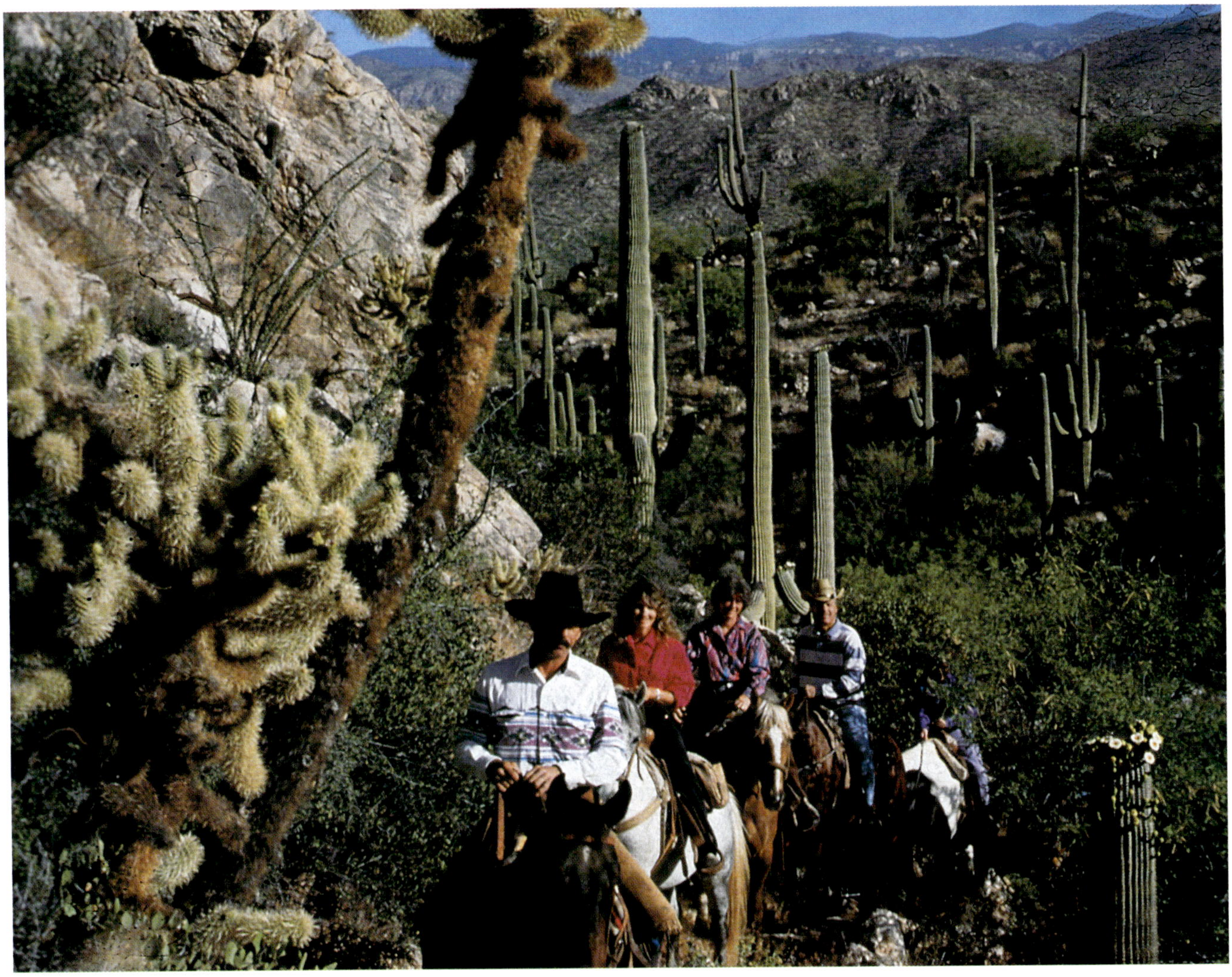

Tanque Verde Ranch

14301 EAST SPEEDWAY, TUCSON, ARIZONA 85748
TEL: 1 520 296 6275 FAX: 1 520 721 9426

This is a unique and striking hotel in the Sonoran Desert. Its name means "Green Tank", for it is where the cavalry stopped to water their horses when fighting the Apache raiders. Tanque Verde has 640 acres bordered by the Coronado National Forest and the Saguaro National Park – the views are spectacular. The dude ranch's adobe buildings are traditional, with beamed ceilings and long verandahs. Accommodation is in cool casitas, with rustic and modern furniture; the bathrooms have attractive Mexican tiles. The various living rooms are spacious, with big stone fireplaces, colourful Indian rugs, inviting sofas and fascinating memorabilia from the region. Stetsons are almost mandatory, indoors or out! Authentic cowboy breakfasts of chilli eggs and blueberry pancakes are prepared out on the range, then its time to 'Ride High' among the tall cacti. At dusk, drinks on the verandahs watching the sunset over the mountains are followed by superb dinners and good wine or a fantastic barbecue, then Country Western dancing. The ranch has a pool, tennis courts, sun terraces, children's area and a boutique with cowboy gear. Golf is nearby. **Directions:** Interstate 10, Houghton Road exit north, turn east on Speedway Boulevard. Ranch driveway at dead end. Price guide: Rooms $260–$350

White Stallion Ranch

9251 WEST TWIN PEAKS ROAD, TUCSON, ARIZONA 85743
TEL: 1 520 297 0252 FAX: 1 520 744 2786

A friendly and welcoming atmosphere envelopes this old Southwestern ranch, surrounded by a 5 mile expanse of desert. The White Stallion Ranch combines the informal ambience of a working cattle ranch with the comforts and conveniences of a holiday resort. There are 35 bedrooms clustered around the ranch in separate buildings. All the rooms are air-conditioned with private bath whilst de luxe suites offer fireplaces, whirlpool tubs and king-size beds. The True family has created a most convivial environment throughout the ranch and this is clearly evident in the popular bar. Here, guests relax in casual attire and enjoy the hors d'oeuvres and drinks at 'Happy Hour'. A full selection of breakfast dishes is served in the attractive dining room. Inviting recipes may be savoured at the buffet at lunch or at dinner, which is also served family style. Outdoor pursuits such as hiking, tennis, basketball, horse-riding and swimming are available on site. Other pastimes include hay rides, playing with the animals at the petting zoo and enjoying the indoor redwood hot tub. Traditional cowboy entertainment is also offered at the ranch and includes moonlight bonfires, hearty barbecues, weekly rodeos and enjoying the native wildlife. Denim and stetsons are very welcome! **Directions:** The hotel is situated on West Twin Peaks road, adjacent to the Saguaro National Park. Price Guide: Rooms $109–$140; suite $130–$170.

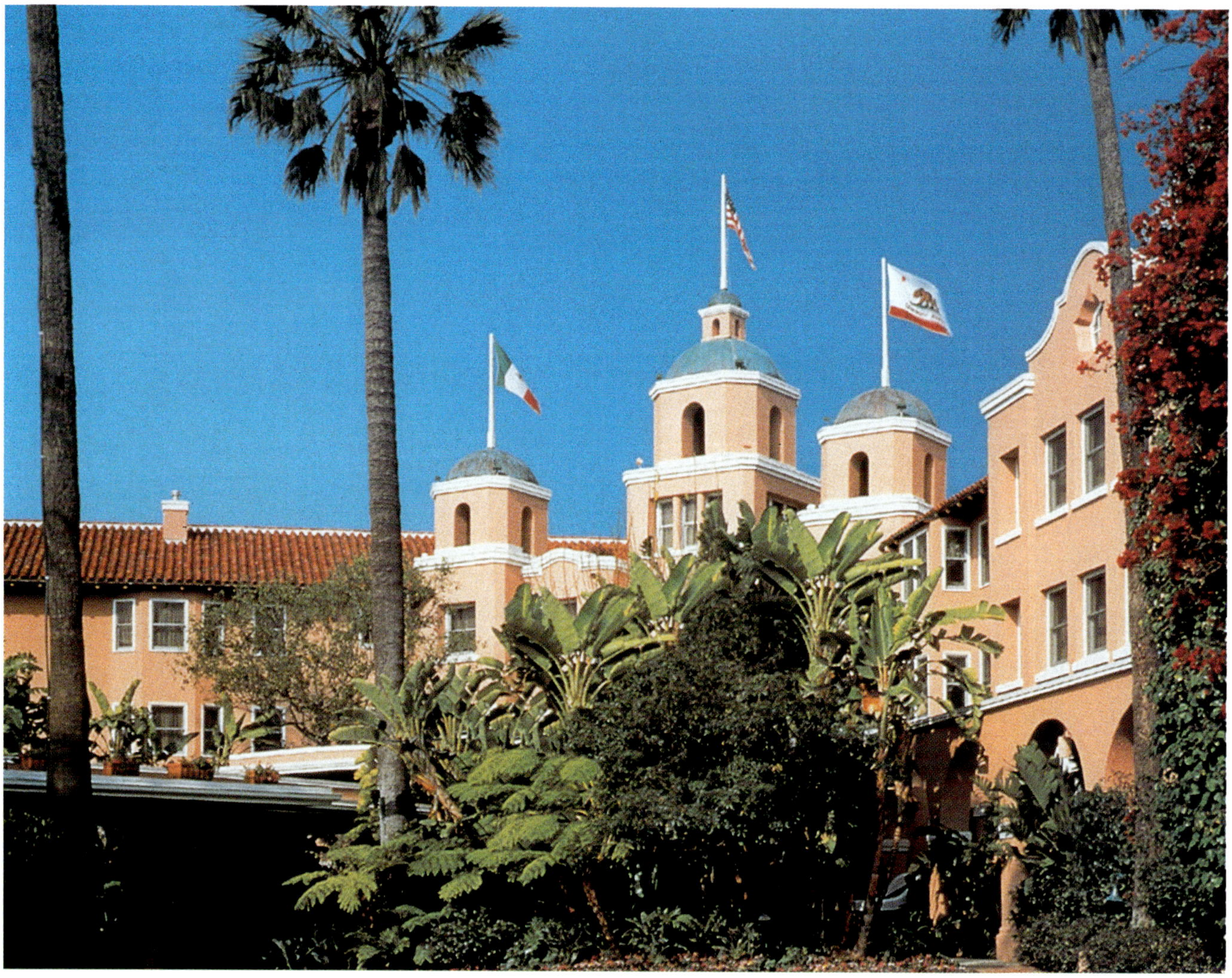

THE BEVERLY HILLS HOTEL & BUNGALOWS

9641 SUNSET BOULEVARD, BEVERLY HILLS, CALIFORNIA 90210

TEL: 1 310 276 2251 **FAX:** 1 310 887 2887 **RESERVATIONS FAX:** 1 310 281 2905 **US TOLL FREE:** 1 800 283 8885

Situated on California's famous Sunset Boulevard, amidst 12 acres of beautiful gardens, The Beverly Hills Hotel offers excellent service and superb accommodation with a touch of glamour. Frequented by Hollywood celebrities, legendary musicians and political figures, the hotel combines art deco furnishings with an elegant style creating a truly luxurious environment. The lobby, with its Venetian glass chandelier and gold leaf ceiling is exquisite and commissioned artwork is visible throughout the property. The accommodation is varied in design and includes 21 unique bungalows. All contain computer modem and facsimile mavhines and a range of up-to-date amenities. The spacious canopied beds are enhanced by the Ralph Lauren linen. Guests enjoy afternoon tea, lights snacks or cocktails in The Sunset Lounge whilst fresh sorbet and other refreshments are available at the poolside Cabaña Café. Fine cuisine is served in the Polo Lounge, popular with the famous and successful. Pastimes include touring the film and television studios, admiring the homes of celebrities and visiting Beverly Hills. Water sports may be practised at the nearby beach whilst those with a passion for shopping will be delighted with the proximity of Rodeo Drive. **Directions:** Take 405 Freeway north to Wilshire Boulevard. Left on Rodeo Drive to Sunset Boulevard. Price guide: Rooms $310–$390; bungalows $360–$385; suite $685–$4,700; bungalow suites $545–$3,595.

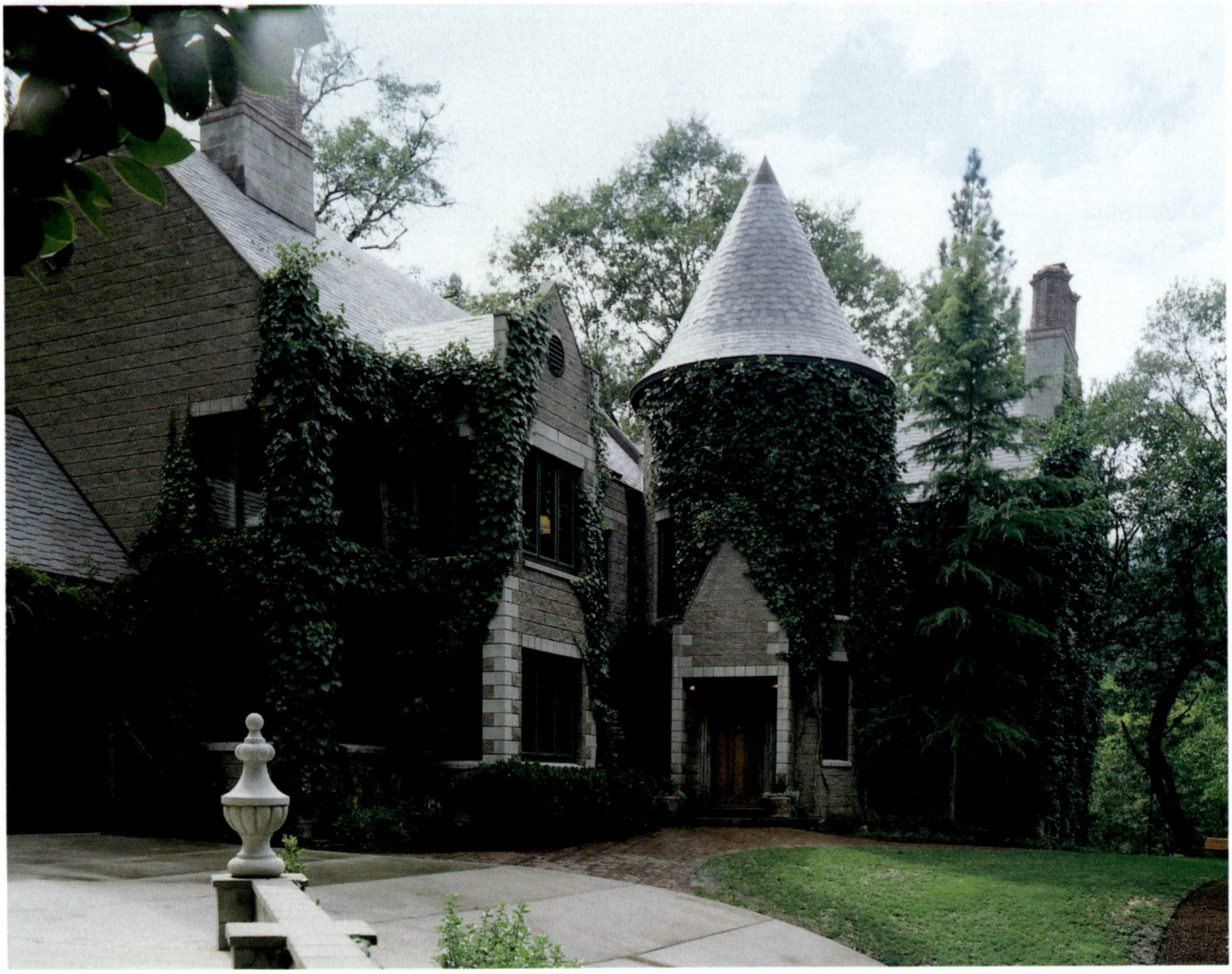

Brigadoon Castle

9036 ZOGG MINE ROAD, PO BOX 324, IGO, CALIFORNIA 96047
TEL: 1 530 396 2785 FAX: 1 530 396 2784 US TOLL FREE: 1 888 343 2836

Located in Shasta County in the northern reaches of California, Brigadoon Castle is at the centre of the region's most beautiful scenery. Its Elizabethan-style manor house is set amid 86 acres of mountain forest and meadow, making it a perfect choice for those seeking a quiet escape from modern day living. There are 5 rooms, each of them unique in its design and offering every imaginable comfort. In the two-level Tyler's Tree Top Room, for example, there is a spacious sitting room on the lower level, with a circular staircase leading up to a bedroom with ivy-covered arrow port windows and murals on the walls. The private bathroom features an Italian slab marble vanity and shower. The Bonny Jean Room provides exquisite accommodation with its Queen-sized, cast-iron bed and marble bath. French doors open on to a balcony with a gothic wrought-iron rail overlooking the gardens and forest. Offering the ultimate experience of seclusion is "The Cottage" guest house, which lies very close to the castle and looks out over mountain creek. A generous breakfast is provided, while weekend rates include a delicious dinner. **Directions:** From Sacramento and San Francisco take I-5 north. Take 299 west to Placer Road and go south to Igo. Left at T-junction into Ronzogg Road and proceed to castle gates. Price guide: Rooms $150–180; cottage suites $210–$285.

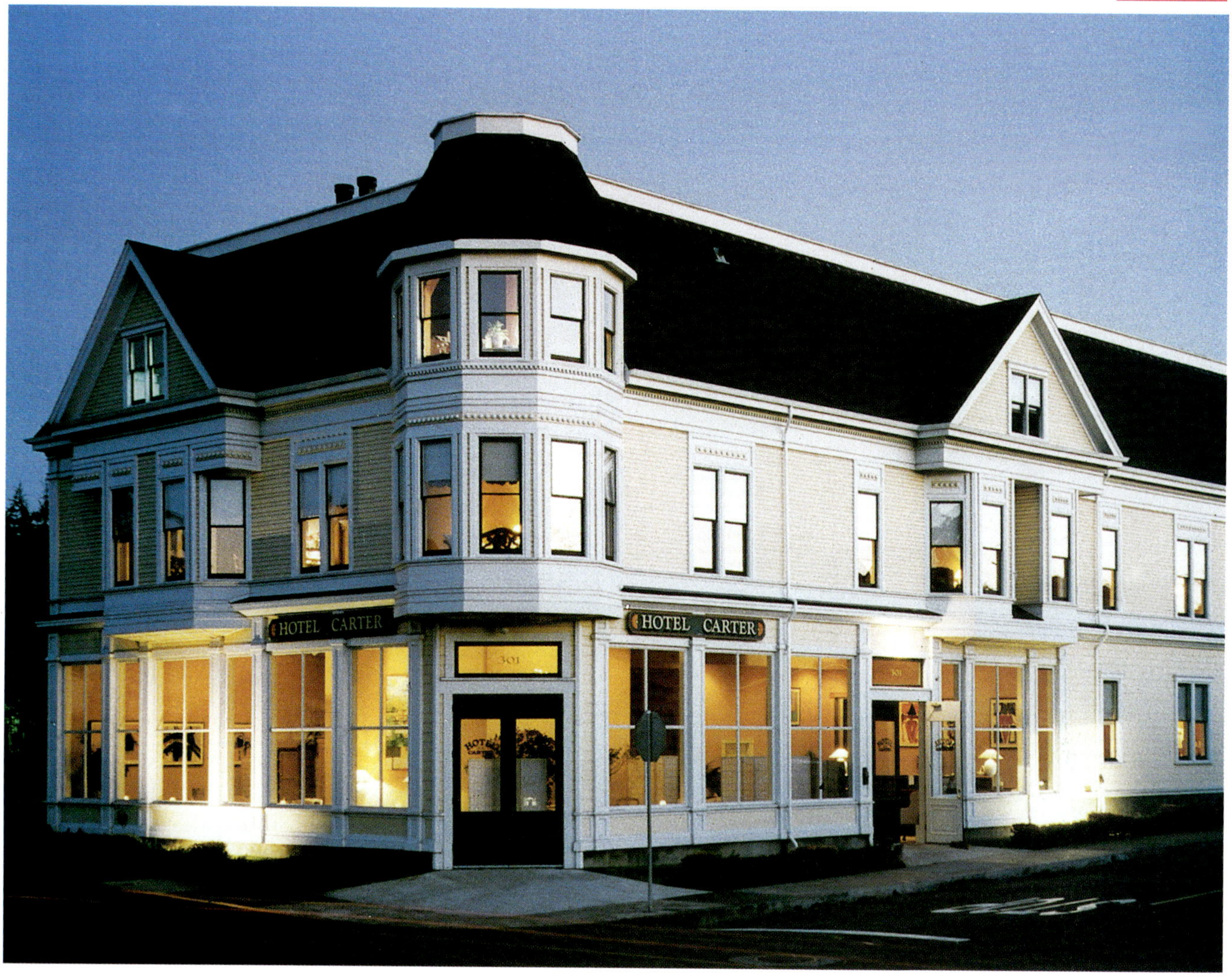

Carter House

301 L STREET, EUREKA, CALIFORNIA 95501
TEL: 1 800 404 1390 FAX: 1 707 444 8067

The architectural charm of the old coastal city of Eureka has earned it the name "The Williamsburg of the West". The Carter House consists of three fine Victorian mansions that embellish the edge of Humboldt Bay at the entrance to historic Eureka's Victorian district: The original Carter House, the Hotel Carter and the Bell Cottage. Each is generously appointed. The attractive interior décor and furnishings are the setting for hospitality of the highest class. Guests are welcomed by an aura of luxury and comfort. Beautiful fabrics, fresh fruit and flowers and a tasteful combination of modern and classical amenities enhance the restful and cheerful atmosphere. Guest rooms are delightfully equipped with every aid to relaxed enjoyment. Extra services are instantly at hand. Breakfasts and dinners are a gastronomic experience – fresh produce and culinary skills bring wide-spread renown to Restaurant 301. The award-winning wine list is selectively comprehensive. Gaps before and after evening meals are filled with hors d'oeuvres, cookies and other nourishments. Things to do and see locally include sailing, rowing, golf, tennis, riding, walking, going to the theatre, the concert, the Avenue of the Giants, the Redwood National Park and the Sequoia Park and Zoo. **Directions:** Off highway 101, a long drive north of San Francisco. Price guide: Rooms $105–$185; suite $195–$500.

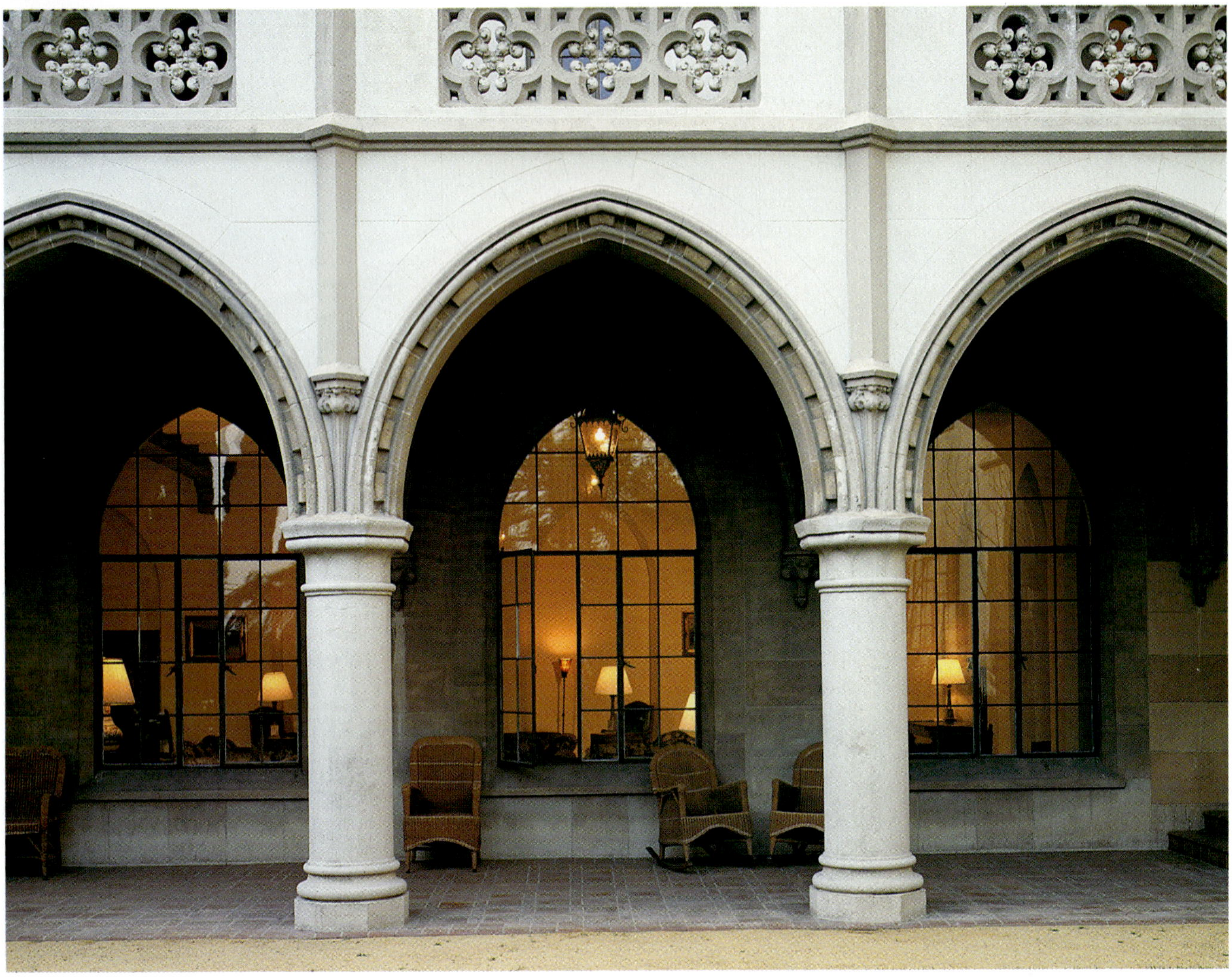

PrimaHotels

CHÂTEAU MARMONT

8221 SUNSET BOULEVARD, HOLLYWOOD, CALIFORNIA 90046-2413
TEL: 1 323 656 1010 FAX: 1 323 655 5311

Inspired by a French château in the Loire Valley, The Château Marmont was built as fashionable apartments in 1929. The building was later sold as a hotel and the imaginative new owner purchased extravagant furnishings from Depression era estate sales to please his discerning guests. Behind its wonderful Gothic portico, Château Marmont very quickly became the discreet hideaway of everyone who was anyone in Hollywood and the hotel enjoyed the loyalty of its devoted guests for many years. In 1990 André Balazs purchased the property and has skillfully blended its attraction as an urban oasis with its essential sense of history. The rooms are classically proportioned and feature a layered look, mixing furnishings of different styles and periods. Within the walled gardens are private cottages and bungalows, most equipped with kitchens and ideal for complete seclusion. Offering hilltop panoramic views Château Marmont is only minutes from Beverly Hills, Century City and the heart of the entertainment industry. Menus feature French and American dishes. Meals may be enjoyed in the dining room, the garden or at the poolside, a comprehensive 24 hour room service menu is also available. Private trainers and massage therapists can be arranged. **Directions:** The Château is situated on Sunset Boulevard. Price guide: Rooms $210; suite $280–$1900

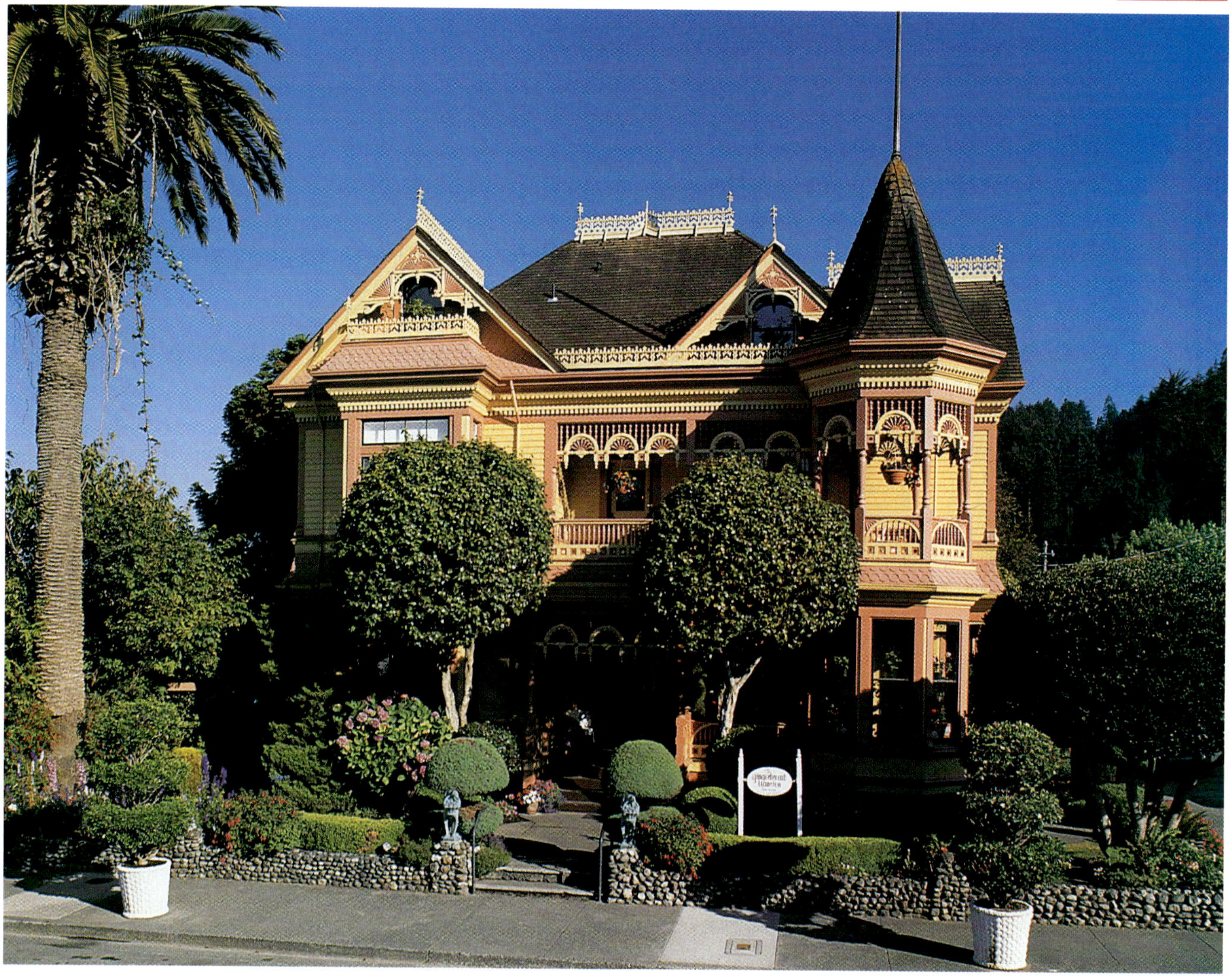

GINGERBREAD MANSION INN

400 BERDING STREET, FERNDALE, CALIFORNIA 95536
TEL: 1 707 786 4000 FAX: 1 707 786 4381 US TOLL FREE: 800 952 4136

Built in 1899, the Gingerbread Mansion Inn retains many of its original features such as exquisite turrets and carvings. A unique combination of Queen Anne and Eastlake styles, the house is elaborately trimmed with ornate gingerbread decorations. The interior has been carefully restored and features plush carpets, rich Victorian wallpaper and cosy fireplaces. The eleven en suite bedrooms are furnished with an individual touch and are enhanced by lace comforters, claw foot bath tubs or tiled fireplaces. The warmth of the hospitality extended at the inn is shown in the small nuances such as the robes and bedside chocolate at turndown. Afternoon tea is served in the four Victorian parlours and comprises freshly baked cakes, biscuits, pastries and other delights. An extensive menu of home-made dishes is served in the elegant Dining Room at breakfast. There are excellent restaurants within easy walking distance. Guests may explore the Pacific coast and the Giant Redwoods; just a ½ hour drive away. Ferndale is a State historical landmark, with well-preserved Victorian homes, old-fashioned boutiques and grand English gardens. **Directions:** The hotel is 5 hours north of San Francisco, take the 101 Freeway. Then 5 miles to centre of town, turn left at bank. Take the Ferndale exit. Price Guide: Rooms $140–$200; suite $230–$350.

Le Parc Suite Hotel

733 NORTH WEST KNOLL DRIVE, WEST HOLLYWOOD, CALIFORNIA 90069
TEL: 1 310 855 8888 FAX: 1 310 659 8508

Le Parc Suite Hotel enjoys a tranquil location, despite being within a short drive of the fashionable shopping streets and nightclubs of the Beverly Hills area and downtown Hollywood. The beach lies just 30 minutes' away. All of the 152 suites are tastefully decorated with fine art prints and offer an impressive range of facilities including a kitchenette with fridge and microwave, minibar, multi-line data phones and a television with a choice of movies and video games. A twice-daily maid service ensures the highest standards are maintained. On the third floor there is a charming breakfast area where guests can choose from an extensive menu of continental and typical American fayre, while in the café, there is a choice of meat or fish entrées and delicious desserts. A marvellous range of recreation and fitness facilities includes roof-top heated pool and cabanas, whirlpool spa, floodlit tennis court, a fitness centre with sauna and circuit training equipment. To take maximum advantage of these, a private tennis instructor, athletics trainer and masseurs are also available. Pastimes include shopping in Hollywood and visiting the nearby restaurants, museums and Beverly Hills. **Directions:** 1 block west of Lacienega Boulevard between Santa Monica Boulevard and Melrose Avenue. Price guide: Suites $300–$400.

152 rms     other  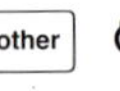  40         

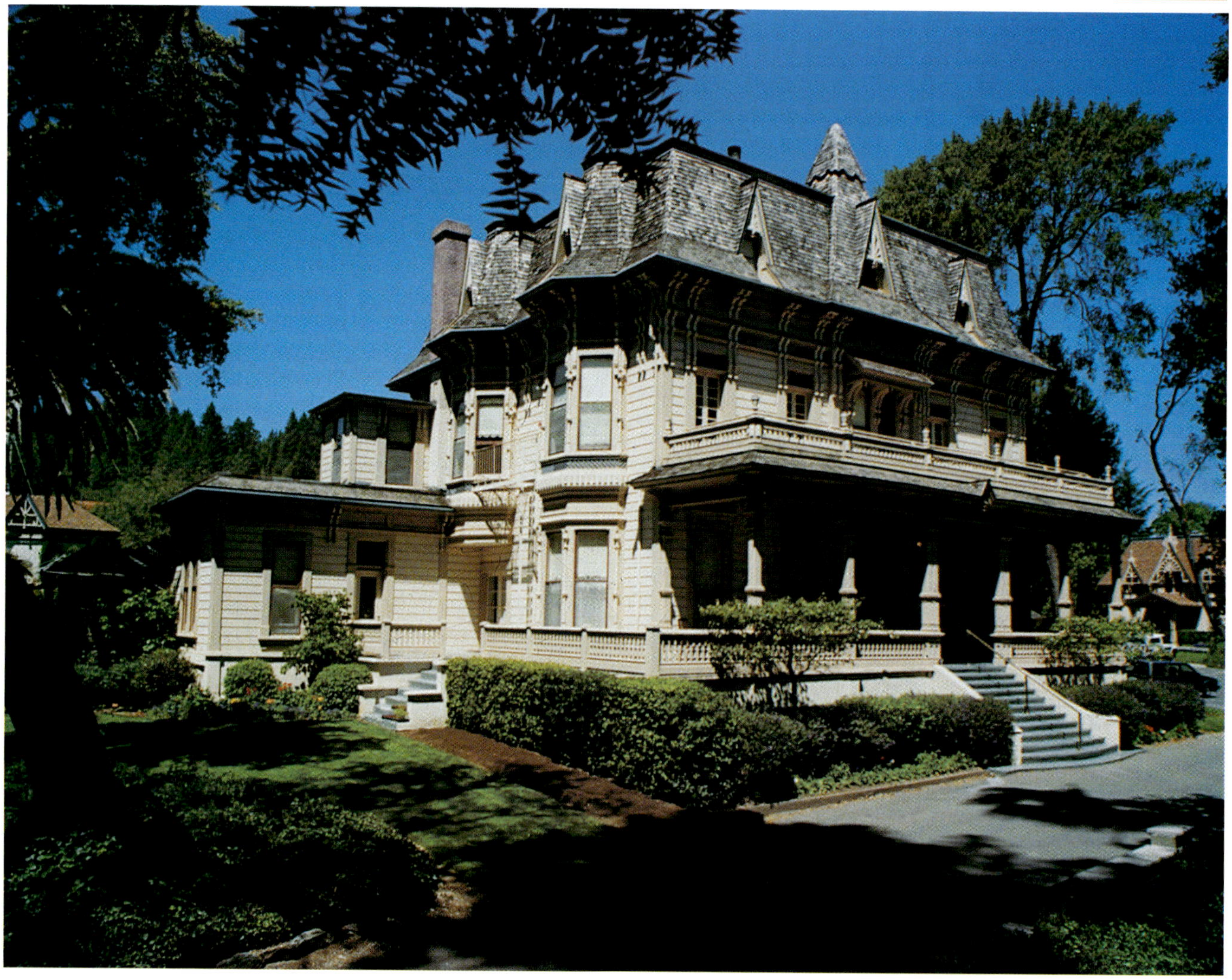

MADRONA MANOR

1001 WESTSIDE ROAD, HEALDSBURG, CALIFORNIA 95448
TEL: 1 707 433 4231 FAX: 1 707 433 0703

This grand Victorian Mansion dates back to 1881. It was built by the craftsmen of Healdsburg and the town was justifiably proud of it. One of the earliest Sonoma wineries was added a few years later. Today Madrona Manor is an impressive country house hotel, standing in extensive, well tended gardens, and an important landmark for the Sonoma Wine Trails. It is now on the National Historic Register of Historic Places and has won a Gold Medal for its wine list. The Victorian emphasis has been maintained, and the house has been decorated and furnished with meticulous attention to ensure that it is an appropriate setting for the fine antiques, many in mahogany, oil paintings, Persian carpets and mirrors so popular in that era. The bedrooms, some located in the Carriage House or Garden Cottage, are delightful, all having soft, restful colour schemes. Guests enjoy a glass of wine in The Music Room while glancing at the scrapbook, before dining in great style – inspired Californian dishes and exquisite wines. (No spirits available. There is a non-smoking policy in restaurant). European breakfasts. Wine-tasting, golf, exploring the Pacific Coast, swimming and strolling in the grounds are recommended recreations. **Directions:** Highway 101, taking Healdsburg Central exit. Left at 2nd stop light (Mill Street becomes Westside Road.) Price guide: Rooms $155–$210; suite $210–$255.

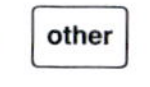

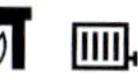

MANKA'S INVERNESS LODGE & RESTAURANT

30 CALLENDAR WAY, PO BOX 1110, INVERNESS, CALIFORNIA 94957
TEL: 1 415 669 1034 FAX: 1 415 669 1598 US TOLL FREE: 1 800 585 6343

Manka's Inverness Lodge and Restaurant comprise a number of buildings, but at its heart is a simple and rustic hunting and fishing cabin. During the daytime its first floor is the place in which to enjoy a quiet read, while at night this area becomes a restaurant where food is grilled on the open fire. Each room in the main house is distinctive; one has an inviting pedestal bath tub and a shower beneath the stars, a second room offers stunning views of Tomales Bay whilst two further rooms place you high above the trees. Those seeking more privacy must book one of the original cabins in the grounds of the Lodge. The 'rustic' cabins have their own personal style and offer all the comforts of a luxury retreat in the heart of nature. The imaginative cuisine served throughout will never disappoint. It includes such gourmet delights as Californian quail, with a centre of garden sage rum raisin dressing, grilled in the fireplace and nestled in bolinas spinach with a wild game jus dotted with pine nuts. Vegetarians must sample the roly-poly squash with a centre of roasted red peppers and local crescenza, served with porcini mushroom risotto and a yellow boy tomato sauce. Inverness is an excellent location for anyone seeking a range of activities, such as hiking, fishing, sailing or surfing. There is a Shakespeare festival in the summer. **Directions:** From San Francisco take Highway 101 north, then Sir Francis Drake drive to Highway 1 north. Turn left for Inverness. Price guide: Rooms $145–$425.

MARTINE INN

255 OCEANVIEW BOULEVARD, PACIFIC GROVE, CALIFORNIA 93950
TEL: 1 831 373 3388 FAX: 1 831 373 3896 US TOLL FREE: 1 800 852 5588

The Martine Inn, built in 1899, is a unique hotel in a superb setting, overlooking Monterey Bay. Its proprietors have ensured that its past is its present – it has a quintessential Victorian era ambience, yet white walls add the Mediterranean influence favoured by a past owner. Guests are instantly impressed by the courtesy of the staff, reminiscent of bygone days, as they are taken to their elegant bedrooms, with delicate wall coverings and drapes, the finest period furnishings. The bathrooms are joyous – claw feet tubs and brass fittings. Downstairs handsome antiques are in evidence, a traditional library – and every evening guests assemble in the parlour for wine and hors d'oeuvres (there is no spirits licence) reminiscent of a fin-de-siècle houseparty. The table settings are enhanced by exquisite china, the finest crystal and handsome old silver. The Martines have an enviable collection of vintage autos, the games room has a 1917 nickelodeon and pool table. Nearby are golf, every water sport, tennis and fascinating places to explore (splendid well-filled picnic hampers can be ordered). Directions: Highway 1 to Pebble Beach turnoff, Highway 68 to Pacific Grove, Righthand lane to ocean (Forest Avenue), then right into Oceanview Boulevard. Price guide: Rooms $150–$300.

20 rms MasterCard VISA AMERICAN EXPRESS other M 20

MOUNTAIN HOME INN

810 PANORAMIC HIGHWAY, MILL VALLEY, CALIFORNIA 94941
TEL: 1 415 381 9000 FAX: 1 415 381 3615

World famous San Francisco is an exciting city and if you wish to experience both city and countryside head for this idyllic country hostelry. It really is a mountain inn, high up, 1000ft above the town of Mill Valley and has a magnificent view over the Bay and across to Mount Diablo. The hotel has incorporated the local redwood trees in its design, with big windows to maximise on its spectacular surroundings. First sight of the hotel is the splendid sun terrace, where new arrivals join fellow guests for a glass of the local nectar – this is a great area for wine. The comfortable bedrooms are pleasantly furnished and the bathrooms well designed, some having Jacuzzis. The bar is rustic and fascinating, with redwood pillars stretching up to the vaulted roof. Midday meals can be enjoyed alfresco on the terrace whilst in the evenings residents dine indoors. The menu is deliciously cosmopolitan. There are wonderful walks and hiking trails through state parks, grasslands and forests, whichever route you choose the scenery will be heavenly. It is a short drive down to the beaches or up to the top of the mountain. **Directions:** Highway 101N, exit on right at Stinson Beach (Highway 1). Turn left after ⅔ miles, then right after 2½ miles onto Panoramie Highway. At the intersection take the High Road and the inn is 8 miles on right. Price guide: Rooms $139–$259.

PELICAN INN

HIGHWAY 1, MUIR BEACH, CALIFORNIA 94965
TEL: 1 415 383 6000 FAX: 1 415 383 3424

English visitors arriving at this enchanting inn follow in the footsteps of Francis Drake, who landed here some 400 years ago in his ship 'The Pelican' – hence its name. Just 20 minutes from the Golden Gate Bridge, yet it stands in a traditional flower-filled cottage garden, with honeysuckle climbing up the walls. A slate roof and mullioned windows add to The Pelican's 16th century ambience. The interior maintains this historic theme – a magnificent collection of antiques and memorabilia from that era, big fireplaces, oak beams, white walls and a charming 'Snug' for residents. The bedrooms are also reminiscent of the period – guests may sleep in a half-tester canopy bed, with colourful rugs on the floor, a decanter of sherry by the bed and start the day with a true English breakfast. All rooms have an en suite bathroom. The convivial bar, its panelled walls decorated with brasses and a dartboard, serves ales, sherries, wine and port. A wide range of traditional British pub food is offered. Dining at authentic refectory tables in the attractive restaurant, guests appreciate a more sophisticated menu. Muir Beach is sheltered by trees and encompassed by the woods, scented with pine trees – the essence of relaxation. **Directions:** Leave Golden Gate on Highway 101, taking Highway 1, Stinson Beach exit. Price guide: Rooms $158–$180 (includes full English breakfast).

7 rms      M 50  

Pine Inn

PO BOX 250, CARMEL, CALIFORNIA 93921
TEL: 1 831 624 3851 FAX: 1 831 624 3030 E-MAIL: info@pine-inn.com

Set in the heart of the village of Carmel, this historic inn is surrounded by charming shops, a number of art galleries and lovely hidden courtyards. Built in 1889, the elegance and refined ambience of a bygone age has been carefully re-created throughout. A choice of standard, superior or de luxe bedrooms is available, as well as suites of varying sizes. Each room is tastefully decorated with European and Far Eastern nuances, while the restaurant, Il Fornaio, is furnished in a classically Italian style. Here, guests can enjoy the special traditions of Italy, choosing authentic food and wine from an imaginative menu and watching the cooks prepare the dishes in the open kitchen. As well as exquisite local pasta dishes, there is a good selection of entrées prepared on either a mesquite grill, in a wood-burning oven, or on a traditional rotisserie. Guests must indulge in the hearth-baked house breads, prepared from old Italian recipes. Popular activities include shopping and revisiting the past in the historic missions, while golf enthusiasts can take advantage of some of the world's most famous courses. Sun-worshippers must watch the beautiful sunsets from Carmel's sandy beach! **Directions:** The inn is only 7 miles from Monterey Airport. Take Highway 1 south to Ocean Avenue, Pine Inn lies between Lincoln and Monte Verde. Price guide: Rooms $95–$230; suites $230.

49 rms other 100

Red Castle Inn Historic Lodging

109 PROSPECT STREET, NEVADA CITY, CALIFORNIA 95959
TEL: 1 530 265 5135 FAX: 1 530 265 3560 USA: 800 761 4766

The intriguing name of this legendary hotel in Nevada City – known as the Queen City of the Northern Mines – is indicative that the ambiance is that of nostalgia for the gold rush '49ers. The house is exquisite, red brick and ornate white filigree paintwork, set against cedar trees. The interior reflects its fascinating past, the decor and furniture authentic to the era, and delightful memorabilia, paintings and books have been carefully researched and chosen. The gardens are terraced with fountains playing, and planted with traditional roses and honeysuckle. There are no televisions, old time traditions prevail and there are storytellers, sometimes music, and the art of conversation is cherished. The guest rooms are wonderfully romantic, with exquisite chintz and wallhangings, and open onto verandahs or the garden. The Red Castle is a 'B&B', it has no restaurant nor bar. Breakfast is a feast of old-fashioned dishes and homemade breads which guests enjoy in the 'grand parlour', garden or their rooms. A full Victorian afternoon tea is another delight. For those requiring something stronger, the local supplier will deliver. Picnics can be arranged by the creek and historic Nevada City is down the garden path. There is good skiing close by. **Directions:** Leave Highway 80 for 49 or 20. The Red Castle is two blocks from the town centre. Price guide: Rooms \$115–\$145; suite \$110–\$150; exclusive use \$979.

SHUTTERS ON THE BEACH

ONE PICO BOULEVARD, SANTA MONICA, CALIFORNIA 90405
TEL: 1 310 458 0030 FAX: 1 310 458 4589 US TOLL FREE: 1 800 334 9000

Shutters On The Beach, a truly luxurious hotel, is the only Santa Monica property set on the golden sands of the beach front. The elegant style of the hotel is delicately understated whilst the ambience is reminiscent of the beach homes frequented by celebrities in the 1930s. Upon entering, guests admire the cosy fireplaces in the lobby, relax in the intimate conservation areas or enjoy the glorious views afforded from the spacious balcony. Original artworks, ornaments and lithographs add character to the public rooms. The guest rooms, most of which offer a panoramic vista across the Pacific coastline, are the essence of opulence, with sliding shutter doors letting in the fresh ocean air. All have en suite facilities, soft bathrobes and toiletries, private bar and an array of modern conveniences. There are two superb restaurants; guests may enjoy modern American flavours in One Pico or enjoy the relaxed atmosphere of Pedals, built in the style of an Italian Trattoria. Santa Monica, with its historic pier, is ideal for strolling, biking or skating. Sun-worshippers may laze on the beach whilst the more energetic may try some of the many water sports on offer. Exploring the sites of the film industry or touring the nearby studios are a must for media moguls. **Directions:** Take Freeway 405 north to Santa Monica Freeway 10 west. Exit 4th Street to the left, then right onto Pico Street. Price guide: Rooms $330–$550; suite $750–$2,500.

THE STERLING HOTEL

1300 H STREET, SACRAMENTO, CALIFORNIA 95814
TEL: 1 916 448 1300 FAX: 1 916 448 8066 US TOLL FREE: 800 365 7660

This glorious example of Victorian architecture has, while preserving much of its character, been transformed into an exclusive and immaculate hotel, with a distinguished clientele. Guests enter through a grand porchway into an ambience of sophisticated simplicity. The spacious foyer has a marble floor, art deco chandeliers, Chinese rugs and is an ideal venue for meeting friends or colleagues. The lounge is classical, with Oriental overtones – perfect for enjoying a quiet coffee. The skills of a talented designer are reflected in the bedrooms, which have beautiful contemporary furniture and are thoughtfully appointed. The bathrooms are opulent, with marble tiles, showers with glass and brass doors and Jacuzzis. The pièce de résistance is the Chanterelle, an exquisite (reservations are recommended) four-star restaurant which extends onto an attractive patio. The inspired Californian dishes with a strong French influence, mellow wines, elegant surroundings and impeccable service ensure that dining here is a memorable occasion. A recent addition is a grand Ballroom, ideal for corporate events or private celebrations. Guests enjoy trips down the Sacramento River and visiting the Crocker Art museum, Sutter's Fort and other fascinating historic buildings, many dating back to the Gold Rush. **Directions:** Exit on H Street from I.80, heading downtown. Price guide: Rooms $179; suites $225.

16 rms     other  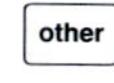  25      

THATCHER INN AND RESTAURANT

13401 SOUTH HIGHWAY 101, HOPLAND, CALIFORNIA 95449

TEL: 1 707 744 1890 FAX: 1 707 744 1219 US TOLL FREE: 1 800 266 1891 E-MAIL: info@thatcherinn.com

Two hours south of San Francisco, the Thatcher Inn and Restaurant is a historic gem in the heart of the Mendocino's wine country. The completely refurbished, turn of the century building is an architectural marvel that reflects the Victorian era. The differing guest rooms have traditional wallpapers and floral quilts in harmonious colour schemes, antiques and huge bathrooms. The fireside Library is a handsome retreat for a quiet read or pensive moment. Early evening cocktails are enjoyed in the Mahogany Lobby Bar. The shelves hold the finest collection of single malt whiskies on the West Coast. The Restaurant serves outstanding Italian and Continental cuisine. Lunch and dinner are served daily in the Grand Dining Room, evocative of the past, with its brass rails, marble tables, ceiling fans and formal seating, or on the garden patio. The ambience combined with the hosts', Don and Marlena, warm hospitality make a most memorable stay. The Inn is ideally located for visits to Mendocino's wine country, the lakes and the redwood forests. **Directions:** From San Francisco drive north on Highway 101 for 100 miles. Price guide: Rooms $130–$180.

San Francisco

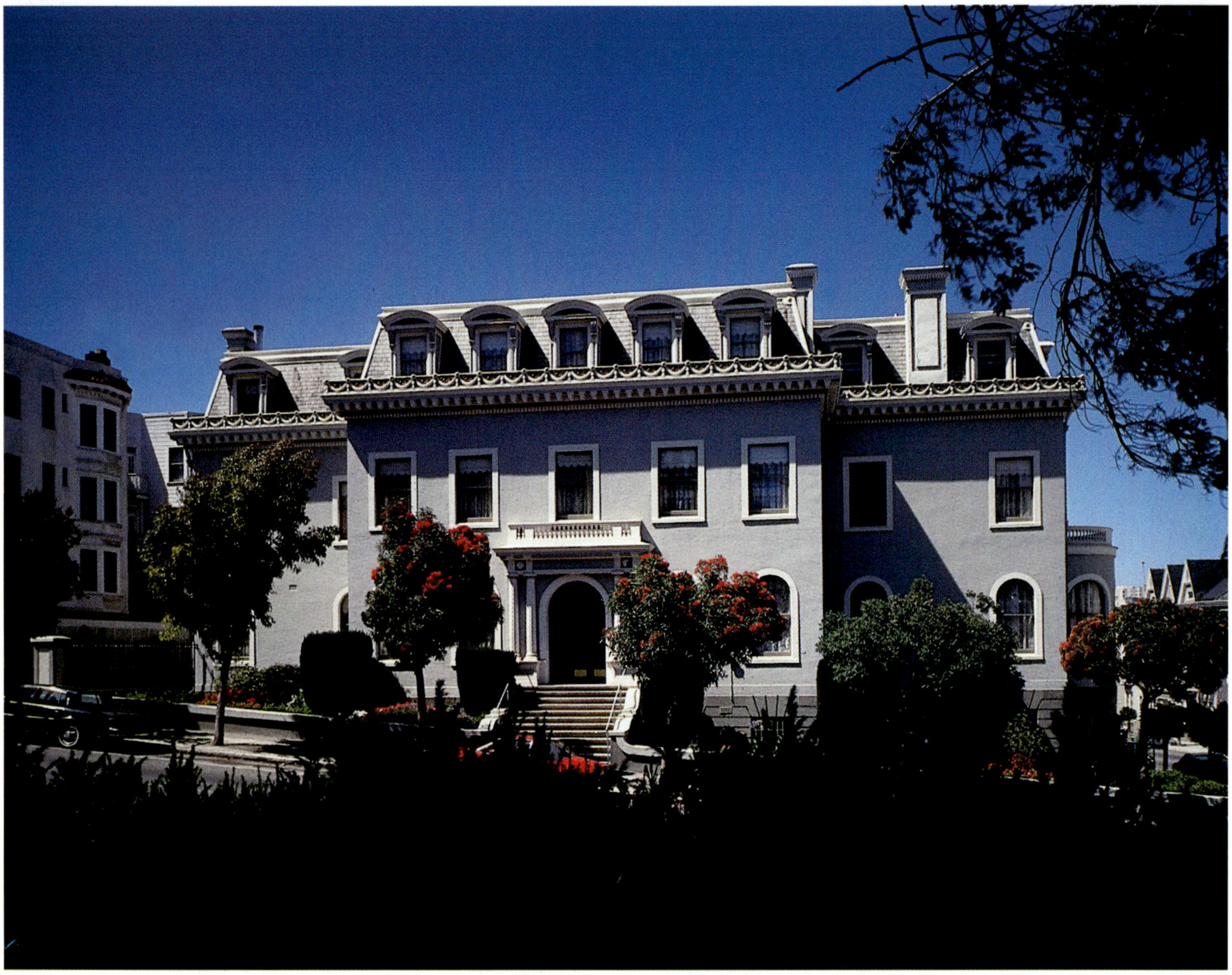

ARCHBISHOP'S MANSION

1000 FULTON ST, SAN FRANCISCO, CALIFORNIA 94117
TEL: 1 415 563 7872 FAX: 1 415 885 3193

Situated in Alamo Square overlooking the beautiful park, this Victorian inn, built in 1904, is one of San Francisco's historic landmarks. With its stucco façade, the Archbishop's Mansion resembles a French château whilst inside, the public rooms are furnished in an elegant style. Oriental rugs complement the wooden floors of the lounges and the original antiques and cosy fireplaces add character to the rooms. The spacious bedrooms are named after renowned operas such as Tosca and Don Giovanni and are individually appointed. Vestiges of the Victorian era are evident in the embroidered linens and antique ornaments whilst the amenities include some of the latest comforts such as cable television and videos. Continental breakfasts are served in either the bedrooms or the grand Dining Room and gastronomes will be delighted with the cheese and wine evenings. Upon arrival, guests are provided with all the latest information on the nearby entertainment. A personalised tour booklet, based on their interests, is then created for each guest by the friendly owners. Evenings are often spent in the city centre which, with its restaurants, theatres and other attractions, is only minutes away. **Directions:** From airport take 101N. Exit at Fell Street. Drive 4 blocks on Fell Street, turn right onto Steiner Street. After 3 blocks turn left onto Fulton Street. The hotel is situated on the corner of Fulton and Steiner. Price Guide: Rooms $139; suite $399.

THE MAXWELL HOTEL

386 GEARY ST, SAN FRANCISCO, CALIFORNIA 94102
TEL: 1 415 986 2000 FAX: 1 415 397 2447

Originally built in 1908, The Maxwell is a 13-storey theatre-deco style building which has been tastefully renovated to offer the highest standards of comfort. It has been beautifully decorated and furnished throughout, with an emphasis on velvet and brocades in strong rich colours such as red, green and gold. The 153 rooms include two penthouses with panoramic views, roof decks and two bathrooms. Reproductions of the work of American painter Edward Hopper, hand-painted deco lampshades and tiled vanities are common features. All the rooms have been fitted with two telephones, voice mail, computers links, writing desks, individually-controlled heat and air-conditioning and in-room movies. Gracie's Restaurant serves good American brasserie fare in an upbeat atmosphere. From the hotel's small but tastefully appointed lobby, theatres, shopping and sightseeing are just steps away. The Maxwell has thoughtfully designed a menu of services and amenities to suit different types of shopping – the Panoramic, Antique, Urban and Spiritual packages! The services include shipping of all purchases made, four hours' complimentary limousine to the city's eclectic shopping districts and 20 customised tour guides. High-tech foot spas are also available for post-shopping trauma! A cable-car will take visitors to Chinatown, North beach or Fisherman's Wharf. **Directions**: On Union Square, a short taxi ride from airport. Price guide: Rooms $145; Suites $650.

153 rms MasterCard VISA AMERICAN EXPRESS other M 150

NOB HILL LAMBOURNE

725 PINE STREET, SAN FRANCISCO, CALIFORNIA 94108
TEL: 1 415 433 2287 FAX: 1 415 433 0975 US TOLL FREE: 1 800 274–8466

Connoisseurs of hotel life call the downtown Nob Hill Lambourne "San Francisco's Healthiest Hotel" because of its collection of rejuvenating spa services and amenities which have left them feeling healthier than when they arrived. Its 20 luxurious and tastefully appointed bedrooms embody an innovative concept for both the leisure and business traveller. Each guest room and suite is designed to function as an office as well as an elegant place to spend the night. Each has a mini-kitchen and exotic bath bar, a personal computer, fax machine, voice mail, a complete library of San Francisco-based movies – and luxurious fluffy mattresses and down pillows which many guests insist on purchasing when checking out. Exercise equipment is in every suite, there is an Oriental-inspired spa treatment room, a variety of spa packages, aromatherapy bath amenities and a natural remedy bar for the ailing traveller. For all its executive and healthy living trimmings the Lambourne is far from computer driven. It has quiet, efficient service and stylish comfort. There is a relaxing lounge and breakfast room and although there is no restaurant, there are many dining areas close by. Valet car parking service. **Directions:** In downtown San Francisco within easy reach of the Powell Street and California St cable car routes. Price guide: Rooms $190–$210; suites $225–295.

20 rms · MasterCard · VISA · AMERICAN EXPRESS · other · M 10

Hawaii

THE
HAWAIIAN
ISLANDS
KAUA'I
Hā'ena
Wailua
Po'ipu
Pu'uwai
NI'IHAU
KAUA'I CHANNEL
O'AHU
Hale'iwa
Kahuku
Kāne'ohe
Mākaha
HONOLULU
KAIWI CHANNEL
MOLOKA'I
Kalaupapa
Hālawa
Kahului
MAUI
Lāna'i
City
Kihei
Hana
LĀNA'I
PACIFIC
OCEAN
ALENUIHĀHĀ CHANNEL
HAWAI'I
Kawaihae
Hilo
Kea'au
Kailua-Kona
Captain Cook
Kalapana
Mauna
Loa
38
Kilauea
Caldera
Nā'alehu

CHALET KILAUEA – THE INN AT VOLCANO

BOX 998, WRIGHT ROAD, VOLCANO VILLAGE, HAWAI'I ISLAND 96785, HAWAII
TEL: 1 808 9677786 (OFF ISLAND TOLL FREE: 800 9377736) TOLL FREE FAX: 1 800 577 1849

Tucked away in the fern forest of Volcano Village – just a mile from the main entrance to Volcanoes National Park – stands Chalet Kilauea - The Inn at Volcano. This stylish cedar-shingled inn is set in lush landscaped gardens and offers the standard of amenities and hospitality only found in the world's most exclusive resorts. A multitude of treasures from around the globe are scattered throughout the spacious living areas and bedrooms. The latter are themed – 'Out of Africa' and 'Oriental Jade' feature marble bathrooms with Jacuzzi and indigenous artworks, while 'Continental Lace' has been decorated and furnished with honeymooners in mind. Original Turner and other examples of fine art adorn the 'Owner's Suite', while the 'Treehouse Suite' is dominated by a spiral staircase. 'Haapu'u Forest Suite' is a separate, elegant, mountain cabin. All the bedrooms contain personal extra touches, including tropical flower arrangements and chocolates on the bed. Luxury is a byword, with the day starting off with a three-course candlelit gourmet breakfast and ending with star-gazing from the Jacuzzi, overlooking the gardens. A selection of 6 one or two bedroomed cottages and vacation homes are available for families, groups or those seeking a more private retreat. Activities include lava-viewing, biking, swimming and bird-watching. **Directions:** From Hilo Airport take highway to Hawaii Volcanoes National Park. Price guide: Homes $125–$225; rooms $135–$155; suites $175–$395.

12 rms MasterCard VISA AMERICAN EXPRESS other

MOËT
BRUT IMPÉRIAL
BRUT IMPÉRIAL
MOËT & CHANDON
CHAMPAGNE
BRUT
ÉPERNAY
FRANCE
75cl
FONDE EN 1743
The first choice at
every Johansens
Recommended Hotel

Washington and Oregon

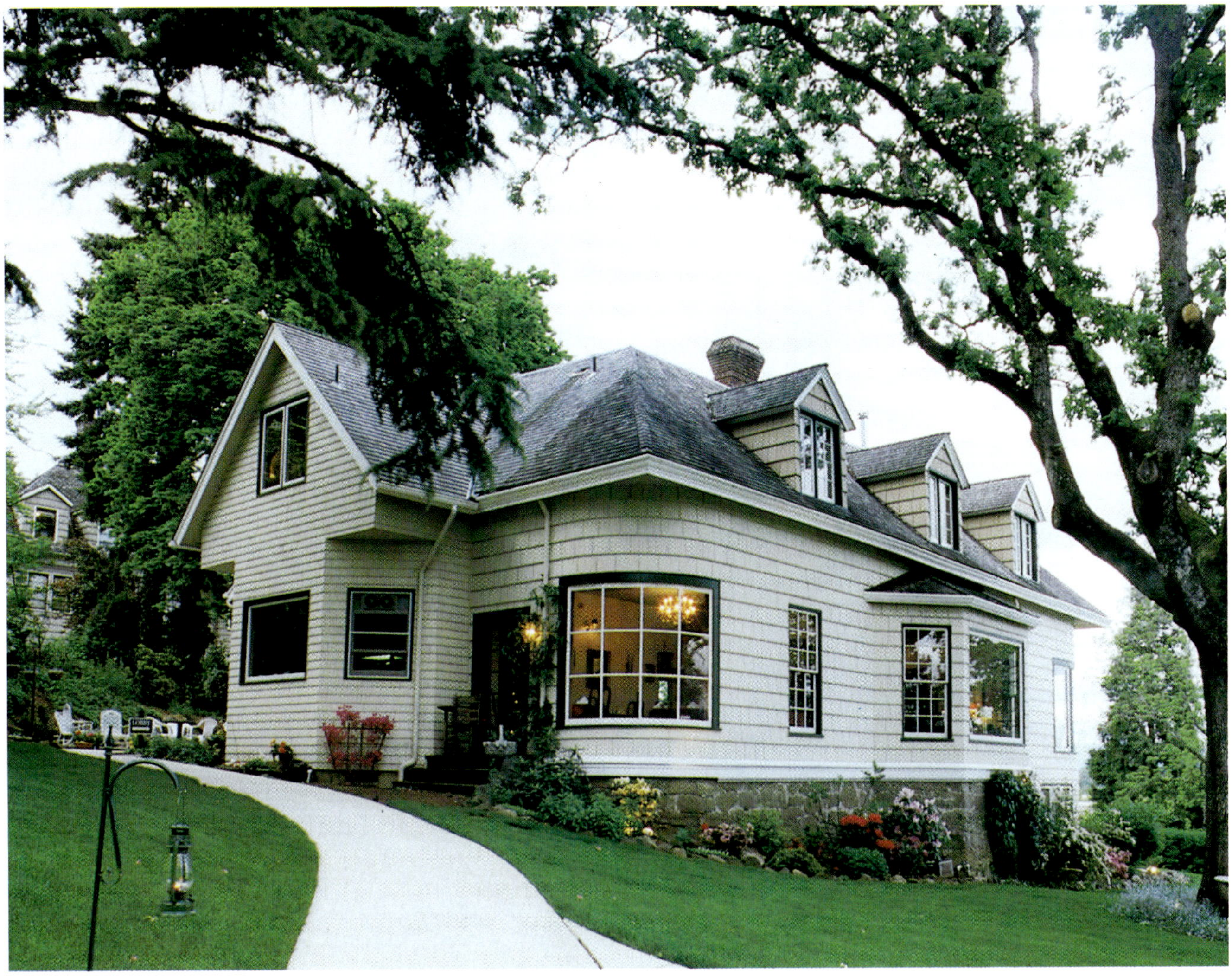

THE CAMPBELL HOUSE – A CITY INN

252 PEARL STREET, EUGENE, OREGON 97401
TEL: 1 541 343 1119 FAX: 1 541 343 2258 US TOLL FREE: 1 800 264 2519

This is a large and gracious Victorian inn standing serenely in the heart of historic Eugene, midway between the majestic Cascade Mountain Range and the Pacific Ocean. Built in 1892, the property has been sympathetically restored in the tradition of a fine European hotel. The Campbell House has all the amenities the discerning traveller seeks: timeless elegance, tasteful décor and excellent service. The well-equipped bedrooms are all en suite, some offering a gas fireplace, four-poster bed, air conditioning and Jacuzzi. Complimentary coffee can be enjoyed in the guest rooms and wine is served in the hotel during the evenings. The hotel has a no-smoking policy. The Campbell House is within easy walking distance of a variety of excellent restaurants, antique shops and boutiques, the Hult Centre for the Performing Arts and the bustling, 5th Street Public Market. For the more active, the renowned "Pre's Trail" jogging path is just half a mile away and there are many riverside paths for cyclists. Challenging whitewater rafting and several public golf courses are within easy reach. **Directions:** From I-5, exit at 194B. Follow Coburg Road-Downtown (Exit 2) City Centre Mall signs to East 3rd Street to Pearl Street. Price guide: Rooms $80–$185; suites $159–$350.

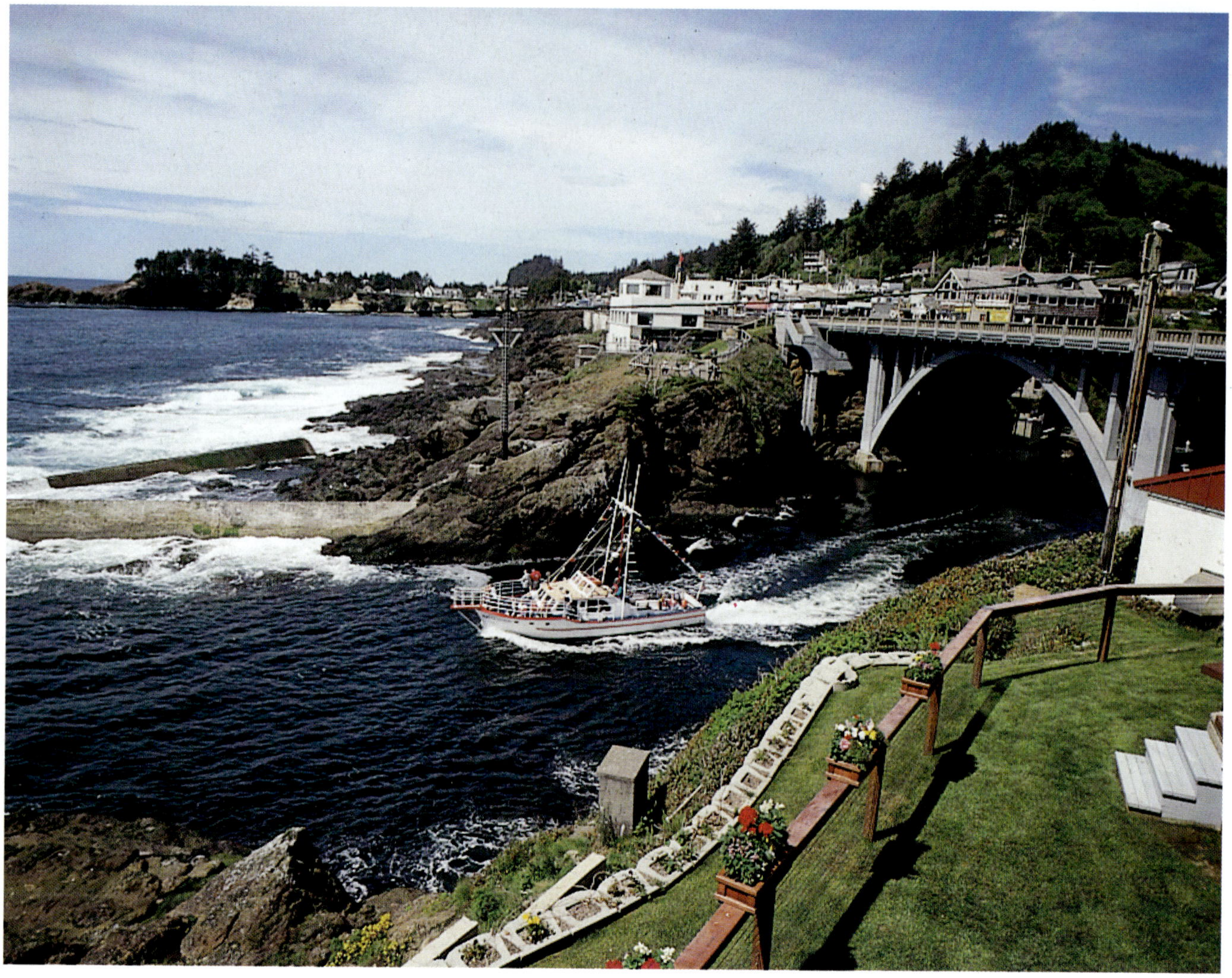

CHANNEL HOUSE INN

35 ELLINGSON STREET (PO BOX 56), DEPOE BAY, OREGON 97341
TEL: 1 541 765 2140 FAX: 1 541 765 2191 E-MAIL: cfinseth@newportnet.com

The Channel House Inn offers all the comforts of a first class hotel with the congeniality and enchantment of a small country house. Situated high on a cliff above the Pacific Ocean on the rugged coast of Depoe Bay it provides guests with panoramic views over deep blue waters, abundant with pods of whales. Glorious sunsets and enthralling winter storms complete the idyllic setting. The interior is bright and beautiful, decorated in cool, pastel shades and furnished shipboard style with fishing trophies, nautical antiques and brass fittings. The 14 spacious en suite bedrooms and suites have every amenity to make a visitor's stay memorable, from queen-size beds and gas fireplaces to large, ocean front, wooden deck balconies where guests can soak in their own private whirlpool and watch the amazing sunsets. Some of the rooms have fully-equipped kitchens. Hearty breakfasts are served buffet-style in a cosy dining room which overlooks the bay. Whilst there is no restaurant, many fine venues specialising in excellent, local seafood dishes are within walking distance. Activities include whale-watching, exploring the coastline and the surrounding forest area, deep sea fishing and golf at the nearby course. A non-smoking hotel. **Directions**: Just off Highway 101. One block south of Depoe Bridge turn left into Ellington Street. Price guide: Rooms $150; suites $195–$225.

Columbia Gorge Hotel

4000 WESTCLIFF DRIVE, HOOD RIVER, OREGON 97031-9970

TEL: 1 541 386 5566/1 800 345 1921 FAX: 1 541 387 5414 E-MAIL: cghotel@gorge.net

The mighty, snow-white craggy heights of Mount Hood soar majestically over this opulent hotel which is situated atop an ice cold waterfall tumbling 210 feet to the swirling Columbia River below. Huge firs enclose acres of landscaped gardens and grounds. It is a setting of unsurpassed beauty that has drawn thousands of visitors looking for a unique experience to the hotel: among them US Presidents Roosevelt and Coolidge and film star legends such as Myrna Loy, Jane Powell, Shirley Temple and Rudolph Valentino, after whom one of the elegant lounges is named. Opened in 1921 on the site of a former Indian meeting ground, the Columbia Gorge is a gracious, secluded and memorable retreat. All 40 en suite guest rooms are distinctive, featuring beautiful antique furniture and offering fine views. The speciality rooms have polished brass or canopy beds and some of the larger suites have open fireplaces. Dining is an impeccably serviced experience. Meals are a gastronomic delight and the restaurant has won many accolades including best breakfast and best restaurant in Oregon. Columbia Gorge has every sporting and leisure activity available. For the adventurous, there is mountain biking, windsurfing, fishing, rafting, skiing on Mount Hood, viewing the stars at Goldendale Observatory or touring Bonneville Dam. **Directions:** Take exit 62 off the I 84. Turn left and left again. The hotel is on the right. Price guide: Rooms $150–$275; speciality rooms $295–$365.

40 rms · MasterCard · VISA · AMERICAN EXPRESS · other · M 200 · 12

Ann Starrett Mansion

744 CLAY STREET, PORT TOWNSEND, WASHINGTON 98368
TEL: 1 360 385 3205 FAX: 1 360 385 2976

The Ann Starrett Mansion is a wonderful place to stay for two special reasons; firstly it is a genuine old inn and secondly it houses an amazing accumulation of curios and objects of virtue. The building was erected in 1889 by George Starrett who gave it, as a wedding present, to his new bride Ann. On the outside she added gables, porches and an octagonal turret. She adorned the interior with the best and the latest features of the era. Today, the mansion is a beautifully preserved tribute to the gentle and cultured style of living at the turn of the last century. The intrinsic character of the bedrooms and suites is ornate and welcoming, the common rooms embellished with pictures and furnishings from an earlier golden age. Breakfast is a delight. On a rainy day you need never leave the mansion, as there is a fascinating collection of memorabilia to discover and to study. Port Townsend, with its host of excellent galleries, shops, museums, restaurants and after sundown night spots must be explored. Outside, there are challenges on the tennis court, on the golf course and at sea where you can go canoeing or even watch the whales in Puget Sound. **Directions:** 1½ hours from Seattle. Take Bainbridge Island ferry to the Olympic Peninsula, then SR305, SR3 and SR104 into Port Townsend. Price guide: Rooms $90–$225.

DOMAINE MADELEINE

146 WILDFLOWER LANE, PORT ANGELES, WASHINGTON 98362
TEL: 1 360 457 4174 FAX: 1 360 457 3037

This charming romantic getaway, set in the picturesque town of Port Angeles with its breathtaking landscape of mountains, tall evergreens and flowers, is ideal for those seeking a peaceful retreat. Every possible modern comfort is found at the Domaine Madeleine whilst John and Madeleine Chambers are the perfect hosts and cater to their guests' every need. The interior is furnished in a blend of European and Asian styles and the five bedrooms are filled with many thoughtful extras such as exquisite perfumes, Christian Dior bathrobes and a wide range of videos and compact discs. The outstanding five-course breakfast is legendary, comprising freshly baked French breads and pastries, exotic fruit, cheeses and specialities such as chicken crêpes and salmon Florentine. Enthusiasts of outdoor pursuits will be delighted with the range of sports available nearby such as backpacking, sailing, kayaking, rock-climbing, cycling, badminton and volleyball. There are many scenic areas to explore including Lake Crescent, Sol Duc Hot Springs, Hoh Rain Forest and Hurricane Ridge. **Directions:** The hotel is two hours from Seattle via Bainbridge Ferry. Follow signs to Sequim, three miles past the fifth traffic light, turn right onto Carlsborg. After nearly two miles, turn left onto Old Olympic Hwy and then right onto Matson. Turn left onto Finn Hall and drive one mile to the Domaine Madeleine sign. Price Guide: Rooms $135–$175.

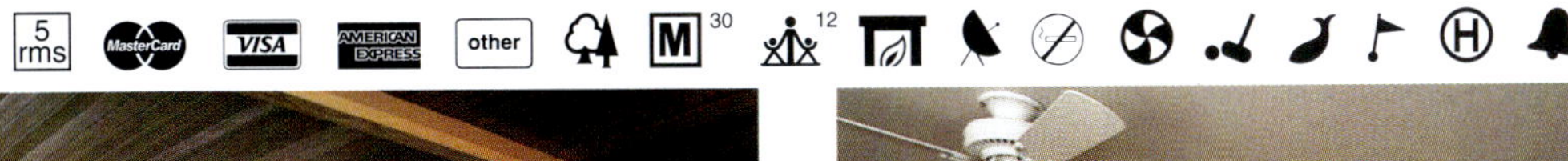

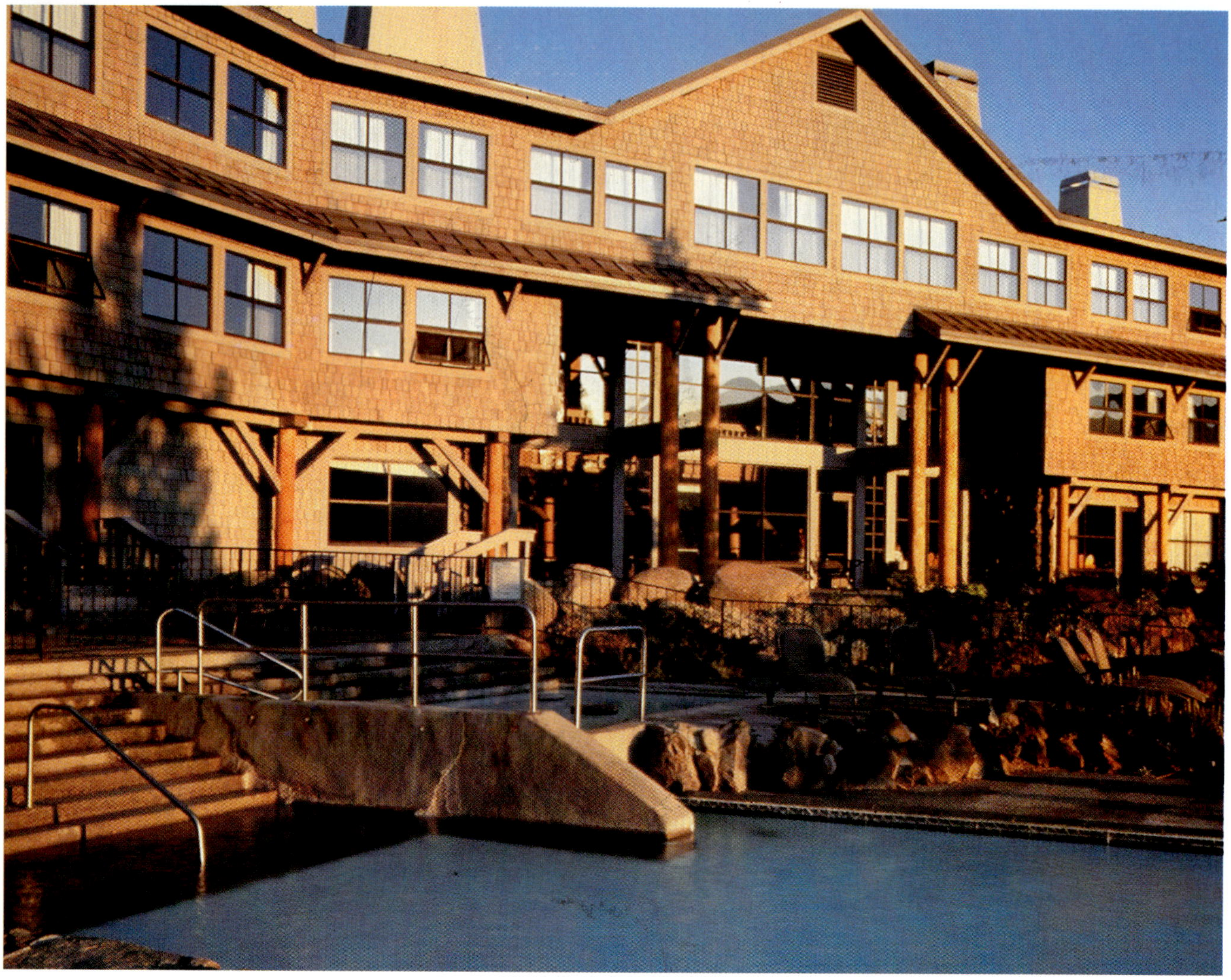

SUN MOUNTAIN LODGE

PATTERSON LAKE ROAD, WINTHROP, WASHINGTON 98862
TEL: 1 509 996 2211 FAX: 1 509 996 3133

This magnificent hotel, high above the Methow Valley, has been designed to blend into the beautiful surroundings. It is open all year round, a fabulous cross country ski resort in winter and proud of its environmentally friendly programme the other three seasons. The Lodge is at the summit of its private mountain, overlooking glorious countryside with rivers and a sparkling lake. The skills of local craftsmen are evident in the split log and carved furniture, stone work, folklore paintings and ornaments. The dramatic lobby has big welcoming overstuffed armchairs. The guest rooms, some in the adjacent lodges, have a rustic elegance and luxurious modern comforts – no televisions, they are deemed unnecessary. Drinks on the terrace or in the atmospheric bar preface an imaginative feast in the gorgeous restaurant, overlooking the valley, enhanced by splendid wines, many available by the glass. Children have their own programme and facilities, while families enjoy the substantial Buckeroo Breakfasts. Winter sports are catered for and hot water is ready for aching muscles or in summer saddle sores, otherwise guests play tennis, fish, golf, swim in the hotel pool, sail on the lake, bike downhill and get a lift back, or relax on a sunny bench communing with nature. **Directions:** In summer take scenic Highway 20, in winter Stevens Pass (2) or Snoqualmie Pass (90). Price guide: Rooms $110–$250; suite $185–$515.

TURTLEBACK FARM INN

CROW VALLEY ROAD, EAST SOUND, ORCAS ISLAND WASHINGTON 98245
TEL: 1 360 376 4914 FAX: 1 360 376 5329

Turtleback Farm stands in 80 acres of forest and farmland within the shadow of Turtleback Mountain on the island of Orcas, considered one of the loveliest of a chain dotting the sparkling waters of Washington State's San Juan archipelago. Fir trees frame open fields which produce hay for the resident sheep whose wool is made into guest-room comforters. Built in the late 1800s, this historic inn has been sympathetically renovated. While preserving the integrity and character of the original "Folk National" farmhouse, it has been enhanced by the addition of warm woods, a fresh, uncluttered décor and the 20th century amenities discerning guests expect. The living room has a beautiful Rumford fireplace, comfortable seating and a games table. The large dining room has a convenient bar. Each bedroom has a private bath and is furnished with a blend of fine antiques and contemporary pieces. Breakfast is served in the polished wood floor dining room or on the expansive deck overlooking the picturesque valley below. New last year is the Orchard House, a separate barn-style building with four king-bedded rooms, complete with sitting and dining areas. **Directions:** Six miles from the ferry landing and four miles from Eastbound, the island's principal village. Price guide: Double from $70–$160; Single $10 less; The Orchard House $210.

The Woodmark Hotel On Lake Washington

1200 CARILLON POINT, KIRKLAND, WASHINGTON 98033–7351
TEL: 1 425 822 3700 FAX: 1 425 822 3699

The Woodmark Hotel enjoys a striking location on the magnificent shores of Lake Washington. Situated just seven miles east of Seattle and minutes from the high-tech corridors of Microsoft and Nintendo, it offers a perfect retreat for travellers and business people alike. There are 100 contemporary-style bedrooms, including 21 suites – more than half of these provide an enthralling view of the lake and imposing Olympic Mountains. An extensive range of amenities includes a bar with a selection of foods and beverages, bathrobe, hairdryer, iron and ironing board, pay-per-view movies and Nintendo entertainment system. Afternoon tea is served in the peaceful setting of the Library Bar, which is also the place to enjoy a pre-dinner cocktail. The hotel restaurant Waters, a lakeside Bistro, serves delicious Northwest cuisine in a relaxed setting. The hotel prides itself on offering the highest standards of service and a host of facilities includes a courtesy van to local attractions and businesses, daily newspaper delivery and same-day laundry service. Those wishing to be pampered must visit the adjoining spa with its vast array of health and beauty treatments. Just steps away from the hotel's entrance is a central plaza with an excellent selection of shops and restaurants. **Directions**: The hotel is situated on Lake Washington. Drive across the floating bridge from Seattle. Price guide: Rooms $195–$245; suites $275–$1,400.

100 rms 200

Seattle

UNION BAY
PORTAGE BAY
LAKE UNION
520
5
99
10th Ave
Washington Park Arboretum
Seattle Centre
Space Needle
Clothes
Madison St
E. Union St
19th Ave
50
E. Cherry St
Seattle Art Museum
Aquarium
E. Yesler Way
Wing Luke Museum
ELLIOTT BAY
Pioneer Square
Kingdome
90
S. Lake Way

SORRENTO HOTEL

900 MADISON STREET, SEATTLE, WASHINGTON 98104–9742
TEL: 1 206 622 6400 FAX: 1 206 343 6155

The name Sorrento conjures up elegant Italy and this elite hotel in the centre of Seattle meets such expectations. New arrivals enter through wrought iron gates flanked by palm trees and drive past a decorative fountain to reach the grand portico of this graceful curved establishment with its fin de siècle embellishments. This hotel, renowned for its courteous staff and impeccable style, has a subtle European influence – the tiled murals over a fireplace, flowers in the niche of a brick wall, the charming patio at the back of the building, a "je ne sais quoi" which adds to its charm. The guest rooms are luxurious, traditional mahogany furniture and gorgeous fabrics side by side with high technology – with oversized bath towels and bed-warmers among the many lavish comforts! Peaceful afternoon tea in the attractive Fireside Room or sophisticated cocktails in the fashionable Bar end the day before dining superbly in the Hunt Club Restaurant, delightfully evocative of Tuscany. Special celebrations or distinguished corporate events are held in the exciting Top of the Town Room. The hotel has complimentary town cars to the waterfront, Pike Place Market and the convention centre. Boat trips round the harbour are fun – in the hotel there is a Nautilus fitness centre. **Directions:** Interstate 5 brings you to the city centre. Valet parking. Price guide: Rooms $190–$230; suite $230–$1500.

76 rms MasterCard VISA AMERICAN EXPRESS other M 80

Colorado and Wyoming

Historic Castle Marne

1572 RACE STREET, DENVER, COLORADO 80206
TEL: 1 303 331 0621 FAX: 1 303 331 0623 E-MAIL: themarne@ix.netcom.com

Historic Castle Marne, a Victorian property transformed into a bed and breakfast inn, is both charming and elegant with a unique atmosphere. Many vestiges of the castle's past are scattered throughout the rooms such as hand-rubbed woods, family heirlooms and ornate fireplaces. Following a careful restoration, original features dominate the interior, which is enhanced by rococo gilt mirrors and fine antiques. The individually decorated bedrooms are stylish and display nuances of the period. Guests are made to feel extremely welcome by the friendly and hospitable owners. The comfortable parlour is ideal for reclining and reading a book beside the beautifully carved fireplace. Special private six-course candlelight dinners can be arranged. Guests may indulge in scrumptious breakfasts and afternoon tea. House specialities include stuffed tomato with egg and spinach purée topped with parmesan and Jack cheeses and the home-baked cakes and biscuits at teatime are a delight to the palate. There are several museums and historic sites clustered around the area. Other attractions include the zoo, botanical gardens or perusing the shops at 'Cherry Creek'. **Directions:** From DIA, Pena Boulevard head to I–70 west, exit Quebec Street. Travel south (left) to 17th Avenue, turning right to York Street. Turn left into 16th Avenue and then right into Race Street. Price Guide: Rooms $85–$180; suite $220.

9 rms · MasterCard · VISA · AMERICAN EXPRESS · M 12 · 10

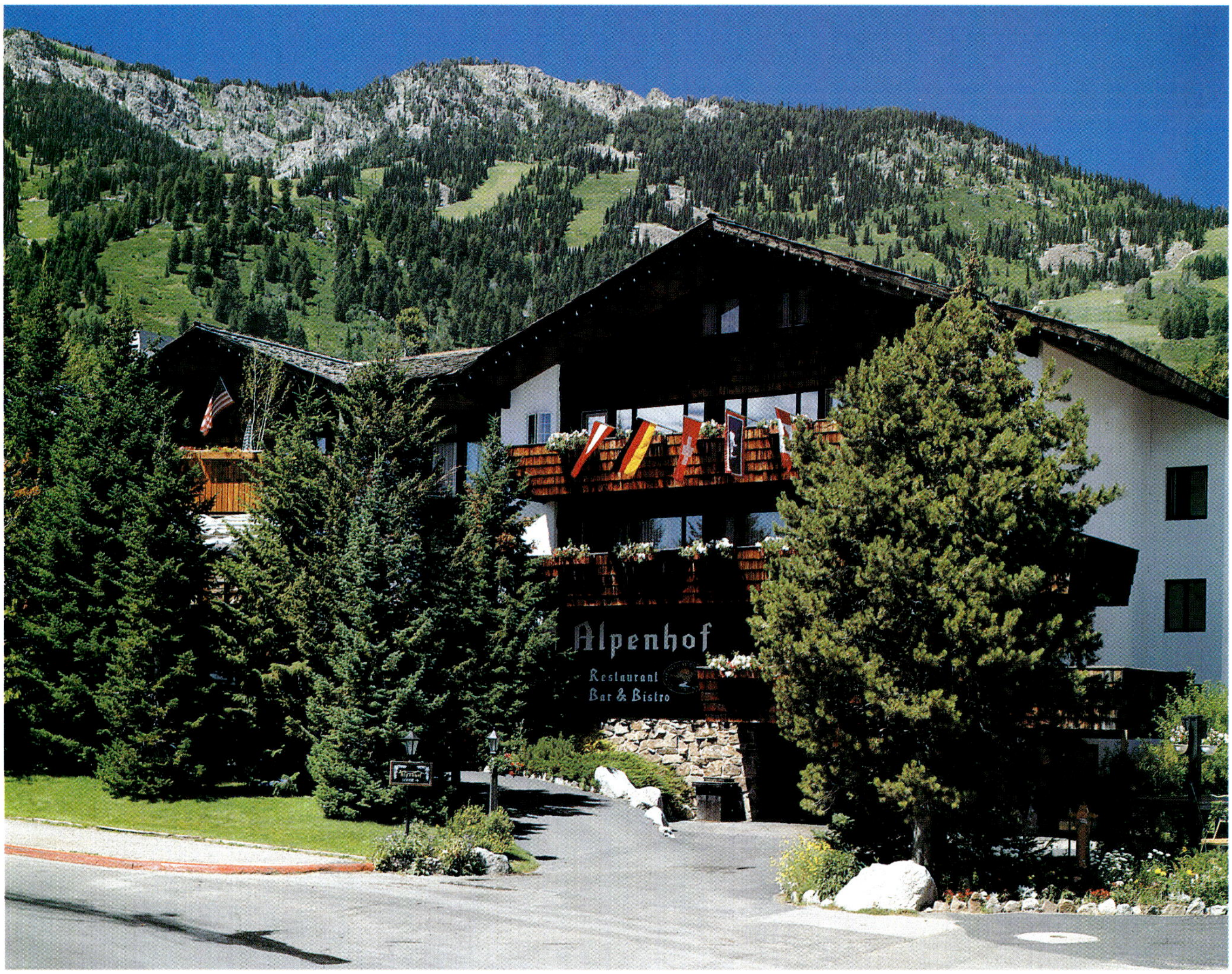

THE ALPENHOF LODGE

TETON VILLAGE, JACKSON HOLE, WYOMING 83025
TEL: 1 307 733 3242 FAX: 1 307 739 1516

It is delightful to find this magical Bavarian hotel at the foot of the Teton mountains, adjacent to the ski-lifts in the heart of Jackson Hole, the popular Wyoming ski resort – close to the small town of Jackson in an area busy throughout the year with visitors to Yellowstone National Park and the scene of Wild West rodeos and shoot-outs in summer. The Alpenhof Lodge is a traditional chalet, with its wooden façade, window boxes and shutters. The elegant interior displays many fine examples of Bavarian wood-carving. The welcoming reception area is filled with flowers; the staff are friendly and helpful. Hand-built furniture from Europe features in many of the spacious, light and airy bedrooms – some with balconies. Efficient bathrooms ensure that plenty of hot water is available after a hard day's skiing (and après-skiing!). Expansive windows, sun terrace and warm fireplace are dominant upstairs in the Alpenhof Bistro serving the best lunches, après-ski snacks and drinks and creative dinners. Downstairs, the elegant Alpenhof Dining Room, Jackson Hole's only 4 star restaurant, is renowned for its gourmet menu, including wild game and award-winning wine list. In winter, alternatives to skiing are snow mobiles into Yellowstone and sleigh rides through the Elk Refuge. In summer, ballooning, golf, hiking, fishing, river rafting, climbing, riding and swimming. **Directions:** Jackson Hole is signed from Highway 22. Price guide: Rooms/suite $128–$398.

Michigan and Wisconsin

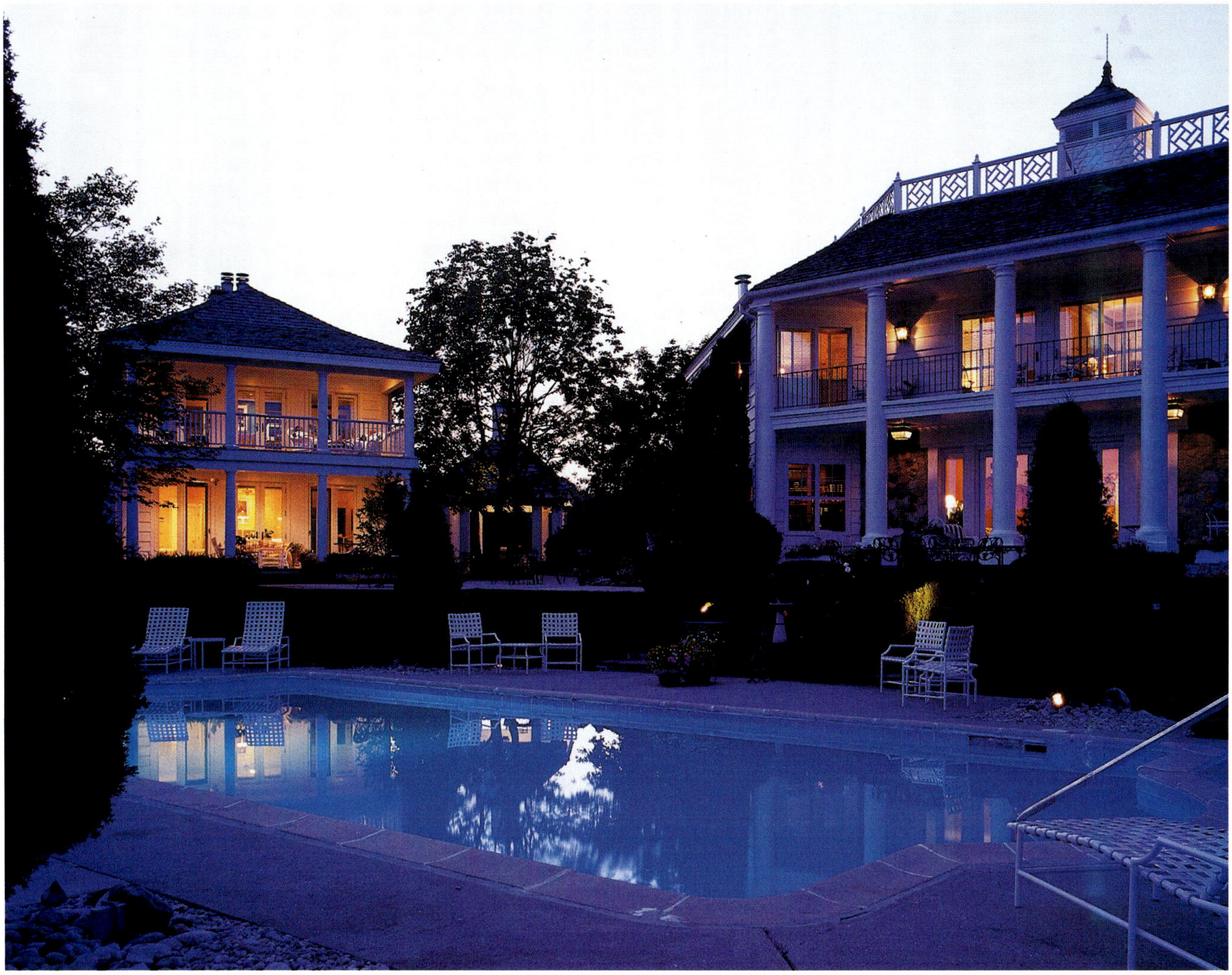

Kimberly Country Estate

2287 BESTER ROAD, HARBOR SPRINGS, MICHIGAN 49740
TEL: 1 616 526 7646 FAX: 1 616 526 8054

This gracious plantation home with verandah and terraces overlooks the Wequetonsing Golf Course and offers guests the ultimate in comfort and relaxation. Each of the well-appointed bedrooms has en suite facilities and is individually decorated. Fresh flowers, sherry and chocolate truffles are just a few of the many thoughtful extras that help create the sense of pampering. Breakfast may be enjoyed in either the dining room, on the terrace or beside the cosy fire in the library, with a daily-changing menu reflecting the very best of the seasonal fruits and berries. In the late afternoon, refreshing beverages, wine and hors d'oeuvres are provided. During warm summer months the pool, well sheltered by a hedge of cedars, is particularly inviting. A comfortable room with television, dartboard and games tables provides entertainment during inclement weather. Fitness facilities include a steam room, sauna, hot tub, exercise equipment and a massage therapist. A range of activities in the area includes golf, biking and hiking. Little Traverse Bay is the place to head for sailing and charter fishing, while winter sports including cross-country skiing are available at Boyne Highlands or Nub's Nob, just a ten minute drive from the inn. **Directions:** From Petoskey take the M-119 and turn right up Hoyt Street. Then take the second right into Bester Road. Price guide: Rooms £165–$190; suites $250–$300.

STAFFORDS PERRY HOTEL

BAY AT LEWIS STREET, PETOSKEY, MICHIGAN 49770
TEL: 1 616 347 4000 FAX: 1 616 347 0636

Petoskey is a small city on Lake Michigan's Little Traverse Bay. It has a fin de siècle appeal, with its Victorian street lamps and elaborate summer homes built by the Midwestern tycoons of that era. Particularly fascinating is the Gaslight District, – the artists' quarter, abounding with galleries, boutiques and home to The Perry Hotel. This attractive residence has a graceful facade, with a grand entrance, a verandah, a Rose Garden and spectacular views over the Bay. The charming guest rooms – some with balconies – are decorated with floral drapes and wallpapers, the furniture blending perfectly. The bathrooms are modern. Guests rendezvous in the elegant Victorian Salon for evening drinks, enjoyed on the verandah in clement weather. Meals are served in the uniquely named H.O. Rose Room, a sophisticated restaurant facing the Lake, where a pianist plays at weekends. The imaginative cosmopolitan menu includes American 'comfort foods'. Over 100 excellent wines are listed. Informal meals, beer and good jazz or folk music can be found in the basement Noggin Room Pub. This is a golfer's paradise, with 8 challenging courses nearby. Excursions to Mackinac Island and Tahquamenon Falls are entertaining. Visitors enjoy the beaches in summer and ski in winter. **Directions:** Leave the US31 at Lewis Street. Ample parking. Price guide: Rooms $75–$185.

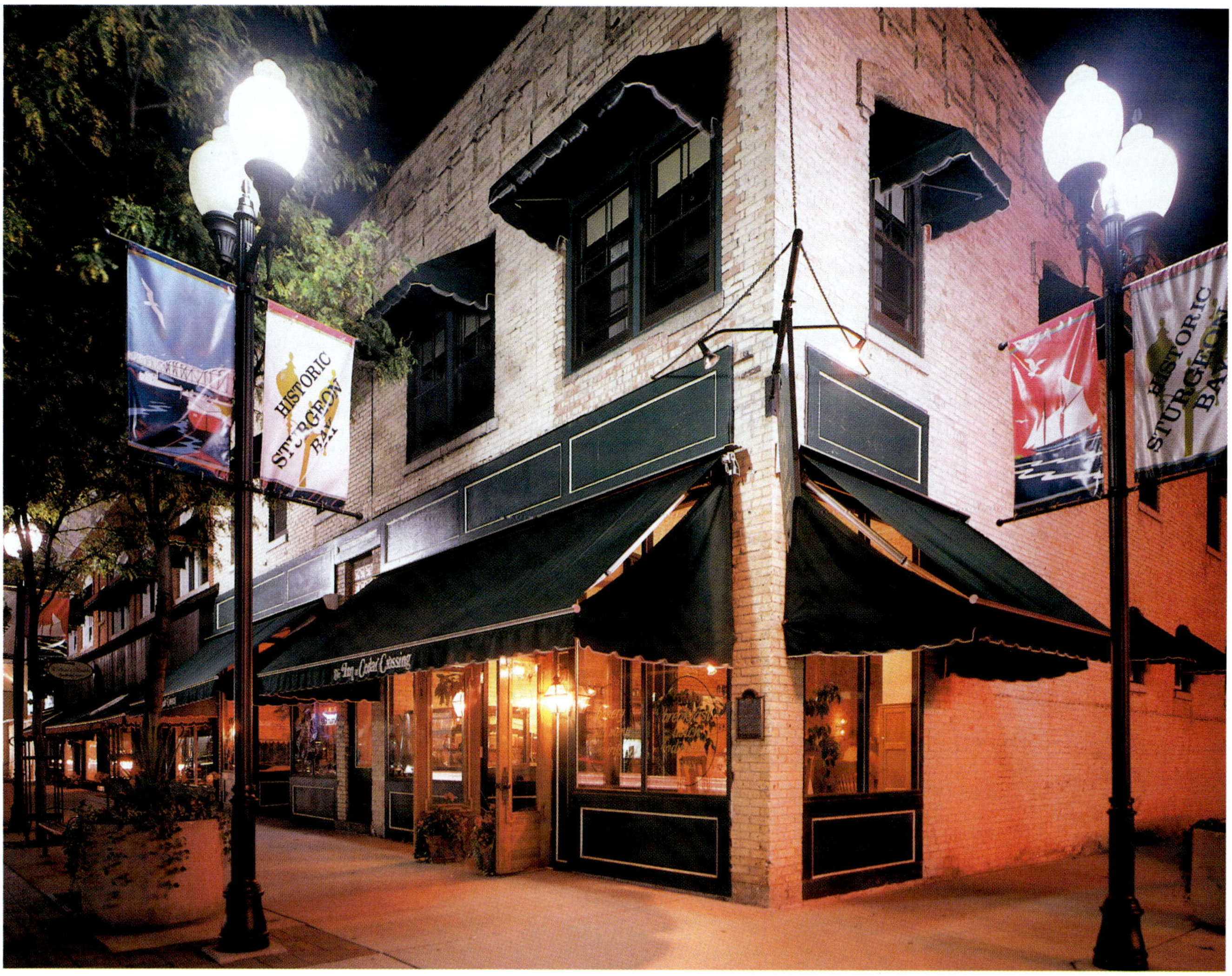

INN AT CEDAR CROSSING

336 LOUISIANA STREET, STURGEON BAY, WISCONSIN 54235
TEL: 1 920 743 4200 FAX: 1 920 743 4422

Built in 1884, the Inn at Cedar Crossing is the result of careful restoration, carried out with sensitivity and enthusiasm. Listed on the National Historic Register, this charming inn reveals its past in the open banister staircase, pressed tin ceilings and a majestic fireplace. Despite its age, however, the inn offers every modern comfort and amenity. Each of the nine bedrooms is furnished with interesting antiques and ornaments and many offer a fireplace, double whirlpool tub or both. The exquisite taste of the inn's owners is much in evidence in the choice of beautiful décor, fabrics and wallpapers. Hearty breakfasts, generous lunches, and dinners featuring imaginative local cuisine, are all served in the elegant dining rooms, reminiscent of the Victoria era. Specialising in fresh fish and seafood, the dinner menu includes mesquite smoked rack of lamb, lobster brodette, grilled beef tender loin napolean, toasted cumin seed pork loin, and nightly fresh catch. Muffins, scones and coffee cakes, served straight from the oven, and some of the many luscious desserts are designed to please those with a sweet tooth. An impressive wine list features both New World and Continental vintages. While Sturgeon Bay has plenty to offer, including interesting boutiques, galleries and museums, further afield lies the enthralling beauty of Door County with its superb and varied landscape. **Directions**: From Milwaukee north on I43 rte 57N to Sturgeon Bay. Price guide: Rooms $95–$155.

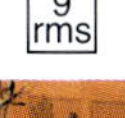

THE WHITE GULL INN

4225 MAIN STREET, PO BOX 160, FISH CREEK, WISCONSIN 54212
TEL: 1 920 868 3517 FAX: 1 920 868 2367 E-MAIL: innkeeper@whitegullinn.com

In the tiny coastal town of Fish Creek, on Wisconsin's famous Door County Peninsula, at the end of the maple-shaded main street, lies White Gull Inn. The inn was founded by a Dr Welcker in 1896 and examples of his excellent taste in furniture are still much in evidence – the walnut, oak or iron beds in several of the rooms may have been his acquisitions. In recent years, the rooms have been beautifully decorated with co-ordinating prints and fabrics which recapture the flavour of the turn of the century. Many of the latest amenities have been added to ensure high standards of comfort and convenience. Late risers need have no fear of missing out on the delicious breakfasts that are served at the White Gull – Eggs Benedict, hash browns and buttermilk pancakes with maple syrup are all available until noon. Similar care is taken to provide good lunches, including home-made soups, sandwiches, omelettes, salads and tempting desserts from the bakery. At dinner, the freshest produce is used in the regional specialities. A menu of delicious desserts often features the apples and cherries for which Door County is famous. The area is a centre for the performing arts with professional theatre, music festivals and a new auditorium. Leisure activities include cross country skiing, windsurfing and exploring the antique stores and galleries. **Directions**: From Milwaukee, take I-43 north to Green Bay then HWY 57 north to Sturgeon Bay, then HWY 42 north to Fish Creek. Price guide: Rooms $99–$190; cottage/house $162–$261.

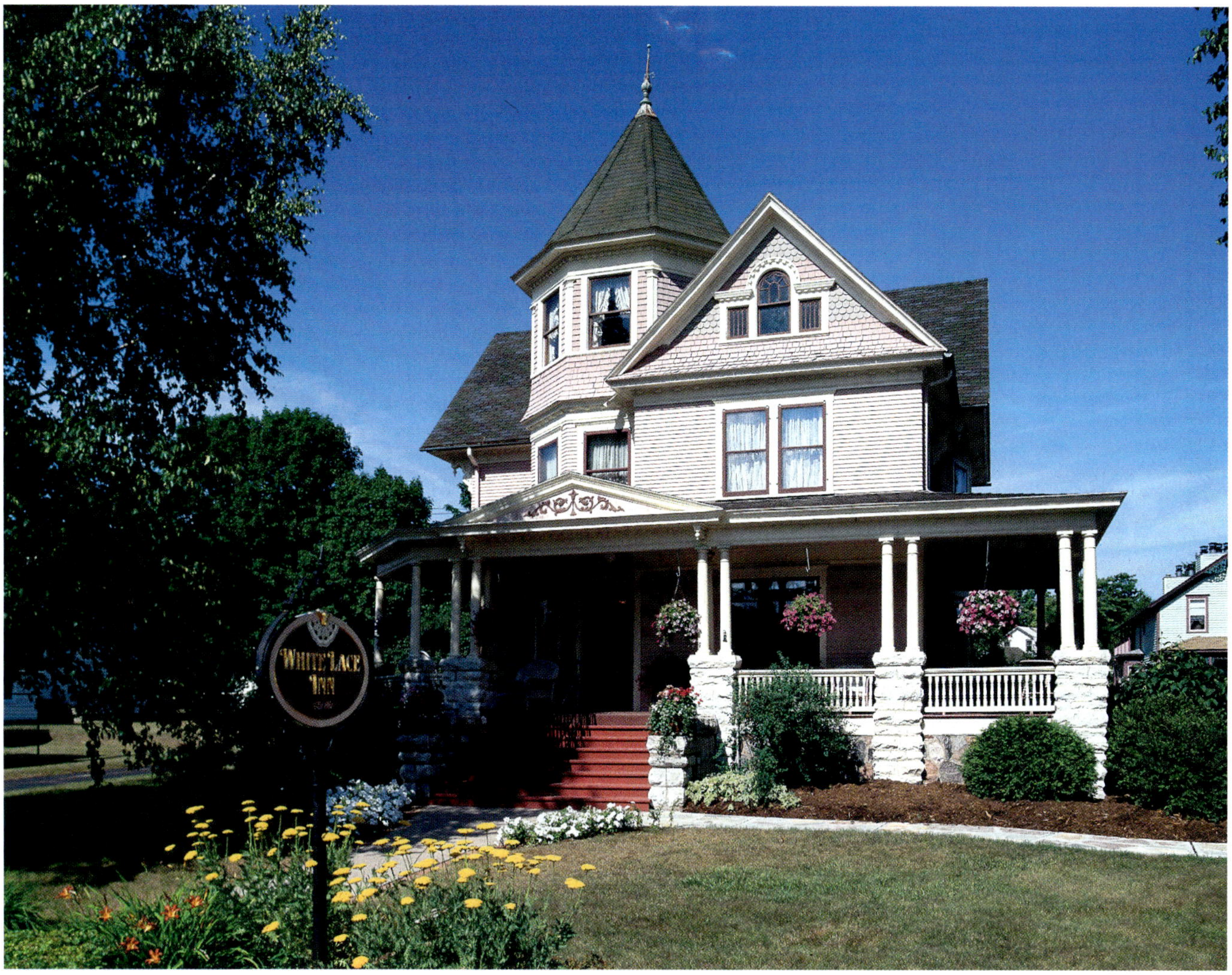

WHITE LACE INN

16 NORTH 5TH AVENUE, STURGEON BAY, WISCONSIN 54235
TEL: 1 920 743 1105 E-MAIL: romance@whitelaceinn.com

Standing in a quiet residential neighbourhood of Sturgeon Bay, these charming Victorian homes, bordered with whimsical picket fences, comprise White Lace Inn. Surrounded by attractive gardens, the inn's location in Wisconsin's famous Door County Peninsula, renowned for its fine artists and galleries, adds to the romance. With over 250 miles of shoreline and five magnificent State Parks, this is an ideal property for those seeking a private retreat. Innkeepers Bonnie and Dennis have participated in and supervised the careful renovation of the houses over a 16 year period and the result is a delightful inn with 18 beautiful rooms and suites. In the Main House there are four opulent rooms, each with a luxurious whirlpool tub. The 'Romantic Retreat' room has a queen-sized canopy plantation bed, a cosy fireplace and a hidden TV/video and stereo system. The most recently restored home is the Hadley House, painted sky blue with a white trim, housing four suites named after each season. Decorated in classic florals, toiles and checks, the suites are the essence of extravagance and feature every possible amenity. Across the gardens, The Garden House offers more modestly priced rooms with a lovely décor that equals the high quality of the suites but on a smaller scale. Enchanting fireplaces, spacious beds and large whirlpools add to the cosy atmosphere in the rooms in Washburn House. **Directions**: From Milwaukee north on 143 rte 57N to rte 42N to Sturgeon Bay. Price guide: Rooms $99–$159; suites $169–$199.

Louisiana and Mississippi

The Dansereau House Restaurant and Inn

506 ST PHILIP STREET, THIBODAUX, LOUISIANA 70301
TEL: 504 447 1002 FAX: 504 447 1003 E-MAIL: dansereauhouse@cajunnet.com

Hidden away in a quiet small town street with a façade incorporating artistic arches, tall, slim columns and an impressive white rooftop tower, Dansereau House is an Italianate mansion rightly recorded in the National Register of Historic Places. Its beauty is accentuated by its lawned surroundings and with a classic exterior mirrored by aristocratic interior grace. Built in the mid-19th century as a large, single storey raised cottage, it has over the years been added to, reconstructed, renovated and refurbished to today's magnificent status. Each of the four air-conditioned bedrooms are distinctively different, charming and spacious. Traditionally furnished with antiques and colourful prints, they have all modern amenities for the occupants' comfort. Large, panoramic windows provide scenic views of the peaceful grounds and give access to a white railed porch around the house where guests can chat and relax over a cool drink or coffee as they watch the sun sink in splendour over the treetops and brilliant green, manicured lawns. The bathrooms are equally large and elegant yet simply furnished. Imaginative Southern plantation cuisine is lovingly produced and served with flair by the attentive staff. Visitors will enjoy exploring the surrounding countryside, searching out antiques in Thibodaux and boat trips down the Mississippi. **Directions:** At Jct LA20 and LA1 turn left. After lights turn left onto West 5th Street. Inn is on the right. Price guide: Rooms $115–$125.

4 rms · other · 16

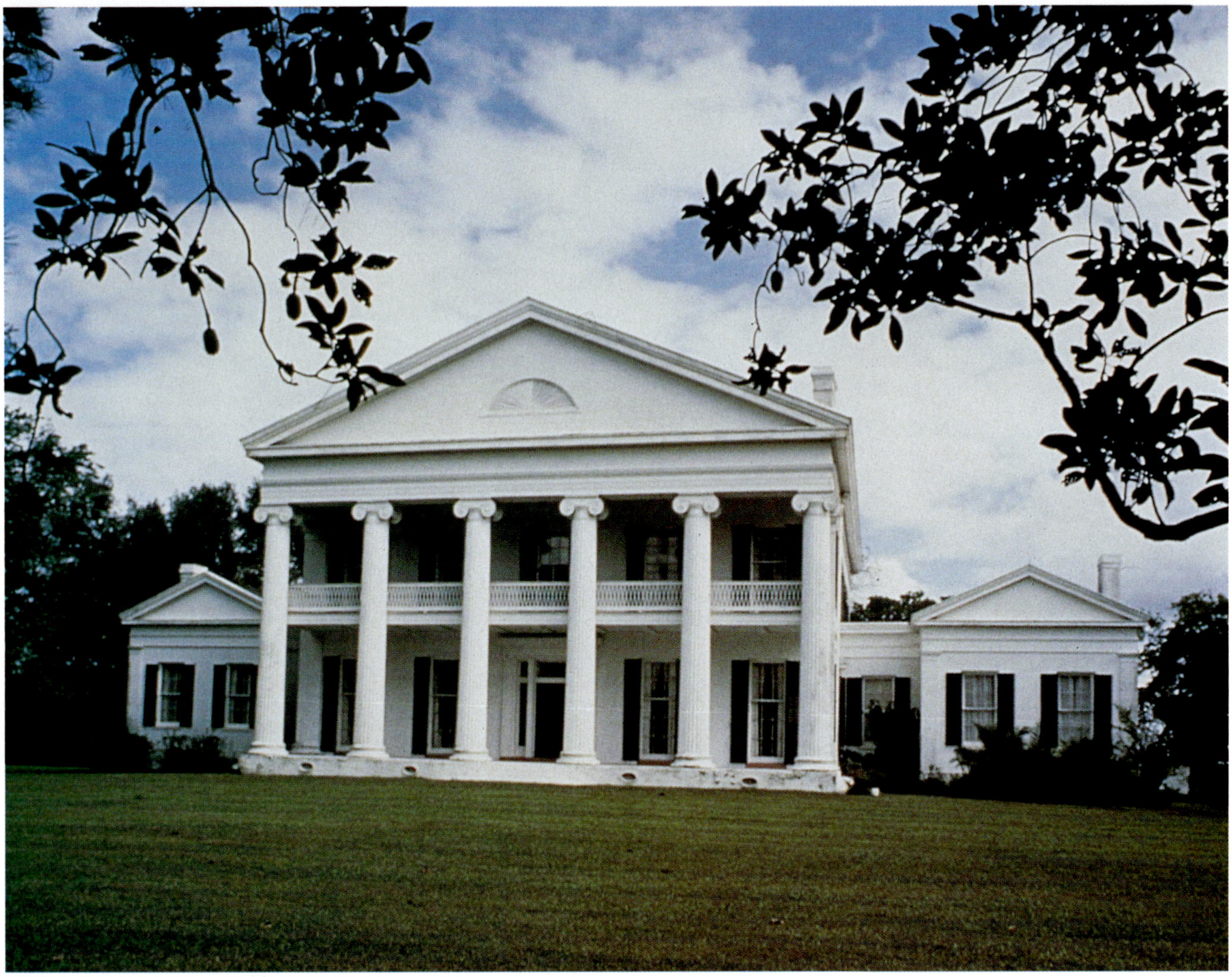

MADEWOOD PLANTATION HOUSE

4250 HIGHWAY 308, NAPOLEONVILLE, LOUISIANA 70390
TEL: 1 504 369 7151 FAX: 1 504 369 9848

Madewood, a great plantation house in Louisiana, has been so authentically restored that several films have been made with the mansion in the star role. A National Historic Landmark, its beauty is accentuated by its setting – extensive parkland encompasses the original slave quarters, kitchen and family graveyard. The classic façade, with its pillars, is magnificent and the interior has the same aristocratic grace. Guests stay in one of the original bedchambers in the main house, where modern facilities blend harmoniously with period antiques whilst retaining the character of the house. Here you will experience a refreshing return to the art of conversation, as there are no televisions or telephones in the bedrooms. Non-smoking prevails throughout. Original artworks from the owner's collection are omnipresent, particularly in the drawing room with its exquisite pieces. Residents gather in the handsome Library at 6.00pm for a preprandial wine and cheese, before a Southern-style dinner, round the immense oak table. Coffee and brandy are served in the Parlour, where guests mingle and converse. Exploring the Bayou country, boat trips down the Mississippi and antique-hunting in shops along the Bayou are popular pastimes. **Directions:** I–10 West, exit 182, cross Sunshine Bridge, then Highway 70 to Spur 70, signed Bayou Plantations. Left for 1 mile then left onto Highway 308. The house is 2.2 miles south of Napoleonville. Price guide (2 persons incl dinner): Rooms $215.

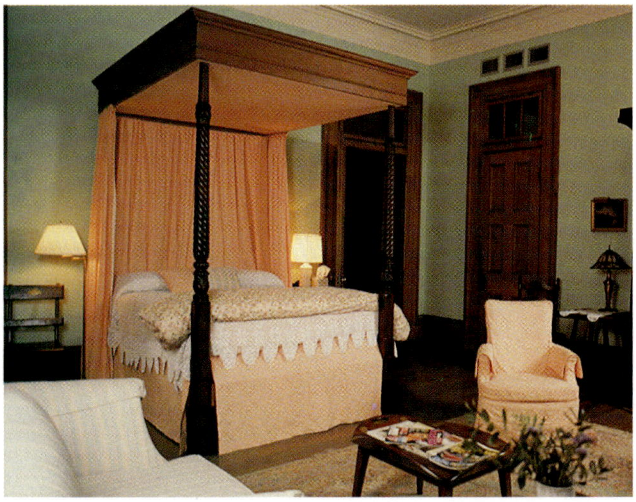

New Orleans

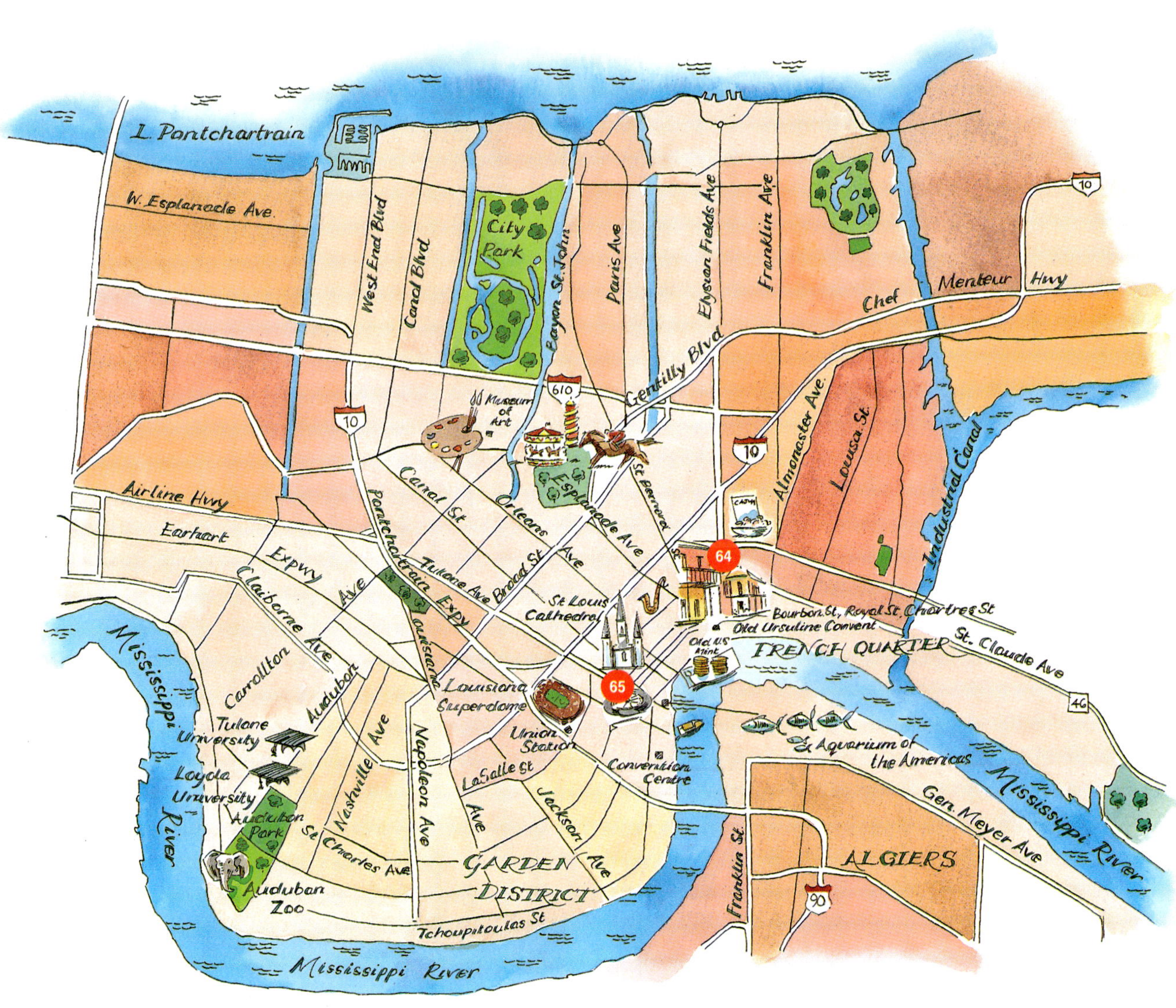

L. Pontchartrain
W. Esplanade Ave.
West End Blvd
Canal Blvd
City Park
Bayou St. John
Paris Ave
Elysian Fields Ave
Franklin Ave
Chef Menteur Hwy
Gentilly Blvd
Museum of Art
Airline Hwy
Earhart Expwy
Canal St
Orleans Ave
Esplanade Ave
St Bernard
Almonaster Ave
Louisa St
Industrial Canal
Pontchartrain Expy
Tulane Ave
Broad St
Claiborne Ave
St Louis Cathedral
Bourbon St, Royal St, Chartres St
Old Ursuline Convent
Old US Mint
FRENCH QUARTER
St. Claude Ave
Mississippi River
Carrollton
Audubon
Tulane University
Loyola University
Audubon Park
Audubon Zoo
Louisiana
Louisiana Superdome
Union Station
Nashville Ave
Napoleon Ave
LaSalle St
Jackson Ave
Convention Centre
Aquarium of the Americas
Gen. Meyer Ave
Franklin St
ALGIERS
St Charles Ave
GARDEN DISTRICT
Tchoupitoulas St
64
65
10
610
90
46

THE CLAIBORNE MANSION

2111 DAUPHINE STREET, NEW ORLEANS, LOUISIANA 70116
TEL: 1 504 949 7327 FAX 1 504 949 0388

This historic, cream and white hotel with its attractive ironwork is situated overlooking the greenery of Washington Square Park in the popular and vibrant French Quarter of New Orleans. Surrounded by art galleries, jazz clubs and restaurants, it has been tastefully restored to its original 1850's Greek Revival style and is listed in the national historic register as an outstanding example of the American-plan house in an urban setting. Its rooms are high and spacious and the décor and furnishings exquisite. Ambience is old world yet upbeat like a jazz ensemble, echoing all that is unique in New Orleans, offering visitors 19th century elegance and style with 20th century comforts and amenities. Soft, comfortable sofas and armchairs, highly polished wooden floors, richly patterned curtains and gentle colourings contribute to a homely, friendly and sophisticated atmosphere. Owner Cleo Pelleteri's attitude is free and easy. Guests may come and go as they please and are even encouraged to tell her when they feel like having their breakfast served. The five spacious en suite bedrooms and two suites are beautifully furnished and have large tester beds. All the facilities are individually controlled including the air conditioning. Guests can relax and enjoy the sunshine in a little garden which surrounds a secluded pool. There is also an adjoining small cottage for those seeking extra privacy. **Directions**: The inn is just off Elysian Field, facing Washington Square. Price Guide: Rooms $150–$300.

7 rms · MasterCard · VISA · AMERICAN EXPRESS

WINDSOR COURT HOTEL

300 GRAVIER STREET, NEW ORLEANS, LOUISIANA 70130
TEL: 1 504 523 6000 FAX: 1 504 596 4513

This award winning hotel offers the most impeccable service you could hope to receive. The hotel has a British theme, hence its name, and the reception rooms are adorned with magnificent works of art. The majority of guest rooms are suites and are stylishly furnished with thick carpets, subtle fabrics and every possible amenity. The marble bathrooms are spacious and feature an array of toiletries and fluffy towels. The stunning open air pool on the fourth floor is ideal for relaxing after a long day whilst the more energetic may wish to make use of the well-equipped fitness centre. The Grill Room is presided over by a French chef who prepares exciting dishes which fuse the finest European flavours with the regional produce of the South. The hotel is beside the French quarter, with its attractive architecture and maze of interesting streets which are filled with antique shops, galleries, boutiques and curio. New Orleans is a wonderful area with a great variety of attractions. The lively nightlife may be experienced in the many jazz clubs, bars and restaurants. For those who wish to explore further afield there is the Bayou region and a fine array of plantation houses, for which the South is famous. **Directions:** Take I–10, east to downtown, Superdome exit (234B exit), right on Poydras Street, down 1 mile, left on South Peters (2nd to last traffic light before Mississippi River), 1 block down, take left onto Gravier Street and left into the hotel courtyard. Price guide: Rooms $250; suite $340–$675.

The Duff Green Mansion

1114 FIRST EAST STREET, VICKSBURG, MISSISSIPPI 39180
TEL: 1 601 636 6968 FAX: 1 601 661 0079

A long, wide stairway leads onto the wrought-iron fenced porch fronting the white doorway of this magnificent mansion situated in the historic district of Vicksburg. Considered to be one of the finest examples of Palladian architecture in the State, it escaped destruction during and after the Civil War's siege by serving as a hospital for Confederate and Union soldiers. Beneath its high ceilings and richly decorated walls of cardinal reds, deep blues and rich greens the polished floors carry bloodstained marks from wounds. In one room, the ceiling beams show where a cannon-ball struck. Original works of art hang throughout and most of the furniture is antique. Duff Green contains seven luxurious bedrooms and suites with amenities to satisfy the expectations of the most discerning visitor. All have an individual character, open fireplaces and porches where guests can relax in the evening air. Guests may also enjoy the free bar in one of the charming reception rooms and during the day can sunbathe on the secluded patio surrounds of a swimming pool. Vicksburg is famous for its battlefield where Civil War skirmishes are re-enacted. It also has regular jazz festivals. **Directions:** From Jackson, take I-20 west and exit at 4B into Clay Street. After approximately 2½ miles turn into Cherry Street. First East Street is on the right. Price guide: Rooms $75–$110; suites £105–$160.

FAIRVIEW INN

734 FAIRVIEW STREET, JACKSON, MISSISSIPPI 39202
TEL: 601 948 3429 FAX: 601 948 1203 TOLL FREE: 888 948 1908

This gracious pillared white house with its sweeping driveway and beautifully landscaped gardens is reminiscent of George Washington's Mount Vernon residence. Situated in the exclusive Belhaven District of Jackson, it is a grand Colonial Revival house listed in the National Register of Historic Places. From the moment guests step into the traditional hallway, the charm and luxurious atmosphere of this property is apparent, with reception rooms to left and right, sparkling chandeliers and polished wooden floors scattered with antique rugs. The Simmons family has owned the house since 1930: there are old family portraits, photographs and crests tracing the history of the family name. The house has two luxurious bedrooms and six opulent suites. All incorporate the original characteristics of 1908 when the house was built combined with every accessory and comfort that today's visitor expects. Two of the suites are very private and have their own entrances and car parking. There is a large, elegant dining room where co-owner Carol Simmons and her French chef serve excellent gourmet meals. The hotel is close to the centre of Jackson and its historical attractions, art galleries, museums and theatres. **Directions**: From I-55 exit at 98A into Woodrow Wilson Drive. Turn left at the first traffic lights into North State Street and Fairview Street is first left after the second traffic lights. Price guide: Rooms $115; suite $165.

8 rms | MasterCard | VISA | AMERICAN EXPRESS | other | M 150

Monmouth Plantation

36 MELROSE AVENUE, NATCHEZ, MISSISSIPPI 39120
TEL: 1 601 442 5852 FAX: 1 601 446 7762

This glorious Greek Revival plantation house is a National Historic Landmark and was once the home of General Quitman. Monmouth Plantation has won many accolades and is considered to be one of the ten most romantic destinations in America. The house is a fascinating testimony to the achievements of General Quitman. The big white mansion stands in 26 acres of landscaped grounds with rose gardens, fountains, a gazebo and bridge over the sparkling lake. The present owners combine the grandeur of the period with their own impeccable taste. The glorious salons feature graceful chairs, magnificent antiques, tapestries and marble fireplaces adorned with elaborate gilt and ormolu clocks. No smoking is mandatory throughout. The guest rooms in the main house are traditional 19th century with tester beds, armoires and other period furniture, while those in the carriage house, cottages and old kitchen reflect a later era. All are sumptuous with plush carpets, comfortable couches and a vast array of personal touches. Towelling robes with the Monmouth Crest hang in the marble bathrooms. The opulent suites have Jacuzzis and elegant living areas. In the evenings guests are invited to meet for hors d'oeuvres and apéritifs in the charming courtyard before enjoying a superb four-course meal in the formal dining room. The Natchez trail is only a short drive away. **Directions:** The house is on Melrose Avenue at the John A Quitman Parkway. Price guide: Rooms $128–$175; suite $155–$350.

28 rms · MasterCard · VISA · AMERICAN EXPRESS · other · M 50 · 14

Florida, Georgia and South Carolina

CHALET SUZANNE

3800 CHALET SUZANNE DRIVE, LAKE WALES, FLORIDA 33853–7060
TEL: 1 941 676 6011 FAX: 1 941 676 1814

This is a small part of heaven in Central Florida – a Swiss oasis! This enchanting small hotel stands in 70 acres of parkland and tropical trees. It has been brilliantly designed, a series of chalets round a paved courtyard ensure that each guest room has its own private entrance and balcony or patio. The rooms are beautifully decorated in joyous colours, each different from the next, air-conditioned and with many luxurious amenities. The bathrooms are mostly vast and several have jet tubs. Splendid hospitality trays await new arrivals! The Hinshaws have been superb hosts for many years and welcomed many prestigious guests. The Little Swedish Lounge (the bar) has an inviting ambience and the Wine Cellar is fascinating. The pièce de résistance is the acclaimed restaurant, with its Art Deco stained glass windows and lovely table settings complementing the absolutely brilliant cooking, always exquisitely presented. Strolling in the park by the lake or a gentle game of croquet is therapeutic. The pool is close to the chalets. The hotel has a boutique, ceramic studio and chapel antiques. Tours of Chalet Suzanne Soup Cannery can be arranged! Florida high life and Disney World are nearby. Good golf is accessible. **Directions:** The Chalet has its own small airstrip. From Interstate 4, take exit 23, go south on US27 for 18.5 miles. Turn left onto Chalet Suzanne Road. Price guide: Rooms $159–$219; suite $219.

30 rms · MasterCard · VISA · AMERICAN EXPRESS · other · M 30

THE CURRY MANSION INN

511 CAROLINE STREET, KEY WEST, FLORIDA 33040
TEL: 1 305 294 5349 FAX: 1 305 294 4093 E-MAIL: frontdesk@currymansion.com

A relaxed and welcoming ambience envelopes this intimate inn, set in the heart of Florida's Key West and listed on the National Register of Historic Places. The Curry Mansion Inn, a charming Victorian home, offers the elegance and refined atmosphere of bygone times. The public rooms are beautifully appointed with an abundance of antique furnishings. Surrounding an attractive courtyard and heated pool, the guest rooms adjoin the mansion and are decorated with soft fabrics and wicker. All offer wet bars, small refrigerators, cable television and en suite facilities. Complimentary breakfast, often including freshly baked muffins and other home-made treats, is served buffet-style around the pool each morning whilst the daily cocktail parties provide guests with an ideal opportunity to mingle and converse. The inn has no restaurant, but is conveniently located in the Old Town area where fine dining establishments abound. Fitness enthusiasts will be pleased with the swimming pool and hot tub. All guests of the Curry Mansion Inn receive complimentary membership at the Marriott's Casa Marina and Pier House's private beach club; both within easy reach. A wide range of water sports may be practised nearby and include snorkelling and scuba-diving. **Directions:** The hotel 150 miles south of Miami, at the southern tip of the Florida Keys. Price guide: Rooms $125–$220; suite $175–$275.

22 rms

HERON HOUSE

512 SIMONTON STREET, KEY WEST, 33040 FLORIDA
TEL: 1 305 294 9227 FAX: 1 305 294 5692

Set in the heart of Florida's Key West, Heron House is refreshingly informal in style and exudes a relaxing and welcoming atmosphere. The result is a peaceful retreat complemented by the polite and unobtrusive staff; ideal for those seeking a quiet weekend or break. The inn has been carefully designed by some of the area's most talented craftsmen and the artistic detail is evident throughout the property, which has won several prestigious awards and accolades. Original watercolours of the Keys adorn the walls of the public rooms. With private decks and balconies, the bedrooms are spacious and enhanced by the use of natural materials such as oak and cedar. The array of thoughtful extras include soft bathrobes and morning newspapers. A generous Continental breakfast is served alfresco-style beside the pool. Guests may relax on the multi-level sun decks or in the cool shade of the Chicago brick patios. Nature enthusiasts can take a stroll through the tropical gardens and admire the brilliant colours emanating from the rare orchids. Heron House is only one block away from the famous Duval Street with its boutiques and galleries. **Directions:** Take the US Highway 1 to Key West and turn right on to Roosevelt Boulevard followed by Truman Avenue. Continue to Simington and turn right. The hotel is 4½ blocks away on the left. Price Guide: Rooms from $119; suite $119–$329.

23 rms MasterCard VISA AMERICAN EXPRESS 12

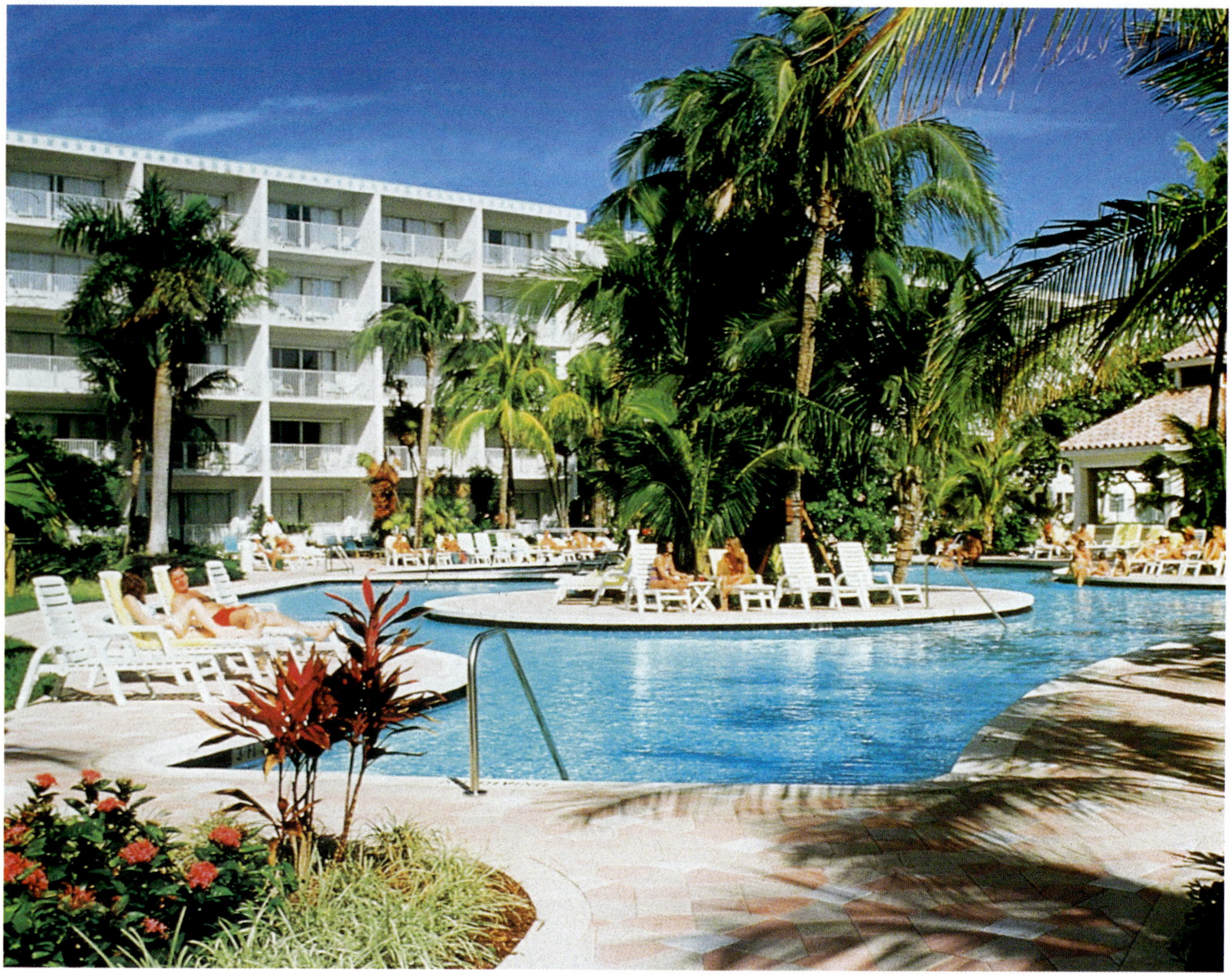

LAGO MAR

1700 SOUTH OCEAN LANE, FORT LAUDERDALE, FLORIDA 33316
TEL: 1 954 523 6511 FAX: 1 954 524 6627

The traditional legacy of warmth and hospitality combined with excellent service has continued through three generations of the Banks family, resulting in a most charming property. The gardens are enchanting with palm trees, a lagoon, an arched footbridge and beautiful colours emanating from the hibiscus, alamanda and bougainvillaea. The spacious bedrooms are the essence of luxury, affording views over the ocean, lake or gardens. Comfortable furnishings and dining areas are complemented by the vast range of modern amenities. The attractive Lounge is enhanced by hand-painted table tops and an elegant grand piano and is often frequented by those seeking a pre-dinner drink. Continental and American cuisine with a hint of Caribbean flavours can be savoured in the formal restaurant or enjoyed in the coffee shop, grill or terrace. Sports enthusiasts will enjoy the two swimming pools, miniature golf course and four tennis courts, overlooking either the lakes or the ocean. Water-taxis are available to take guests to the many nearby attractions. The cruise ships at Port Everglades, the Convention Center and many major sports venues are within easy reach. South Florida is surrounded by several fine restaurants, amusement parks and exquisite shops. **Directions:** The hotel is just 10 minutes away from Fort Lauderdale's International Airport. Price Guide: Rooms $100–$285; suite $285–$600.

Ocean Front Hotel

1230–38 OCEAN DRIVE, MIAMI BEACH, FLORIDA 33139
TEL: 1 305 672 2579 FAX: 1 305 672 7665

Nestling on the foot of the beach and ocean, this charming hotel boasts a Mediterranean façade and an interior enhanced by Art Deco original pieces, typical of properties in the Miami Beach area. Service is an important criterion and the friendly and enthusiastic staff aim for excellence. French and English antiques adorn the public rooms whilst authentic 1930's furniture may be found throughout the house. The 27 bedrooms, all with en suite facilities, contain many thoughtful additions such as a safe, colour television and video, a mini-bar and soft bathrobes. Whirlpools, balconies and private elevators are displayed in the penthouse suites, affording glorious views of the ocean. The convivial restaurant and café, Les Deux Fontaines, offers a creative menu complemented by stylish presentation. Specialising in seafood, popular dishes include local produce and tropical fish such as Mahi-Mahi, lobster and yellowtail. The restaurant is ideal for private dining or banquets, seating up to 400 people. The hotel is just steps away from the beach and sea, perfect for strolls along the warm white sands or a dip in the ocean. Other nearby outdoor pursuits include tennis, water-skiing, golf, fishing or shooting. **Directions:** From Miami airport, take the MacArthur Causeway. Follow the signs to Miami Beach and then on to Ocean Drive. Turn left, proceed 7 blocks and the hotel is between 12th and 13th Street. Price Guide: Rooms $179–$215; suite $275–$325; penthouse $515.

27 rms MasterCard VISA AMERICAN EXPRESS M 40

The Richmond

1757 COLLINS AVE, MIAMI BEACH, FLORIDA 33139
TEL: 1 305 538 2331 FAX: 1 305 531 9021 E-MAIL: reservations@richmondhotel.com

"The Richmond is a modern Art Deco masterpiece". Located directly on the ocean front, the dazzling swimming pool and huge half-moon heated Jacuzzi are surrounded by a nationally honoured tropical garden of indigenous coconut palms, blooming bougainvillaea and a myriad of other exotic foliage. It is idyllic and joyful by day and wonderfully romantic at night. The Verandah Café is beautifully situated overlooking the pools and features a bountiful choice of favourite dishes. There is also a fully-equipped fitness centre. The bedrooms are charming and restful; many with glorious views. Everything is appointed with top line cotton linens. The Richmond is a short walking distance from the Miami Beach Convention Center, Lincoln Road, Ocean Drive, restaurants, clubs and shops. The Richmond considers itself to be more than a hotel; it is the three generations of the family that built the Richmond and continue to personally welcome visitors from around the world. **Directions:** Take Airport Expressway 112 East (direction Miami Beach) to the Toll Plaza. Continue East to I–195 (Miami Beach). Exit on Alton Road South to 17th Street. Left on 17th Street to Collins Avenue (AIA). Left on Collins Avenue. The Richmond is located 3/4 block north on the East Side (Oceanside) Collins Avenue. Valet parking. Price guide: Rooms $170–$275; suite $325–$400.

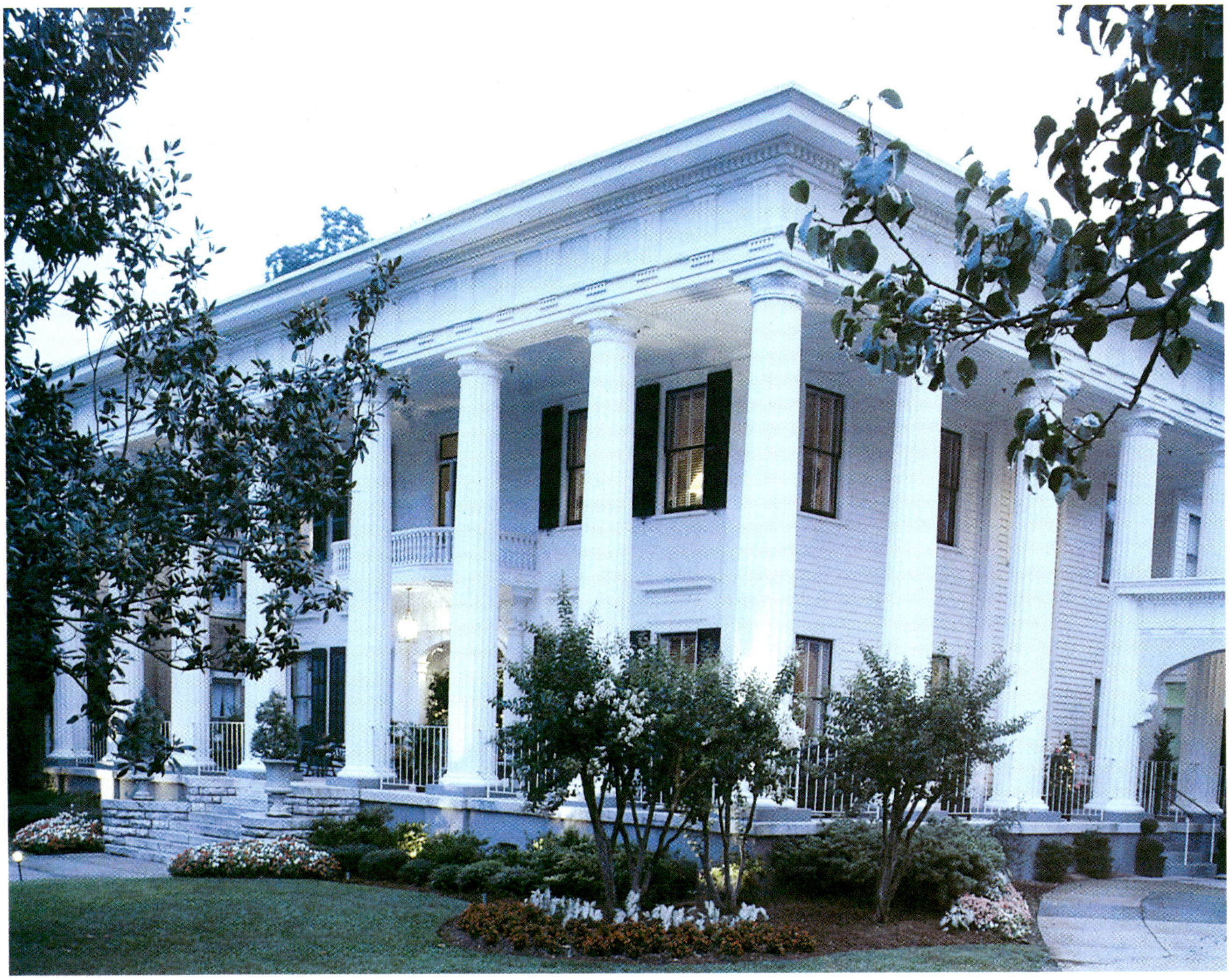

1842 Inn

353 COLLEGE STREET, MACON, GEORGIA 31201
TEL: 1 912 741 1842 FAX: 1 912 741 1842 TOLL FREE: 1 800 336 1842

This imposing townhouse hotel was built in 1842 as the home of the Mayor of Macon. The main building is a dramatic Greek revival house with Palladian columns and the Inn has expanded into an adjoining Victorian carriage house. The two are linked by an unusual courtyard and garden, filled with flowers and amusing statuary. '1842' is on the National Register of Historic Places. The interior is captivating – graceful chandeliers, Adam-style chimney pieces, priceless antiques, elegant drapes and fascinating memorabilia. The bedrooms are delightful, with canopied beds. The bathrooms are twentieth century, as are the luxurious amenities provided. Breakfast is brought to the guest rooms as there is no restaurant – however residents have complimentary membership of an élite private dining and health club and Macon has excellent restaurants. Apéritifs and hors d'oeuvres are available each evening in the Library or on the cool long terrace and nightcaps can be ordered when returning from dining out. Swimming, golf and tennis privileges have been arranged at the River North Country Club. Macon has a fine opera house and theatres. **Directions:** From Interstate 75 take exit 52 downtown, Hardeman Avenue, after two traffic lights turn left into College Street finding the Inn after two further sets of lights. Price guide: Rooms $105–$165.

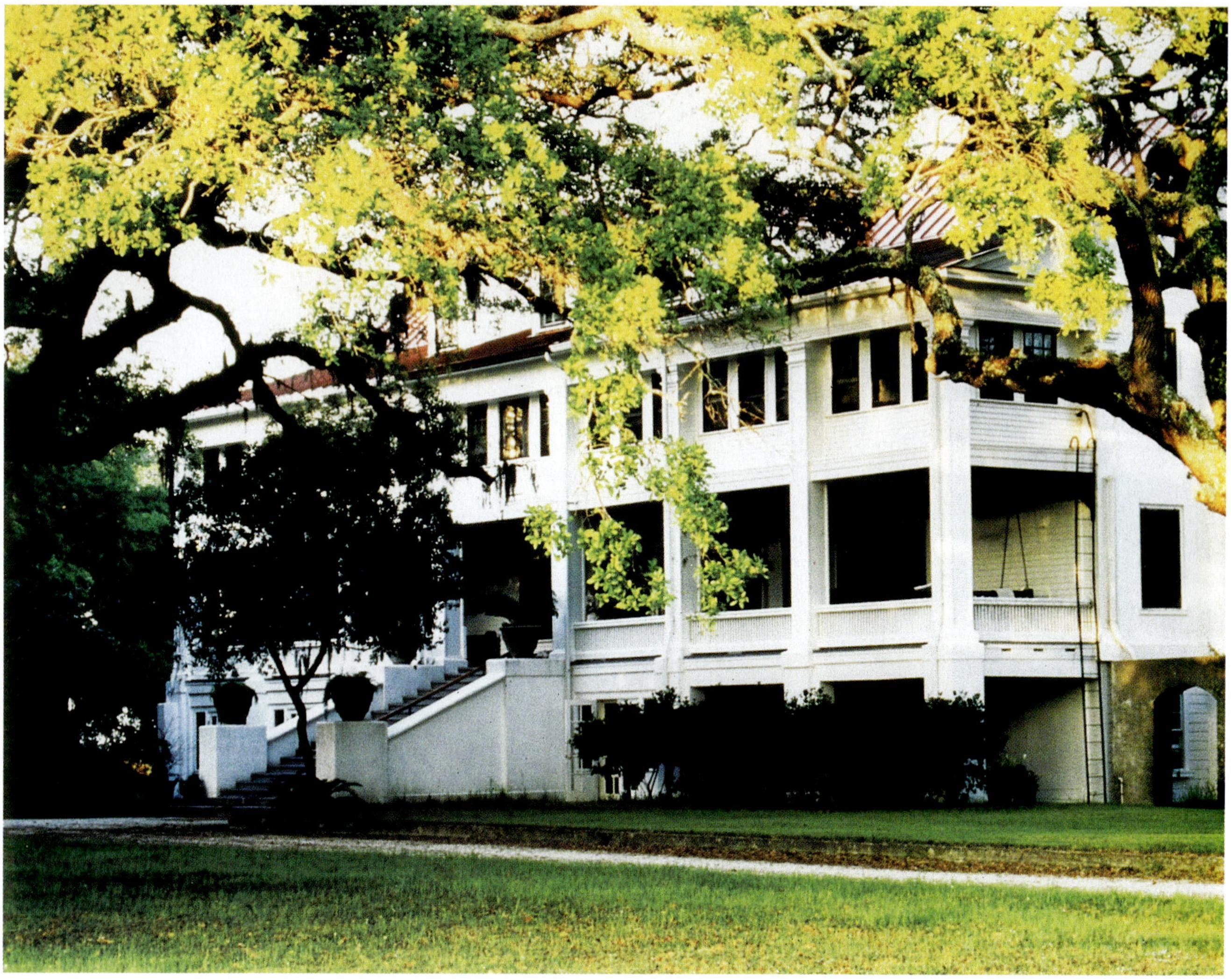

Greyfield Inn

CUMBERLAND ISLAND, PO BOX 900, FERNANDINA BEACH, FLORIDA 32035-0900
TEL: 1 904 261 6408 FAX: 1 904 321 0666

This lovely mansion is located on Georgia's largest and most southerly barrier island, Cumberland Island, although the postal address is Florida! Much of the island has been designated as a National Seashore, protecting it from development. The limited number of visitors allowed daily ensures a peaceful environment for the wild horses, deer, armadillos and numerous species of birds that make their home here. Greyfield's private area includes more than 1,300 acres and guests can spend their days swimming, hiking, beach combing, clam-digging and hunting for sharks' teeth. A memorable breakfast includes orange juice, muffins, fruit pancakes and smoothies. A picnic lunch in a basket is prepared for enjoying on the porch – a favourite place for reading and relaxing – or taking to the beach. In the evening, the gourmet dinner is a more formal affair. It is served in the candlelit dining room, which is decorated with flowers and offers a stunning view of the island's sunsets. The nightly entrée comprises seafood, game hen, lamb or beef tenderloin, home-made breads, fresh vegetables and delicious desserts. A small, but excellent wine list accompanies the menu. Greyfield maintains a well-stocked bar, located in the gun room. The well-appointed bedrooms are air-conditioned. **Directions:** Leave I–95 to exit 129 in Florida, then A1A to Amelia Island to the ferry terminal. Price guide: Rooms £275–£395.

HENDERSON VILLAGE

125 SOUTH LANGSTON CIRCLE, PERRY, GEORGIA 31069
TEL: 1 912 988 8696 FAX: 1 912 988 9009

This is hunting country and Henderson Village is the ideal base from which to venture out with gun and rod to get "the big ones". A collection of charming cottages in the style of 19th century Southern plantation houses, graced with wide shady porches, nestle in the heart of the village which is situated in trophy buck country. Each of the 28 guest rooms and suites is individually decorated with fine fabrics, artwork and antiques. All have luxurious baths and a wide selection of modern facilities. Most have fireplaces. Excellent regional American cuisine prepared by an award winning French chef is served in the attractive restaurant at Langston House and breakfast can be served to guests in their room or on their porch. Serpentine brick paths lead to rolling pastures and formal gardens which feature a swimming pool and twin gazebos. The village is surrounded by 10,000 acres of prime hunting land. There are Booner and Crocket Bucks, wild quails for the wing shooter, boars that can top the scales at 500 pounds and eight ponds stocked with fish such as bass, catfish and bream. Wild boar and turkey hunt packages may be combined with fishing. **Directions:** From Atlanta, take the I-75 south to exit 41. Turn right and travel approximately one mile to the first intersection. Henderson Village is on the right. Price guide: Rooms $145–$185; suite $205.

28 rms · MasterCard · VISA · AMERICAN EXPRESS

THE LODGE ON LITTLE ST. SIMONS ISLAND

PO BOX 21078, ST. SIMONS ISLAND, GEORGIA 31522
TEL: 1 912 638 7472 FAX: 1 912 634 1811 E-MAIL: lssi@mindspring.com

Robinson Crusoe might have loved this perfect place. The Lodge on Little St. Simons Island refreshes and invigorates the soul, placing the visitor firmly and comfortably in touch with nature. The island, the smallest of many that cluster off the coast of Georgia between Savannah and Jacksonville can be reached by private boat through the salt marshes. Nature lovers feel wonderful when they stay at The Lodge, a unique inn on this wildlife sanctuary, a haven of peace and outstanding beauty. Accommodation is in five cabins, with rustic furnishings, nothing elaborate but extremely comfortable, with plenty of hot water for showers after a day's activities. Breakfast is at 9 o'clock and those not wishing to lunch may request picnic baskets. Guests meet for cocktails and canapés early evening and dine together at 7.30, enjoying traditional regional dishes, the wine flows. No smoking indoors! Preservation of the creatures in this environment – and protection of the Lodge residents – is paramount and codes of behaviour have been established. There is so much to do – Interpretive Naturalist programmes, riding, canoeing, swimming, fishing, cycling and there is transport down to the beach. Ornithologists have an opportunity to see the rarest species. **Directions:** Arrive by boat from Hampton Club Marina on St Simon's Island (not far from Brunswick). Price guide: Rooms $325–$550; suite $400–$600. Full Island rental available.

15 rms 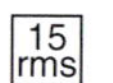    30     

MELHANA PLANTATION

301 SHOWBOAT LANE, THOMASVILLE, GEORGIA 31792
TEL: 1 888 920 3030 FAX: 1 912 226 4585

Melhana Plantation was originally developed as a quail hunting plantation and now comprises 30 historic buildings set in 50 acres. Impressive moss-laden oaks and sweet-smelling magnolias line the entrance to the main house, where elegantly-appointed suites are available to guests. All feature king or queen-sized beds, cable channel television, jacuzzi tubs and fresh flowers. Generous breakfasts, served in the elegant dining room or garden loggia, include delicious breads baked in the kitchen. Afternoon tea is provided in the Hogan Room. There is world class fine dining in the restaurant featuring excellent southern regional cuisine with white glove service.

A heated indoor swimming pool and fitness centre are among the many leisure facilities available, while sightseeing opportunities in the surrounding area abound. Thomasville boasts many architecturally significant structures, including the Museum at Pebble Hill Plantation. The Thomas County Museum of History offers a view of south-western Georgia in the past. **Directions:** From 1-75 take exit 4 to Highway 84 west to Thomasville. From Thomasville travel south on Highway 319 to Melhana Plantation. The inn is located approximately 6 miles south of Thomasville on Highway 319 south. Price guide: Suites $250–$450.

Savannah

SAVANNAH RIVER
Riverfront Plaza
Franklin Sq
City Market
Bay Street
Bryan Street
Barnard Sq
State Street
Oglethorpe Ave
Orleans Sqre
Civic Center
Chippewa Sq
Davenport House
Owens-Thomas House
Colonial Park Cemetery
East Broad Street
Liberty Street
Macon Street
Pecan Pie
Montgomery Street
Barnard Street
Whitaker Street
Bull Street
Drayton Street
West Jones Street
East Jones Street
East Gaston Street
Mercer House
MARTIN LUTHER KING JR. BLVD
16 WEST
16 EAST
83
84
85
86
87

THE ELIZA THOMPSON HOUSE

5 WEST JONES STREET, SAVANNAH, GEORGIA 31401
TEL: 1 912 236 3620 FAX: 1 912 238 1920

The Eliza Thompson House, built in 1847, offers a delightful fusion of past and present times with traditions and customs of the last century and the comforts and amenities of today. Set on a quiet residential street, the house is one of the oldest inns in the heart of Savannah's historical district and is an architectural landmark. Meticulous restoration work has resulted in the superb interior, enhanced by heart pine floors and antique furnishings. Guests may stay in either the 12 stately rooms in the main house or in the Carriage House, which boasts a further 13 rooms. All the bedrooms are furnished in an exquisite style with en suite facilities and colour televisions. In addition, some main house rooms have charming fireplaces. The soft bathrobes and make-up mirrors are thoughtful extras. The breakfast is imaginative and extensive, comprising home-made recipes with fresh, local ingredients. Other delightful traditions include afternoon tea, served in the parlour, or the daily cheese and wine reception in the evening. Guests may relax in the beautifully landscaped courtyard, where the air is scented with southern fragrances and the gentle sound of the Ivan Bailey fountain may be heard. Savannah is a wonderful town to explore with many antique shops, museums and old churches nearby. **Directions:** Travel east on I-16, towards Savannah. Exit at Montgomery Street, turn right at traffic lights on Liberty Street. Turn right on Whitaker Street and left onto Jones Street. Price Guide: Rooms $89–$199.

25 rms MasterCard VISA M 18 12

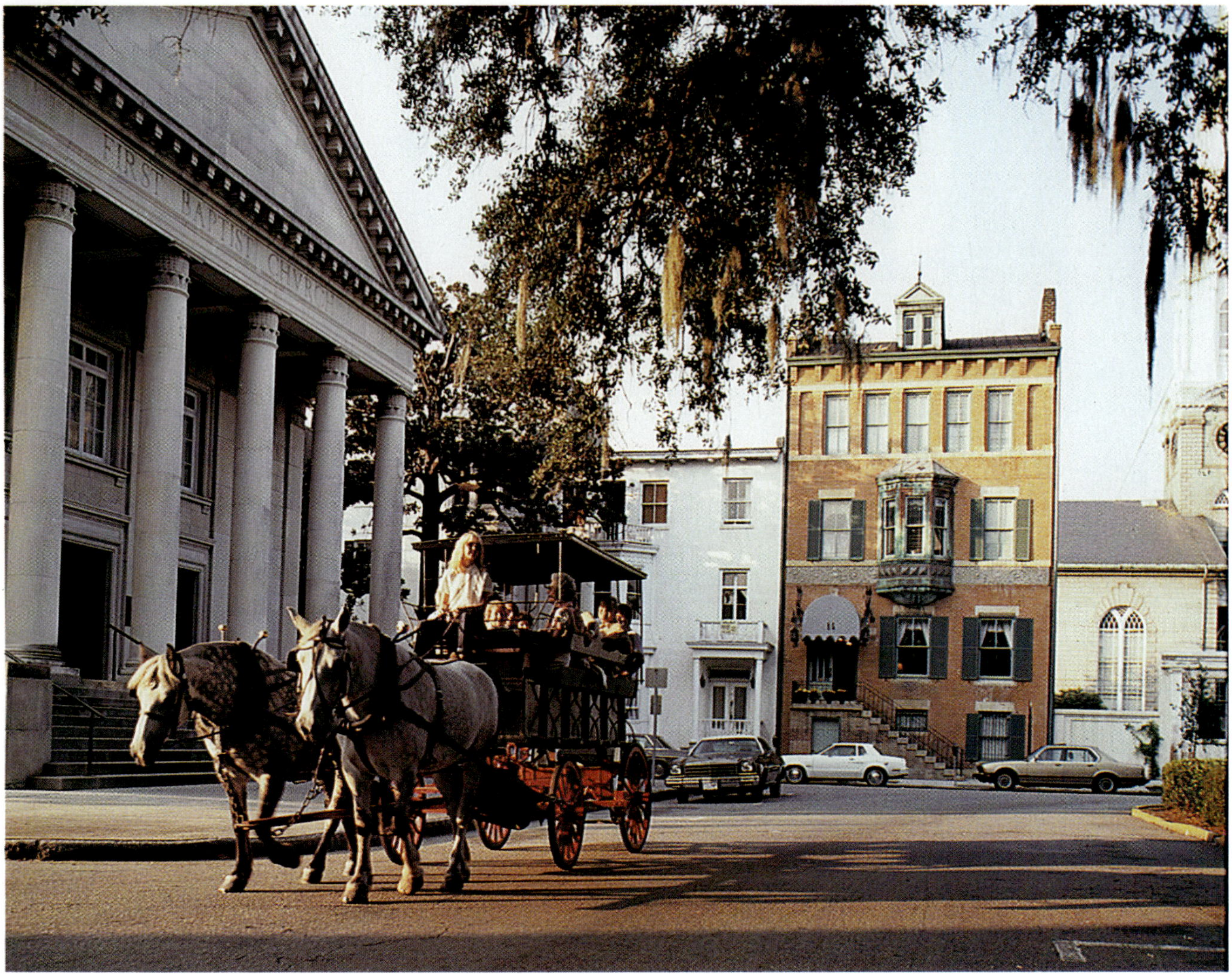

Foley House Inn

14 WEST HULL, CHIPPEWA SQUARE, SAVANNAH, GEORGIA 31401
TEL: 1 912 232 6622 FAX: 1 912 231 1218 E-MAIL: foleyinn@AOL.COM

Savannah is steeped in history, with its port today, as in the past, an important role. The steamship Savannah, built here, was the first to cross the Atlantic. The elegance of the Old Town reflects the gracious way of life centuries ago and it is therefore an immense pleasure to enter the Foley House Inn, a town house which has been carefully and authentically restored by craftsmen, whilst discreetly introducing essential modern comforts. Today it is a prestigious and exclusive inn, offering old world courtesy. The house is approached by a staircase and the canopied entrance features lanterns on either side. Elaborate plasterwork and shutters add to its classical charm. The interior is rather romantic with fine wall hangings, delicate chandeliers, graceful furniture, superb paintings and beautiful flowers. This style extends to the bedrooms (some situated in the adjacent Carriage House). The bathrooms are welcoming, with striking wallpapers, ornate friezes, marble surrounds and gold taps. The Parlour is where guests gather for breakfast, evening hors d'oeuvres, cocktails or a glass of fine wine. Other treats include afternoon tea, coffee and lemonade, during the summer months. The Concierge will suggest where to dine locally and arrange concert or theatre reservations. Exploring Savannah is fascinating, with its waterfront, old churches, parks, museums and galleries. **Directions:** Street parking only. The inn occupies a corner of Chippewa Square. Price guide: Rooms $135–$250.

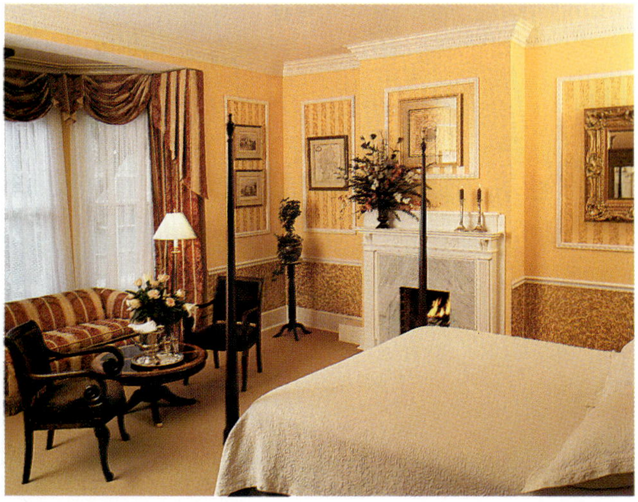

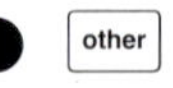

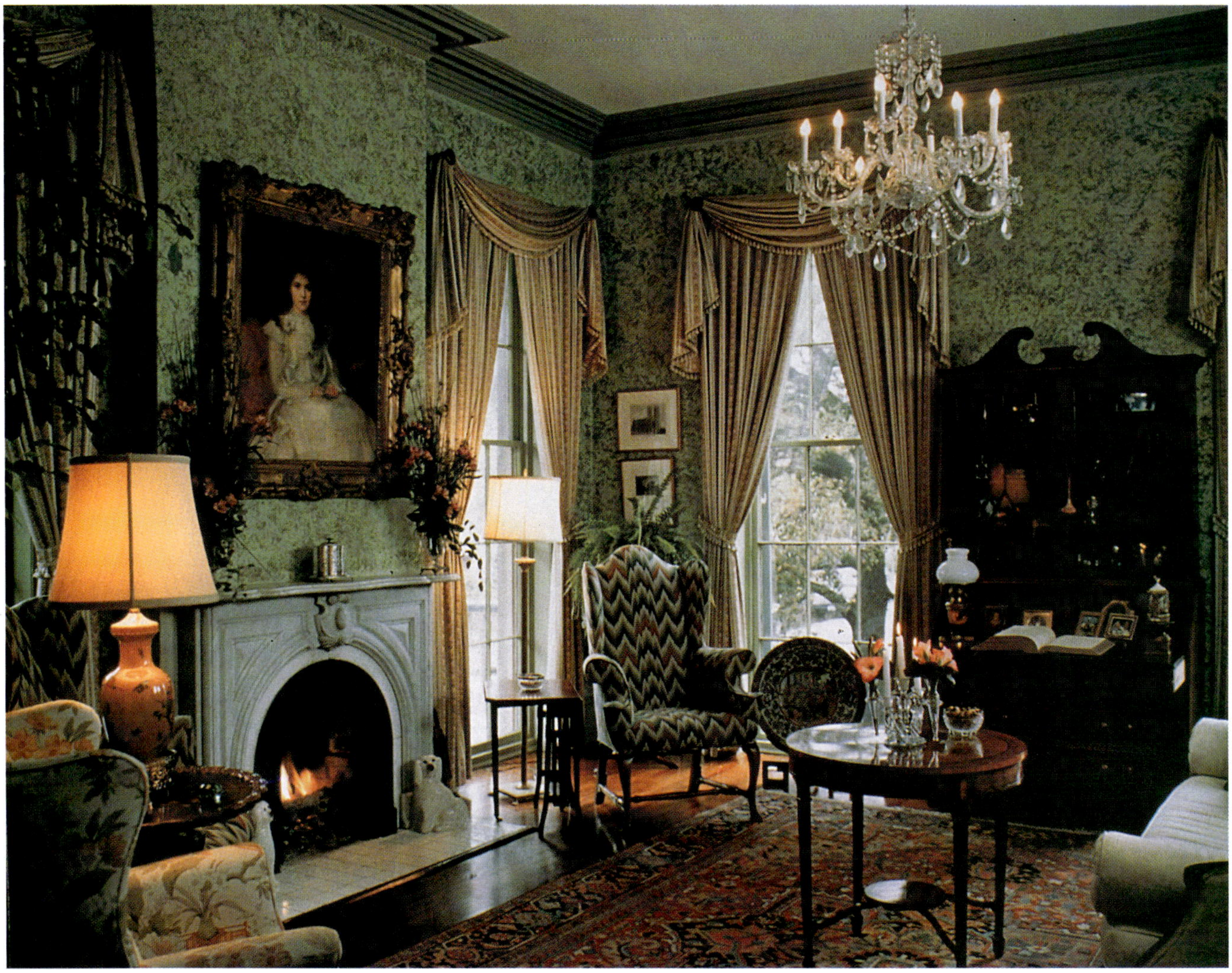

THE GASTONIAN

220 EAST GASTON STREET, SAVANNAH, GEORGIA 31401
TEL: 1 912 232 2869 FAX: 1 912 232 0710 E-MAIL: Gastoniann@aol.com

This graceful inn, with its elegant wrought iron detail enhancing the Georgian facade, was once two fine private town houses, built soon after the end of the Civil War. Inspired reconstruction and renovation has resulted in The Gastonian, an elite and immaculate small hotel in a secluded residential street close to the centre of the town. The interior is dignified, the welcome cordial and the ambience that of good living The wallcoverings and rich hues of the décor reflect careful research into historic Savannah's homes and are perfect settings for authentic Regency antiques and intriguing memorabilia. The guest rooms are flawless, the individual themes being French, Italian, Victorian, Colonial American and Countrystyle. Luxurious towelling robes await residents in the delightful bathrooms – the Caracalla Suite has a draped whirlpool tub for two! The Carriage House at the back of the Inn is now a romantic bridal suite. Breakfast is a feast, afternoon tea a delight and the day ends with complimentary port or sherry in the the Parlour. Excellent restaurants for dining are in walking distance. Savannah offers historic buildings, a fascinating port and a verdant park, reached by horse-drawn buses and trams. **Directions:** The hotel is mid-town, with parking. Price guide: Rooms $200–$375.

THE JESSE MOUNT HOUSE

209 WEST JONES STREET, SAVANNAH, GEORGIA 31401
TEL: 1 912 236 1774 FAX: 1 912 236 2103 E-MAIL: rob@jessemounthouse.com

This historic port and important city played a prominent part in the War of Independence and the Civil War. It was "Gone With The Wind" country! Savannah today is evocative of the past, with its hidden gardens, cobbled streets and elegant architecture and the famed Southern hospitality has lingered on. The Jesse Mount House was built in 1856 surviving those turbulent years to become a legendary inn. The pride of the establishment is the exceptional personalised service and attention lavished on the guests. New arrivals are enchanted by its graceful façade. The parlour is nostalgic – lovely sofas and fine rugs, a chandelier and handsome portraits. The guest rooms are exotic and romantic, furnished with antiques and memorabilia, each unique in style. The bathrooms have whirlpool tubs, towelling robes and other luxuries. The complimentary gourmet breakfast in the jasmine scented courtyard is idyllic; on cooler days it is taken in the exquisite antebellum dining room. Afternoon tea is also served. In the evenings, perhaps after a refreshing drink in their rooms, guests dine in one of the restaurants nearby. Savannah is beautiful, with its port and historic buildings, galleries and Forsyth Park, to view from a horse-drawn bus! **Directions:** Take I-16 to Montgomery Street, turn right on Liberty Street, turn right on Whitaker Street and turn right on West Jones Street. Off-street parking. Price guide: Rooms/suite from $160.

THE PRESIDENT'S QUARTERS

225 EAST PRESIDENT STREET, SAVANNAH, GEORGIA 31401
TEL: 1 912 233 1600 FAX: 1 912 238 0849

Residing on Oglethorpe Square, these authentic Federal-style town houses were constructed by the estate of Andrew Gordon Low in 1855. Fashioned in the likeness of Savannah's Davenport House and as a neighbour of the renowned Owens-Thomas House, The President's Quarters opened its doors in 1987 after a careful restoration. With a long history of famous inhabitants and guests such as Robert E. Lee, each room is individually decorated celebrating 19 Presidents known to have enjoyed Savannah's southern hospitality. The spacious guest rooms feature regal wallcoverings and carefully chosen historic colours exclusive to grand homes of Savannah. Selected suites have balconies, romantic loft bedrooms and hand-painted ceilings. The inn is renowned for its fine service and hospitality. Those accustomed to pampering will enjoy the thoughtful extras such as soft bathrobes, a chilled bottle of wine and a basket of fresh fruit. Other delights include breakfast served in the rooms, sumptuous afternoon hors d'oeuvres and a nightly turndown service with bedside cordials and local sweets. Concierge service is available 24 hours for dining and entertainment suggestions and reservations. The night-life of River Street is only 3 blocks away! The many quaint shops will please those with an interest in curio. **Directions:** Take I-16 to Montgomery, right on Oglethorpe, left on Abercorn, right on York. Off-street parking. Price guide: Rooms $137–$157; suite $177–$225.

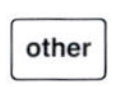

THE RHETT HOUSE INN

1009 CRAVEN STREET, BEAUFORT, SOUTH CAROLINA 29902
TEL: 1 843 524 9030 FAX: 1 843 524 1310 US TOLL FREE: 1 888 480 9530

Dating back to 1820, The Rhett House Inn was once an in-town plantation house; its huge verandahs and white columns still recall the charm and romance of the Old South. All the rooms are individually and exquisitely furnished with every amenity to provide the ultimate in comfort and convenience. Many have Queen or King-size beds, fireplaces and whirlpool bath tubs. Ideally designed for a romantic getaway, guest rooms in the recently renovated historic cottage feature private entrances and porches. A blend of American and English antiques fill the living room, which is the perfect place to relax and read a book. Healthy and delicious breakfasts include fresh fruits, pancakes, savoury French toast and eggs – all served with freshly brewed coffee. Gourmet picnics, available on request, are perfect for the beach, or waterfront and in the evening there is no better way to unwind than by enjoying a glass of wine or a home-made dessert on the verandah. Although biking is the preferred way of sightseeing, the lovely town of Beaufort can also be explored by foot and carriage tours. The welcoming staff are always happy to help arrange golf, tennis, swimming, fishing and kayaking. Hunting Island, Charleston and Savannah are all within easy reach. **Directions:** From the north, 1-95 exit 33 to Beaufort. From the south, 1-95 exit 8 to Beaufort. Follow the signs. Price guide: Rooms $150–$225.

Two Meeting Street Inn

2 MEETING STREET, CHARLESTON, SOUTH CAROLINA 29401
TEL: 1 843 723 7322

This beautiful Queen Anne style mansion, built in the early 1890s, enjoys a reputation as Charleston's most elegant bed and breakfast inn. The first thing guests notice as they approach the building is its unusually irregular exterior – created by fish-scaled turrets, multiple roof lines, bay windows and the curved piazza supported by double columned arches. The garden reflects these graceful contours with curved brick walkways leading through its century-old water oak, dogwood, cherry and tea olive trees. The house was a wedding present from a wealthy local jeweller to his daughter and her groom, Waring P. Carrington, and is now owned and managed with pride by the Spell family. Antiques, oriental rugs and heirloom accessories abound throughout. The entry foyer, with its generous use of carved English oak, panelled walls and cut-crystal Czechoslovakian chandelier quickly establishes the superb character of the house. Two stained glass windows by Tiffany are the exceptional features of the parlour, while the oval shape of the dining room is testimony to the Victorian love of shaped walls. Breakfast is served in the formal dining room/courtyard whilst tea is in the verandah or the formal parlour. Nine spacious and elegantly-appointed bedrooms, all en suite, afford unrivalled luxury. The Governor's House Inn is the family's second equally outstanding property. **Directions:** From 26E, exit Meeting Street, go south to corner of Meeting and South Battery. Price guide: Rooms $155–$265.

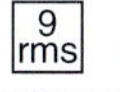   

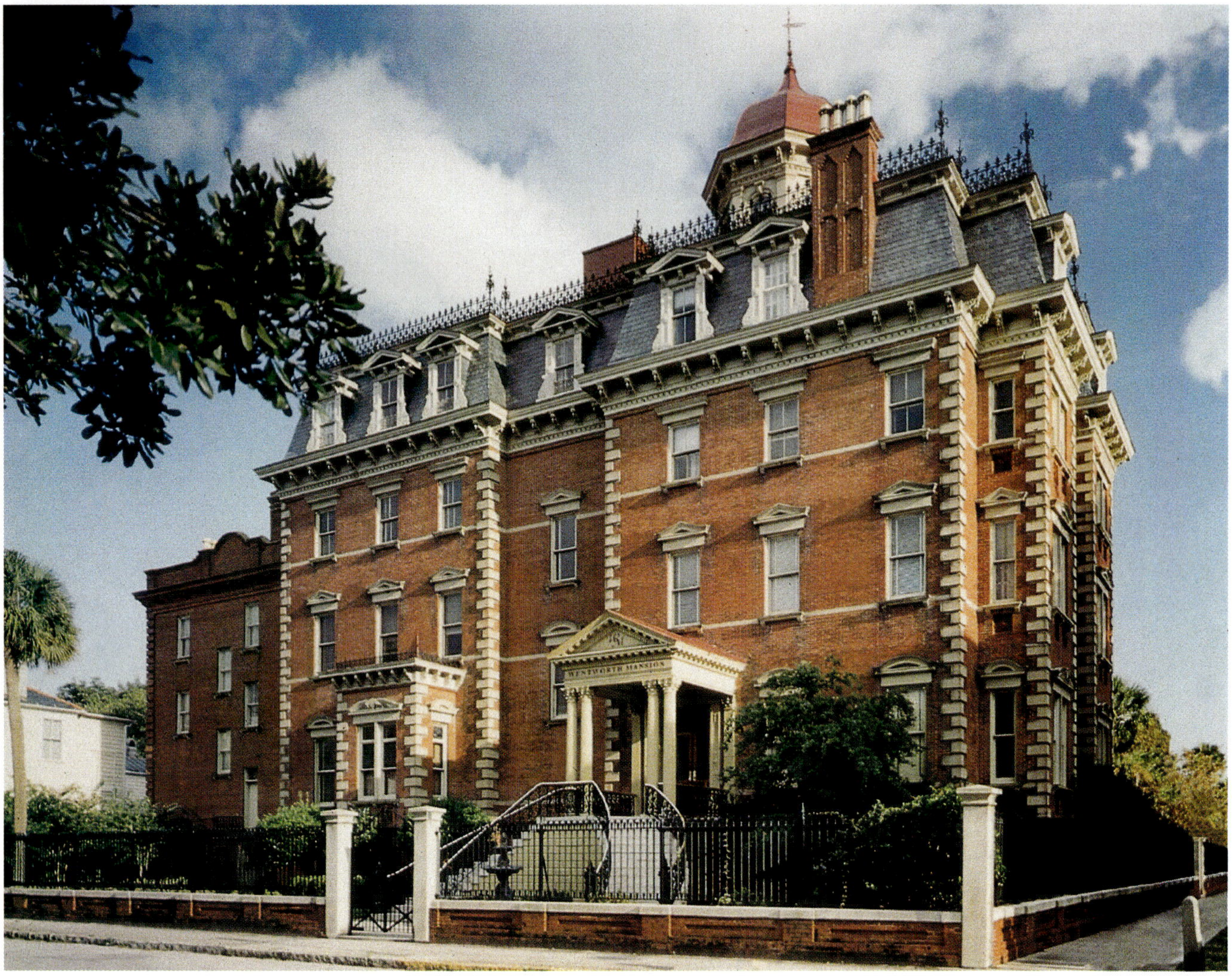

Wentworth Mansion

149 WENTWORTH STREET, CHARLESTON, SOUTH CAROLINA 29401
TEL: 1 843 853 1886 FAX: 1 843 720 5290 E-MAIL: mgr@wentworthmansion.com

Situated in the historic city of Charleston, the Wentworth Mansion evokes the image of America's Gilded Age. This magnificent residence is furnished in a most elaborate manner, with marble fireplaces and beautifully fashioned woodwork. Built in 1886, the house has undergone an extensive restoration, resulting in an excellent property offering fine accommodation and a refined ambience. The spacious bedrooms are adorned with fine antiques and contain luxurious whirlpools and king-size beds. Guests may relax with a book and enjoy the tranquil atmosphere of the Rodgers Library or laze on the sun porch of the Harleston Lounge, sipping a light apéritif. A stunning view of the Charleston skyline may be seen by climbing the spiral staircase up to the towering cupola. Daily events include wine tastings and breakfasts on the sun porch. Delicious treats are served for afternoon tea and feature in the evening turndown service. The hosts aim to recreate the same standard of cuisine in the new restaurant, due to open by the end of 1998. Guests may use the nearby fitness centre and practise a number of sports close by such as tennis and golf. **Directions:** On I–26 take exit Meeting Street, turn right on Meeting Street, then right on to John Street. Turn left onto King Street, then right onto Wentworth Street. The Wentworth Mansion is on the left, before the flashing traffic lights. Price guide: Rooms $275–$475; suite $475–$675.

21 rms     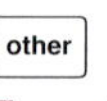    

North Carolina

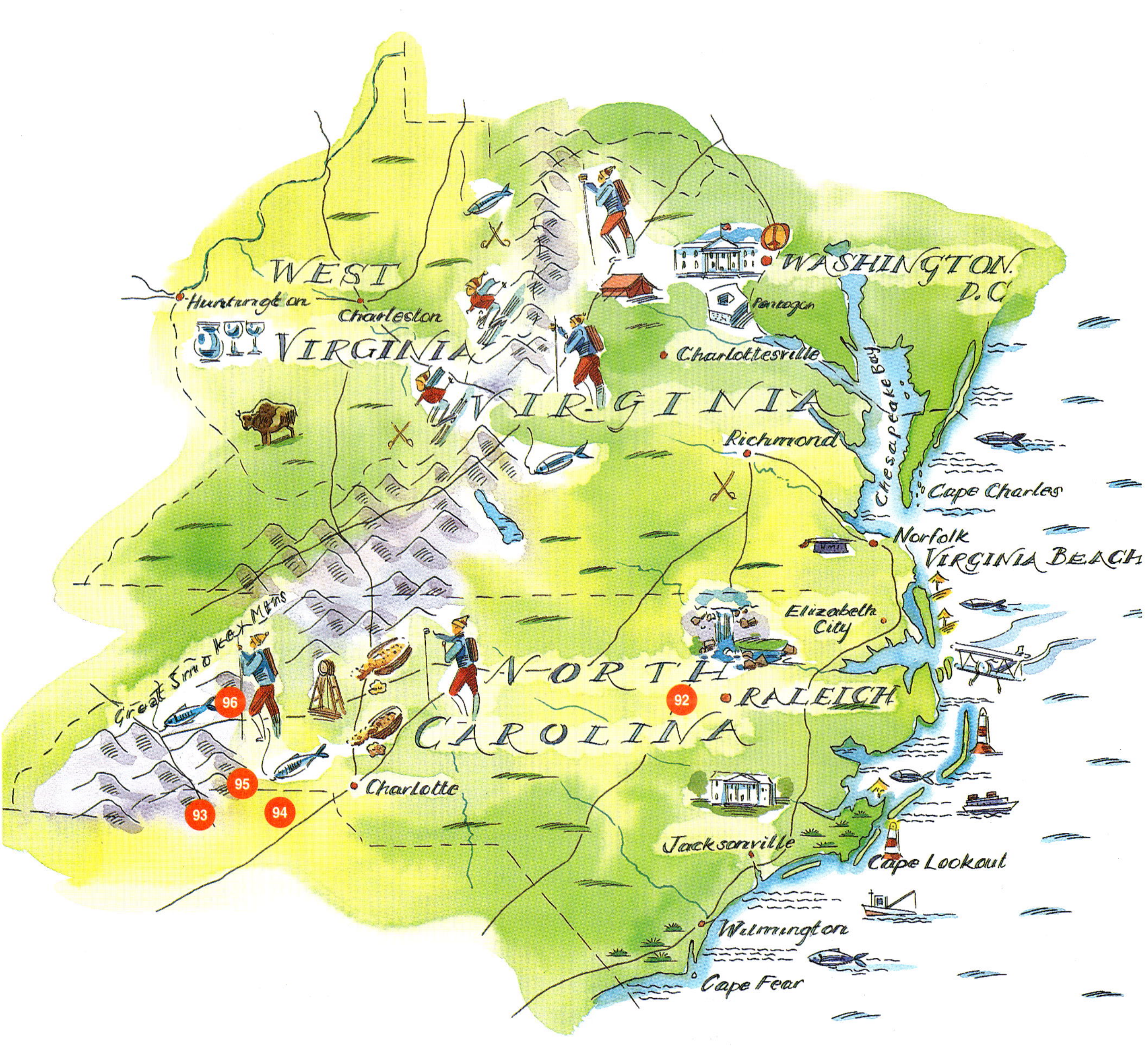

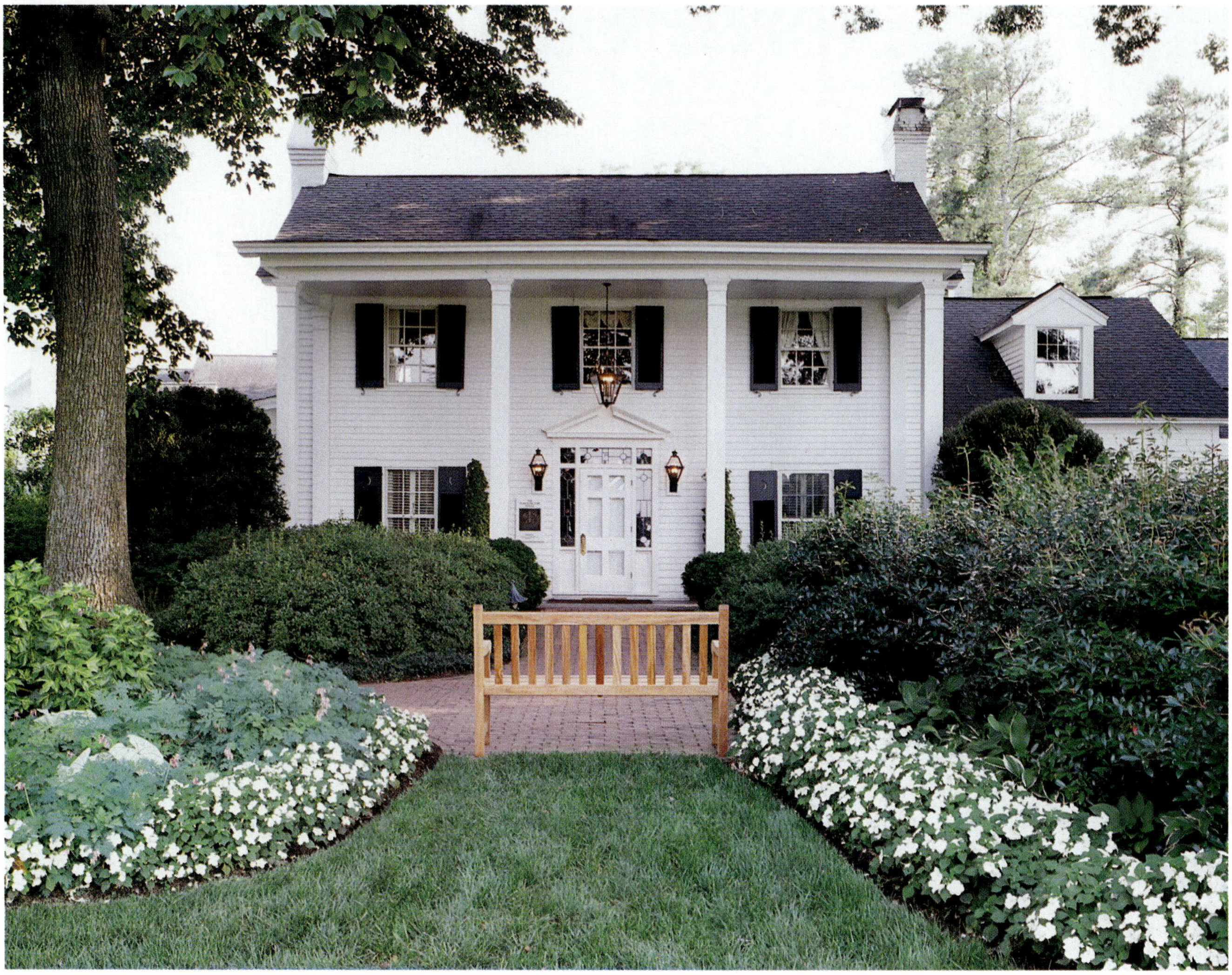

THE FEARRINGTON HOUSE

2000 FEARRINGTON VILLAGE CENTER, PITTSBORO, NORTH CAROLINA 27312
TEL: 1 919 542 2121 FAX: 1 919 542 4202 E-MAIL: fhouse@fearrington.com

Not far from Raleigh, the capital of North Carolina, Fearrington Village is a fascinating community. The inspiration of the Fitch Family who in 1974 purchased a 640 acre farm dating back to 1786. The barn and silo still stand and cows graze in the meadow – but the Village is now home to 750 families. The Fearrington House, rebuilt after a fire in the 1920's, became a restaurant in 1980, with accommodation available next door. It is a beautiful residence, with white walls, green shutters and classical pillars surrounded by well-kept gardens blooming with colourful plants and fine old trees. The charming bedrooms are extremely comfortable, peaceful and very light, filled with old English pine furniture and bowls of fresh flowers. Guests take tea in the elegant Garden House or relax in the Sun Room leading onto the enchanting terrace and rose gardens, later feasting by candlelight in the famous restaurant on magnificent Southern specialities and distinguished wines. Smoking is discouraged in the restaurant. The village is intriguing, with its aura of self-containment. It has craft and garden shops, its own bank, market café, medical and fitness centres; also tennis, croquet, riding and swimming and golf is not far away. **Directions:** From Durham Raleigh Airport take Route 40 to Chapel Hill, then Route 15-501 to Fearrington Village. Price guide: Rooms $175–$325.

THE GREYSTONE INN

LAKE TOXAWAY, NORTH CAROLINA 28747
TEL: 1 828 966 4700 FAX: 1 828 862 5689

A stay at this unique inn is to join a superbly hosted private house party. The Greystone Inn is built near the site of the legendary Toxaway Inn. The setting is idyllic, overlooking the lake and surrounded by luxuriant, verdant gardens. The Inn is a beautiful mansion, built as a private house – the architecture having European overtones. It has been lovingly transformed into a hotel with modern facilities yet old world charm and courtesy prevail. The guest rooms, those in the adjacent Hillmont annex facing the waterside, and the Lakeside Suites are spacious and romantic, furnished with antiques and period pieces, all with charming drapes. The bathrooms are twentieth century, with Jacuzzis. The sun porch where tea is served is evocative of the past, having wicker furniture, and the salons are gracious. Cocktails are sipped in the traditional Library or on the Terrace. Dining is an occasion – inspired interpretations of classical Southern dishes accompanied by mellow wines. Croquet, golf, tennis, fishing, many water sports, hiking and picnics in the lovely countryside, swimming in the pool or lake, relaxing in the spa or just appreciating the tranquility – the days are full. Directions: Take US64 from Brevard, after 20 miles the Inn is signed on the right. Price guide: Rooms $265–$420; suite $350–$525

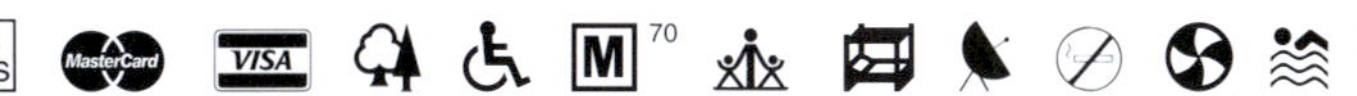

Pine Crest Inn

200 PINE CREST LANE, TRYON, NORTH CAROLINA 28782
TEL: 1 828 859 9135 E-MAIL: info@pinecrestinn.com

Situated at the foot of the Blue Ridge Mountains, this traditional English-style inn was once a popular haunt for some of America's finest 20th century authors including F Scott Fitzgerald and Ernest Hemingway. Its beautiful location makes Pine Crest Inn an ideal choice for enthusiasts of outdoor pursuits. The interior is furnished in a quaint style with stone fireplaces, wooden floors and oriental rugs. The charming British owners have aimed to create a "home away from home" ambience, with books to read beside the fire, games to play and areas for guests to commune. The choice of accommodation is delightfully varied with rooms, suites and cottages; all individually decorated. There is a wide array of amenities such as cable television, telephones, bathrobes and sherry. Guests relax with a drink in the Fox and Hounds Bar before dining in the superb restaurant; serving imaginative dishes and a fine selection of wines. The Pine Inn is renowned for its excellent cuisine and a breakfast is the highlight of every morning, with blueberry muffins, Belgian waffles, eggs Benedict and other specialities. After a hearty meal, guests may wish to ramble through the surrounding woods or explore the many nearby hiking trails. Volleyball may be practised on site whilst golf, tennis, swimming and riding is arranged nearby. **Directions:** From I-26, exit 36 to Tryon. Follow Rte 108/176 to town of Tryon. Turn on New Market Rd. Follow signs to Inn. Price Guide: Rooms $130–$140; suite $140–$200.

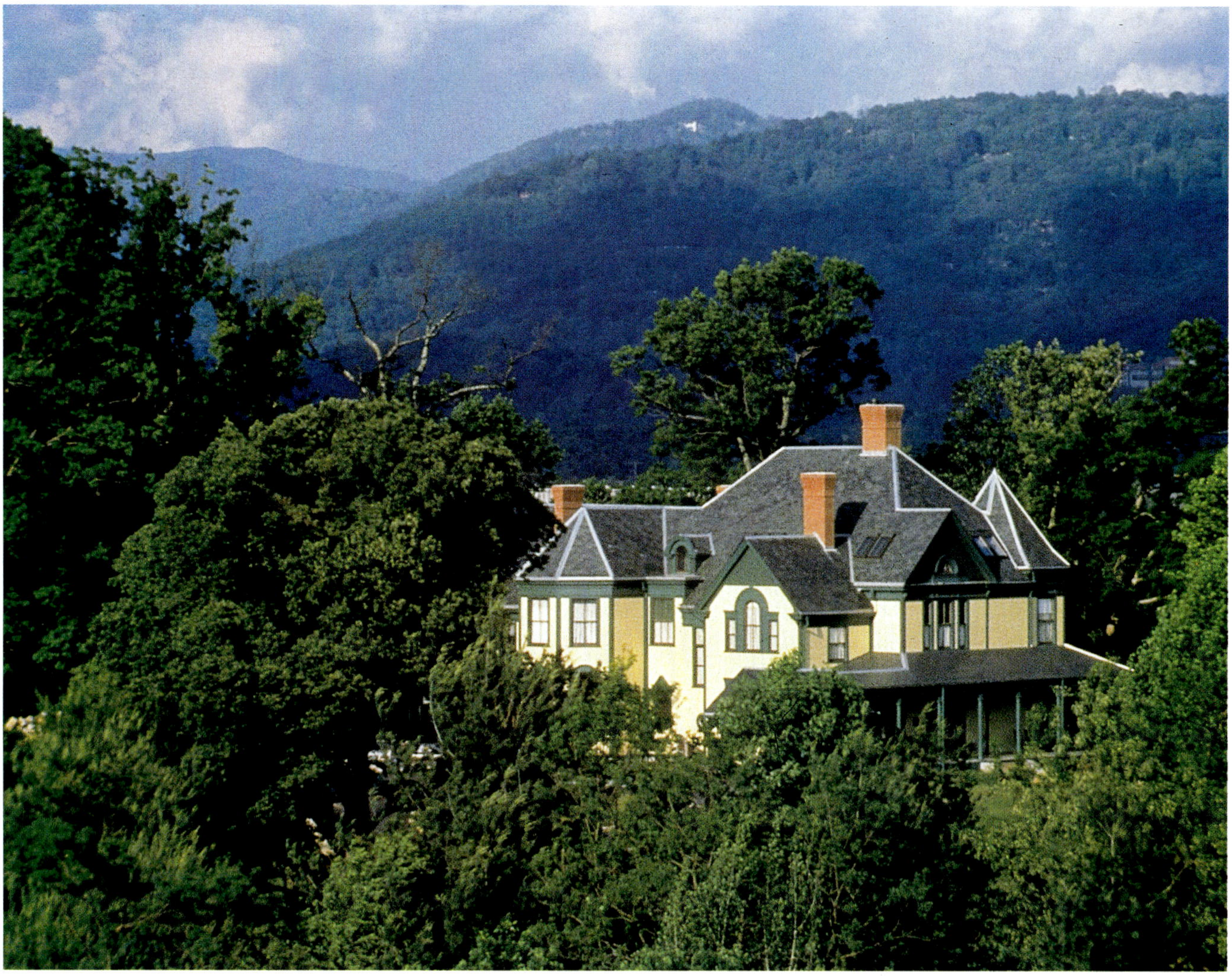

Richmond Hill Inn

87 RICHMOND HILL DRIVE, ASHEVILLE, NORTH CAROLINA 28806
TEL: 1 828 252 7313 FAX: 1 828 252 8726 US & CANADA TOLL FREE: 888 742 4541

Richmond Hill Inn was built by a former congressman and ambassador in 1889 on a hill overlooking the French Broad River and surrounded by extensive gardens, vineyards, orchards and acres of rolling grounds. The present owners have restored this Queen Anne mansion to its original grandeur and it is once again a majestic example of architecture combining classic grace with supreme comfort and social acclaim. It is delightfully furnished with antiques and has regained the charm of its glorious past. With the addition of the Garden Pavilion and nine croquet Cottages, the inn now offers 36 uniquely appointed rooms. Twelve of the luxurious guest rooms are located in the mansion itself, above a magnificent oak panelled hall. The Pavilion has 15 rooms, which overlook the parterre garden and a waterfall. The Croquet Cottages surround a courtyard and feature a front porch with rocking chairs. All are elegantly furnished and have every comfort and convenience. Dining in Gabrielle's restaurant is a gastronomic experience. In the area, enjoy the Biltmore Estate, Blue Ridge Parkway, antique shopping, and fine craft galleries and studios. **Directions:** Located near US Highway 19/23, three miles northwest of downtown Asheville. Take Highway 251/UNC Asheville exit and look for Richmond Hill signs. Price guide: Rooms $135–$315; suites $285–$375.

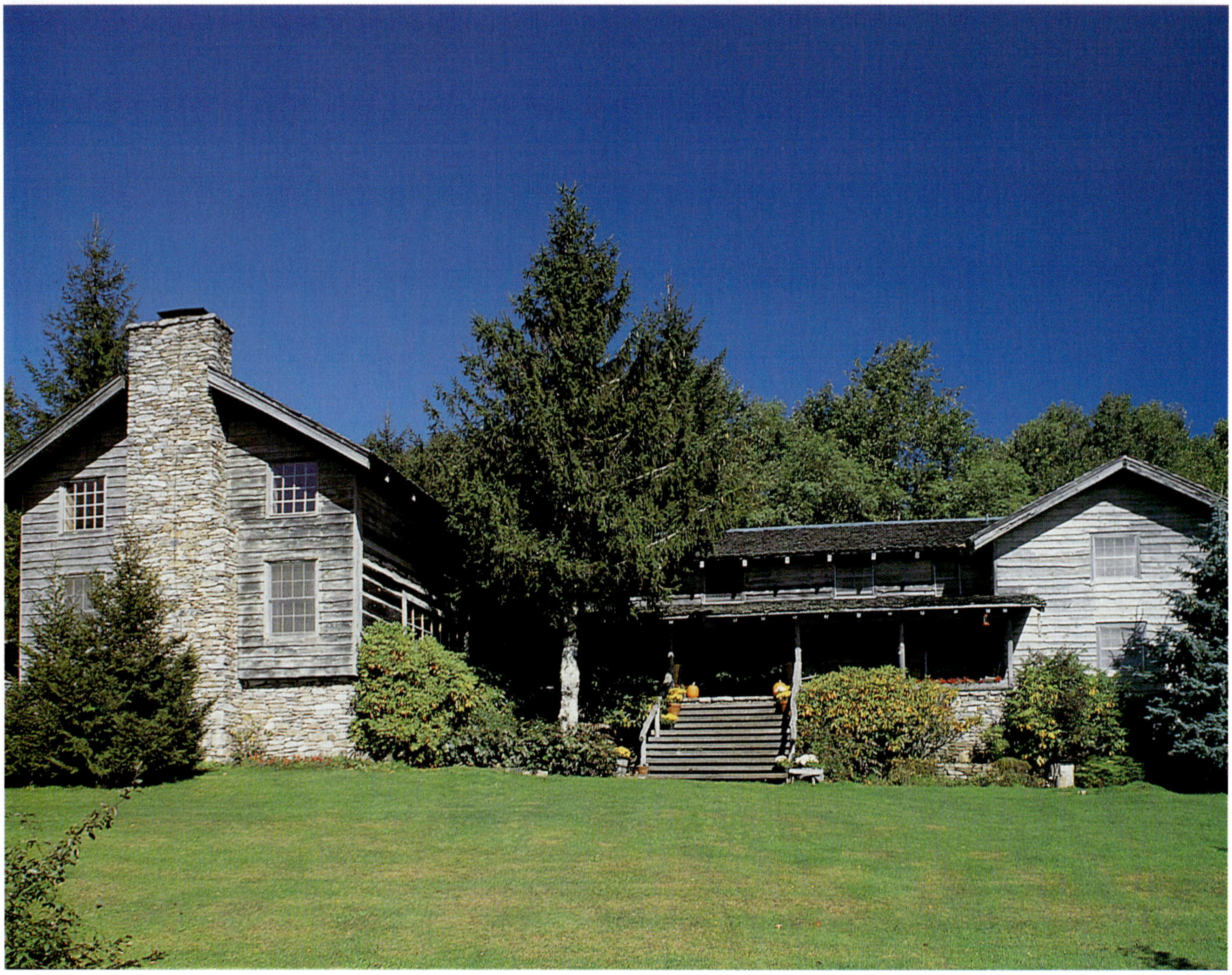

THE SWAG COUNTRY INN

2300 SWAG ROAD, WAYNESVILLE, NORTH CAROLINA 28786
TEL: 1 704 926 0430 FAX: 1 704 926 2036 E-MAIL: letters@theswag.com

A perfect mountain retreat languishing at almost 5,000 feet with direct access to the Great Smoky Mountains National Park. This hand hewn log lodge has breathtaking views and one of the highest croquet lawns in North America! With oak flooring and comfortable furnishings, the sitting room features a chandelier of intricately laced antlers and a massive stone chimney whose log fires have warmed many a convivial gathering. The bedrooms, some in separate cabins, are romantic with stone fireplaces, handmade quilts, local objets d'art and rubber ducks in the bathrooms. Some bedrooms have balconies, The Woodshed has a swing on its porch and The Hideaway is the most romantic suite. Among the many amenities are coffee grinders! Breakfasts are magnificent – try the blueberry pancakes. Superb picnics can be arranged. Guests dine together by candlelight, enjoying a sumptuous 4-course meal. Conversation flows. Special weekends are devoted to wild flowers, birds or starry night skies. When not following the wilderness trails, it is lovely just relaxing in a hammock, or lounging in the spa with its 50 mile view, playing croquet or fishing in the streams. **Directions:** Interstate NCI-40 exit 20, state highway 276 – 2.8 miles to The Swag sign, right into Hempill Road, 4 miles to hotel gate, 2.5 miles up the private driveway. Price guide: Rooms $240–$510.

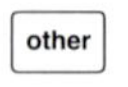

Maryland, New York State and Pennsylvania

ANTRIM 1844

30 TREVANION RD, TANEYTOWN, MARYLAND 21787
TEL: 1 410 756 6182 FAX: 1 410 756 2744 TOLL FREE: 1 800 858 1844

The great plantation houses in Maryland that survived the Battle of Gettysburg are nostalgic of a magical period in America's history. This is the era that Dorothy and Richard Mollett have recreated for their guests at Antrim 1884. Their loving and meticulous restoration of the classic Greek revivial mansion reflects long hours of research. Antiques and authentic wallhangings have been imported from Europe, fabrics are rich, mirrors have ornate gilt frames and the handsome portraits are illuminated by brilliant candelabra. The romantic guest rooms have pristine delicate linens and the luxurious suites are in imaginatively transformed outhouses. Wooden butlers outside each door offer newspapers in the morning and roses at night! On warm evenings guests dine on the enchanting verandah overlooking the formal gardens, on cooler nights in the fascinating Smokehouse Restaurant. The five-course menu is fabulous and the cellar holds magnificent wines. Strolling in the 23 acre estate is therapeutic, the pool has a picturesque gazebo and gentle exercise includes croquet, lawn bowling, target golf and tennis There are special facilities for corporate events and the Pavilion is an elite setting for private celebrations. **Directions:** Route 140 east to Taneytown, cross railroad tracks and bear right at fork. After 150' turn right, parking is signed. Price guide: Rooms $175; suite $300

TYLER SPITE HOUSE

112 WEST CHURCH STREET, FREDERICK, MARYLAND 21701
TEL: 1 301 831 4455

Tyler Spite House is a most delightful inn with a peculiar name which tells you nothing about the charming qualities of this up-to-date hostelry but the name does commemorate its interesting origin. The celebrated eye-surgeon, John Tyler, to thwart a scheme by the town planners, had the building put up virtually overnight in the direct path of the envisaged road extension. The law protected substantial buildings and thus the road-scheme was "spited". The historic inn was taken over in 1989 by Bill and Andrea Myer who have made it a wonderful place to stay while conserving and even embellishing the fine old décor that has given this stately mansion its unique appeal and character. The bedrooms are lavishly comfortable. Breakfasts are served bountifully but formally in the elegant dining room or often, in summer weather, outside on the patio among the flowers by the swimming pool. A rewarding tour of Frederick can be made on foot or uniquely by horse-drawn carriage. Afterwards, high tea is the speciality at the weekend, served in style either in the music room or the library. During the summer months, guests may indulge in strawberries in the garden. **Directions:** From Route 70 follow Market Street into the Historic District, turning left into 2nd Street, then left into Record Street and onward to Church Street. Price guide: Rooms $140–$250.

Asa Ransom House

10529 MAIN STREET (ROUTE 5), CLARENCE, NEW YORK 14031–1684
TEL: 1 716 759 2315 FAX: 1 716 759 2791

Built as a grist mill in 1803, by Asa Ransom, a silversmith, this fine property has been restored and refurbished and the result is a distinctive inn renowned for its charm and character. Set in the heart of Clarence, Asa Ransom House is situated in a peaceful location ideal for those seeking a tranquil ambience. Guests relax in the comfortable library and enjoy a game of chess, checkers or a large jigsaw puzzle. Alternatively, the fine selection of books will delight readers, who may recline in a soft chair beside the fire. The owners' attention to detail is evident in the superb bedrooms, decorated with antique and period furnishings. All offer en suite facilities, television and air conditioning whilst many have fireplaces and balconies. Freshly baked muffins and pastries, fresh fruit and seasonal entrées comprise the delicious breakfast. The Asa Ransom House is renowned for its excellent cuisine and as lunch is served only on Wednesdays and afternoon tea on Thursdays, guests are advised to reserve a table! The two dining rooms are beautifully furnished and the dishes, made with the finest seasonal produce, are complemented by a good wine list. Pastimes include browsing the giftshop, strolling in the herb garden or antique hunting in the quaint shops close by. Lancaster Opera House is nearby; Niagara Falls is only 44km distant. Toronto is 2 hours away. **Directions:** Travellers from the east must take I-90 leaving at exit 49, whilst those from the north must leave at exit 48A. Price guide: Rooms $95–$265.

THE BREWSTER INN

6 LEDYARD AVENUE, CAZENOVIA, NEW YORK 13035
TEL: 1 315 655 9232 FAX: 1 315 655 2130

Surrounded by secluded lawned grounds, The Brewster Inn stands elegantly on the southern shore of Cazenovia Lake close to a quaint village which was founded in 1793. It is a perfect venue for carefree relaxation. The inn was built as the summer home for financier Benjamin Brewster who, with John D. Rockefeller, Sr, established the Standard Oil Company. Its elegance is enhanced by rich décor, fine drapes and impressive woodwork, including solid mahogany and antique quartered oak. Guests choose from bedrooms in the main inn or in the completely renovated carriage house. Each one has a private bath, air conditioning, television and telephone. Four rooms have Jacuzzi baths and there is one three-room de luxe suite. The attractive dining rooms offer dinner menus of superb, classic American cuisine to please every palate. The inn's intimate Tap Room is an excellent spot in which to recline and converse with the other guests. After a complimentary Continental breakfast guests can enjoy a leisurely stroll along the inn's extensive shoreline, swim in the clear lake waters, fish off the private dock or browse around Cazenovia's many shops. Lorenzo is also worth a visit, as are the beautiful grounds of Cazenovia College and the picnic area at the nearby, spectacular Chittenango Falls. **Directions:** The Brewster Inn is on US Route 20, 20 miles east of Syracuse. Price guide: Rooms $130–$140; suite $140–$200.

CENTENNIAL HOUSE

13 WOODS LANE, EAST HAMPTON, NEW YORK 11937
TEL: 1 516 324 9414 FAX: 1 516 324 0493 E-MAIL: centhouse@hamptons.com

This immaculate property, set in the historic town of East Hampton on the corner of Montauk Highway and the Village Pond offers comfortable accommodation and pleasant surroundings. Situated on Long Island, often considered to be a playground for the rich and famous, a sense of casual elegance pervades the interior of Centennial House, where the owners' painstaking attention to detail is evident. The public rooms are enhanced by antiques, period furnishings and a grand piano. Chintz fabrics feature dominantly in the English country parlour, the guest rooms and the secluded cottage. Each room is well-appointed with en suite bathrooms, brocade and interesting ornaments. The extensive breakfast menu comprises fresh fruit, cereals, eggs and house specialities. Pastimes include dining at the many fine establishments nearby, admiring the beautiful mansions and walking along the beaches. **Directions:** Centennial House is about a 2 hours drive from Manhattan. Take the Long Island Expressway to Exit 70; then follow signs to 'Montauk/27 East'. As you enter the Village, you will see a Getty gas station on your left. Proceed through the blinking light for exactly $\frac{4}{10}$ths of a mile and you will see our mailbox on the right hand side of the road. Price guide (including breakfast): Rooms \$250–\$395; The Guest House (weekly) \$2500–\$4500.

ROSE INN

813 AUBURN ROAD, ROUTE 34 NORTH, BOX 6576, ITHACA, NEW YORK 14851–6576
TEL: 1 607 533 7905 FAX: 1 607 533 7908

Ithaca, halfway between New York City and Niagara Falls, is in a major wine growing area. The countryside is glorious, and this is the setting of the Rose Inn, a graceful white house built in the style of an Italian Palazzo, standing in 20 acres of landscaped gardens. Known locally as "The House with the Circular Staircase", this is the pièce de résistance of the hotel. Built by a master craftsman, it spirals up to to an elegant cupola in the roof. The interior of the Inn is exceptionally fine – meticulous attention to detail is reflected in the authenticity of the antiques, old paintings, gilt mirrors and sconces. Unusual objets d'art and eclectic furnishings (comfortable squashy sofas) add to the charm of the formal parlour. The enchanting guest rooms have a luxurious yet historic ambience created by classic period pieces and delicate lace covers. Joyous comforts include big bath robes! Splendid country breakfasts start the day and dinner is a memorable event – exquisite table settings, inspired gourmet dishes and heavenly wines. The region has 40 wineries, lakes, waterfalls, a glass museum and Cornell University to explore. Activities include croquet on the Rose Inn lawn, salmon fishing and other country sports. Golf is nearby. Jazz is played on weekends in the Carriage House. **Directions:** Take Route 34 South from Interstate Highways 90. Price guide: Rooms $100–$175; suite $175–$275

Roycroft Inn

40 SOUTH GROVE STREET, EAST AURORA, NEW YORK 14052
TEL: 1 716 652 5552 FAX: 1 716 655 5345

The Roycroft Inn is in every sense an American National Landmark. It was founded over a hundred years ago by the philosopher and writer Elbert Hubbard to provide congenial accommodation for devotees of the local Arts and Craft movement. His influence and memory live on at the Roycroft, thanks largely to the Margaret L Wendt Foundation who enabled the inn to be renovated and reopened in 1995 in a style worthy of the founder's highest beliefs and aspirations. The décor and furniture are either original or authentic reproduction examples of the celebrated movement of which the inn is a shrine. The bedrooms at the Roycroft conform to the original structure whilst enhancing and conserving the historic character of the entire building. All rooms are furnished in traditional Roycroft style and feature modems, televisions and video equipment. The Roycroft inn restaurant is open for lunches, dinners and on Sunday for brunch. In summer there is dining out of doors. Private facilities are available for meetings and parties for as few as 10 or as many as 200 people. Attractions in the locality are museums, golf courses, nature walks, tennis and in season, many downhill and cross-country skiing areas. **Directions:** From Buffalo follow Route 190 south to Route 90 heading west. Take exit 54 to Route 400 and exit onto route 20A East Aurora, becoming Main Street. Pass through village, turn left into South Grove Street. Price guide: Suite $130–$230.

22 rms MasterCard VISA AMERICAN EXPRESS other M 200

New York City

THE KITANO NEW YORK

66 PARK AVENUE AT 38th STREET, NEW YORK, NEW YORK 10016
TEL: 1 212 885 7000 FAX: 1 212 885 7100

This is where East meets West with a grand flourish – in the heart of New York. The Kitano New York is a splendid reincarnation of the original hotel opened 25 years ago, and by embracing its neighbours, is now an impressive and luxurious hotel, with impeccable multi-lingual staff. The Orient is evident throughout; a splendid bronze Botero 'Dog' guards the marble lobby, with its graceful staircase and contemporary lanterns. The decor is a blend of Manhattan and old Japan – simple uncluttered lines and extremely comfortable – and the salons display a magnificent collection of paintings and objets d'art. The spacious bedrooms look out over the city – but sound proof windows ensure peaceful nights – mostly furnished Western style but the Tatami Suite is authentic Japanese, with its own tea ceremony room. Caviar is available in the sophisticated piano bar and cosmopolitan meals are enjoyed in the sunny Garden Café. The traditional Nadaman Hakubai restaurant is famed for its unique Kaiseki cuisine, served on exquisite Japanese porcelain. The city offers museums and galleries, shops and theatres; the hotel limousine goes to Wall Street each morning; and guests can relax in the New York Sports Club just three blocks away. **Directions:** 35 minutes from Kennedy Airport, close to Central Station, Valet parking. Price guide: Rooms $285–$380; suite $465–$1295

149 rms       50  

THE LOWELL

28 EAST 63RD STREET, NEW YORK, NEW YORK 10021
TEL: 1 212 838 1400 FAX: 1 212 319 4230 E-MAIL: lowellhot@aol.com

Globe-trotting corporate presidents and travellers accustomed to the very best seek to stay at The Lowell when in New York. A hotel with the highest of reputations, it has a touch of romance about it too, with its exciting art deco façade, located on a tree lined avenue – almost a boulevard in Paris! This exclusive hotel continues its European theme in the lobby, with its French Empire furnishings and chiaroscuro walls. Liveried doormen greet new arrivals, the concierge is multilingual and the staff are famed for their old world courtesy. The bedrooms and suites are magnificent, furnished with fine antiques, beautiful brocades and handsome old prints, and have spectacular views over Manhattan. Some have open fires, others private terraces, one has its own gymnasium! There are points for PCs, multi-line telephones and stunning marble bathrooms. The popular Fitness Centre on the second floor is state-of-the art. Several of the suites, each with its own unique style, are ideal for board meetings or special product launches and there are superb venues for private entertaining. **Directions:** Limousines will be sent to meet guests at airports, rail terminals or off ships. The hotel also offers valet parking. Price guide: Rooms \$345–\$445; suite \$545–\$2600.

CLIFF PARK INN & GOLF COURSE

155 CLIFF PARK ROAD, MILFORD, PENNSYLVANIA 18337–9708
TEL: 1 717 296 6491 FAX: 1 717 296 3982 E-MAIL: cpi@warwick.net

Surrounded by 500 acres of magnificent gardens, meadows and a 9-hole golf course, Cliff Park Inn and Golf Course affords captivating views across the Delaware River valley. Built in 1820, this former farmhouse is an idyllic venue for either business or leisure. The interior has retained many characteristics of its 19th century past with wide floorboards, working hearths and family heirlooms. The bedrooms are located in adjacent buildings and feature interesting antiques, en suite facilities and fine furnishings. A delicious breakfast comprises freshly baked scones, cinnamon French toast and other delights, whilst in the evenings, guests savour gourmet cuisine in the Colonial dining room. The varied menu offers an imaginative range of meals from classic American dishes to more exotic flavours. Golfers will be delighted with the 9-hole golf course whilst non-golfing guests may recline on the spacious porch, enjoying a good book or simply admiring the attractive surroundings. Opportunities for outdoor pursuits abound and hiking, cross-country skiing, fishing, rafting, canoeing and hunting may be enjoyed close by. The neighbouring town of Milford is renowned for its antique shops and boutiques. **Directions:** In New Jersey, take Interstate 80W to exit 34B (Route 15N). Proceed on Route 15N for 35 miles into Milford, PA. Proceed straight through traffic light. Go 2 blocks; turn left onto Sixth Street. Go 1-½ miles. Inn on left. Price guide: Rooms $90–$210.

THE FRENCH MANOR

HUCKLEBERRY RD (RTE 191), SOUTH STERLING, PENNSYLVANIA 18460
TEL: 1 717 676 3244 FAX: 1 717 676 9786 E-MAIL: thesterlinginn@ezaccess.net

This exquisite French château was built by wealthy Mr Hirshhorn in 1932, a replica of one he owned and loved in the South of France. It is built in traditional stone, with a slate roof, standing high on a hilltop, surrounded by lush gardens. This is a luxurious hotel. The interior reflects the skills of craftsmen from Southern Europe and the architecture is magical – gothic archways, dramatic vaulted ceilings, grand fireplaces, tower rooms. The guest rooms (four in the charming Carriage House) are enormous, with canopied beds and big plump sofas, ideal for enjoying a glass of champagne. The 'period' bathrooms are very efficient The salons are glorious, with graceful, Louis XV style furnishings and in the romantic flower filled Provençal dining room the chairs upholstered in splendid brocades. Guests sip aperitifs on the verandah then feast on an array of authentic aromatic French dishes accompanied by superb wines. (Reservations are recommended). Fabulous picnic lunches can be arranged. The French Manor has a informal modern sister, The Sterling Inn, and residents share its indoor pool, spa and many sporting facilities. The château estate has trails for hiking, biking and cross country ski-ing. The neighbourhood offers golf, galleries and antique shops. Internet: www.thesterlinginn.com
Directions: The Manor is on Route 191, South Huckleberry Road.
Price guide (B&B): Rooms $120–$180; suites $175–$225

9 rms · MasterCard · VISA · AMERICAN EXPRESS · other · M 20

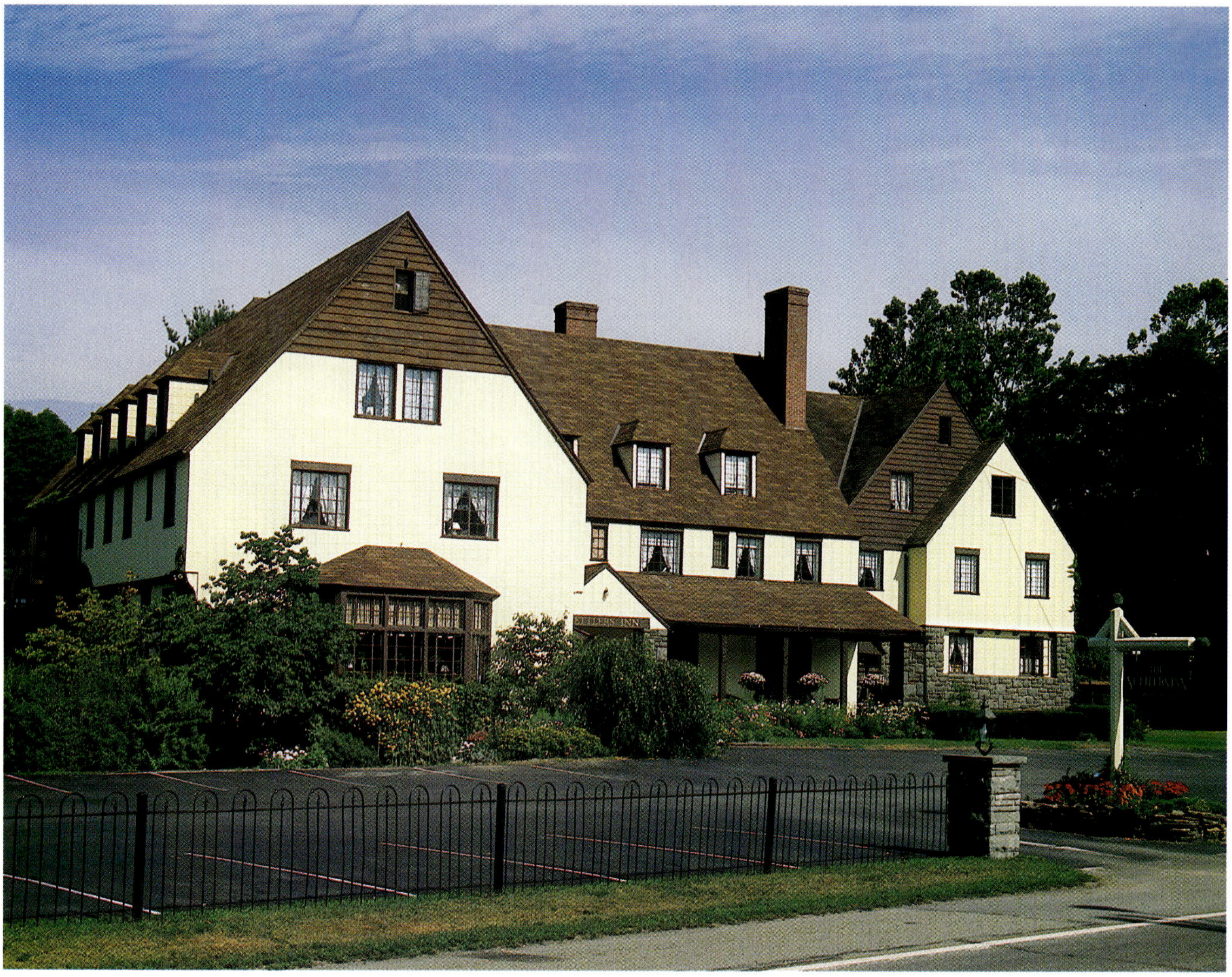

THE SETTLERS INN

FOUR MAIN AVENUE, HAWLEY, PENNSYLVANIA 18428

TEL: 1 717 226 2993 FAX: 1 717 226 1874

The Settlers Inn combines the hospitality and gracious service of a past era with the comforts and conveniences of modern times. This subtle blend results in a charming small hotel offering a welcoming atmosphere, comfortable accommodation and a superb dining experience. The interior, dominated by a magnificent bluestone fireplace, is beautifully appointed with antique furnishings. Freshly baked breads and pastries are served at breakfast whilst the dinner menu features an inspired choice of dishes. A relaxing afternoon may be spent strolling through the herb and flower gardens. A vast array of trinkets and practical items ranging from aprons to elegant windchimes is on sale at The Potting Shed, a charming gift shop set in the beautiful grounds. Popular activities include bird-watching, hiking, photography, golf, sailing and ice-skating. There are several areas of outstanding beauty nearby and these include Bingham Park, Lake Wallenpaupack and the Upper Delaware region. **Directions:** From I-84, take exit 7 to Route 390 North. At Route 507, turn right onto 507 North. At the traffic light, turn left onto Route 6 West and follow through Hawley to Bingham Park. The Inn is on the left. Price guide: Rooms $75–$145.

New Jersey and Delaware

The Inn At Montchanin Village

ROUTE 100 AND KIRK ROAD, MONTCHANIN, DELAWARE 19710
TEL: 1 302 888 2133 FAX: 1 302 888 0389

In a world where time seems to have stood motionless for well over a hundred years lies The Inn at Montchanin Village. Set in the heart of Brandywine Valley, the village grew up as home for labourers who worked at the nearby DuPont powder mills and factories. It comprises eleven buildings, built between 1870 and 1910 and clustered on a gently sloping hillside. Nine of these have been painstakingly restored and transformed into 20 guest units of various shapes and sizes. Selected period and reproduction furniture has been used to add charm and elegance to individual rooms and a meticulous eye for detail is evident in the tasteful décor. All are equipped with a refrigerator and ice-maker, a microwave oven, cable television and telephones. The inn's restaurant, Krazy Kat's, created from the old blacksmith's shop serves delicious breakfasts including Belgian waffles with maple syrup and fresh berries, bagel cream cheese and smoked salmon platter and assorted muffins, breads and cereals. Soups, salads and sandwiches are prepared for luncheon, while dinner includes a choice of five appetisers and an impressive menu of entrées. There are a number places of interest in the near vicinity. These include The Winterthur mansion, the country's premier museum of American decorative art and the magnificent Longwood Gardens. **Directions:** The inn is off Route 100 North and can be accessed from Route 202. Price guide: Rooms $150–$170; suites $190–$400.

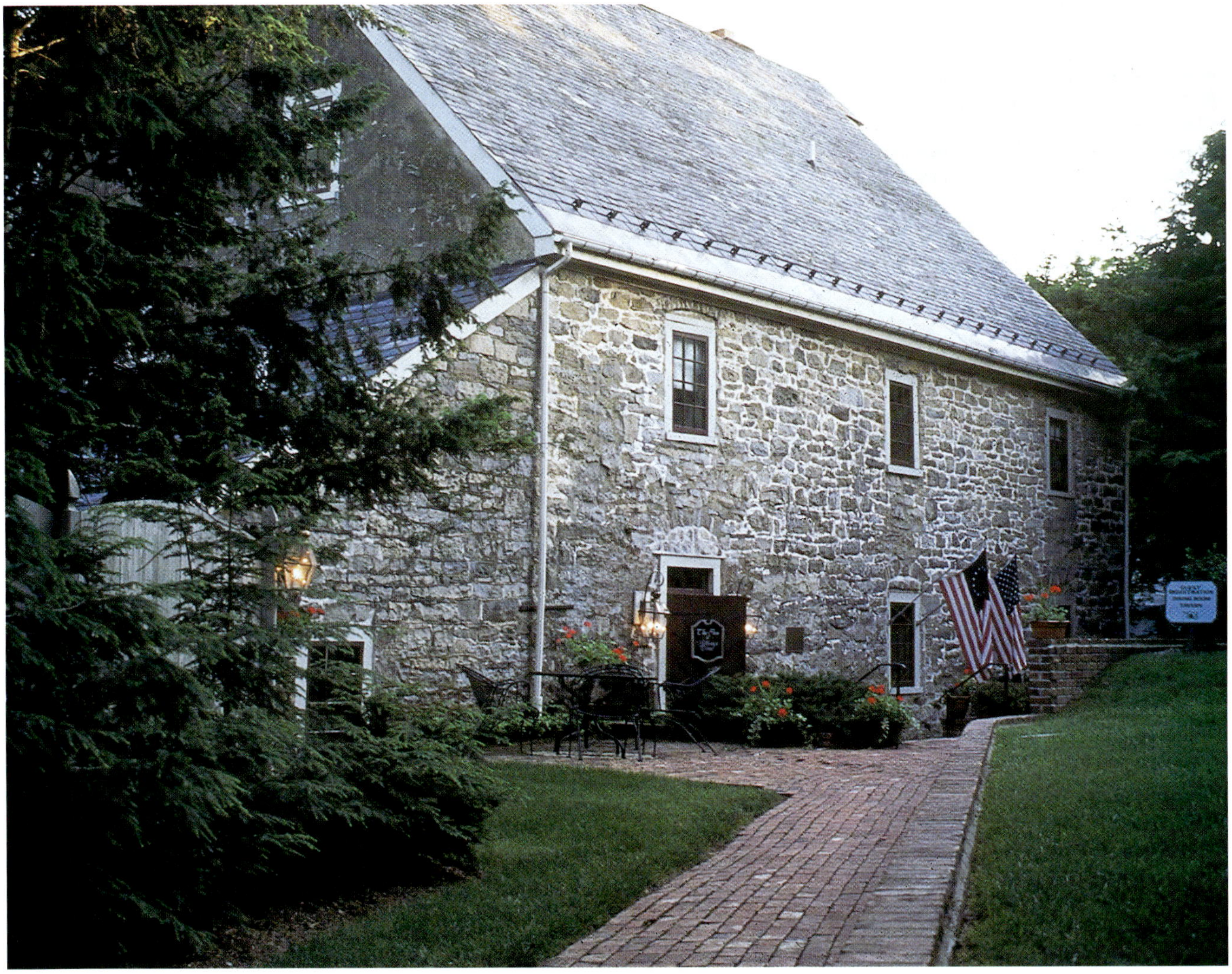

INN AT MILLRACE POND

PO BOX 359, HOPE, NEW JERSEY 07844
TEL: 1 908 459 4884 FAX: 1 908 459 5276

The Inn at Millrace Pond comprises a series of historic buildings gathered round the first ever erected in the little town of Hope, founded in the later part of the 18th century. The superb work of restoration of these original structures has resulted in the creation of a most attractive inn, set in an exceptionally serene location. It is the focal point of the surrounding landscape and of the community. The original mill no longer works, but in the tavern room its relics are on show and the millrace still flows, creating an authentic old world scene. The inn prides itself on its reputation for generous hospitality. In the award-winning restaurant, candlelit dinners are served from an imaginative menu featuring delicacies such as lemon grass poached shrimp and dried cherry and duck confit spring roll. The bedrooms are interestingly furnished and decorated, ideally equipped for comfort and easy living. Energetic visitors can play tennis or golf, go walking, jogging or cycling. Those whose tastes are more idle will enjoy the shops and antique galleries in the nearby towns. During the warmer months, it is said that Charlie, the owner, sometimes takes guests out in his 1921 Cadillac! **Directions:** Leave Route 80 at exit 12, follow Route 521 southward, then left in Hope along Route 519. The Mill will be on your left. Price guide: Rooms $100–$160.

Queen's Hotel

601 COLUMBIA AVENUE, CAPE MAY, NEW JERSEY 08204
TEL: 1 609 884 1613 E-MAIL: qvinn@bellatlantic.net

Owned and managed by Dane and Joan Wells, Queen's Hotel is the up and coming younger sister of her longer established relation, The Queen Victoria, situated just across the road. It began as a gambling house in 1876 and over a hundred years later, in 1995, it was the subject of major restoration and renovation. The result is a fine small hotel, combining modern conveniences with old architecture, set in the historic district of Cape May. Queen's Hotel is in an enviable position, surrounded by over 600 establishments from the Victorian era with the beach only a short walk away. The bedrooms are well-equipped with mini refrigerators, coffee makers, air conditioning and the latest bathroom and shower amenities – the luxury suites have whirlpool baths. House bicycles and beverages are complimentary. Many fine restaurants are located nearby. There are also interesting shops and various entertainments including concerts, a food and wine festival and a Victorian Christmas in December. The surrounding area is one of the most renowned bird-watching areas in North America. Fishing, golf, riding and tennis are also practised close by. **Directions:** Drive south on the Garden State Parkway to exit 0, continue straight over bridge to Lafayette Street. At first stop light turn left into Madison. Proceed 3 blocks, turn right at water tower into Columbia Avenue, go ½ mile to first stop light. The hotel is on the right. Price guide: Rooms $90–$255.

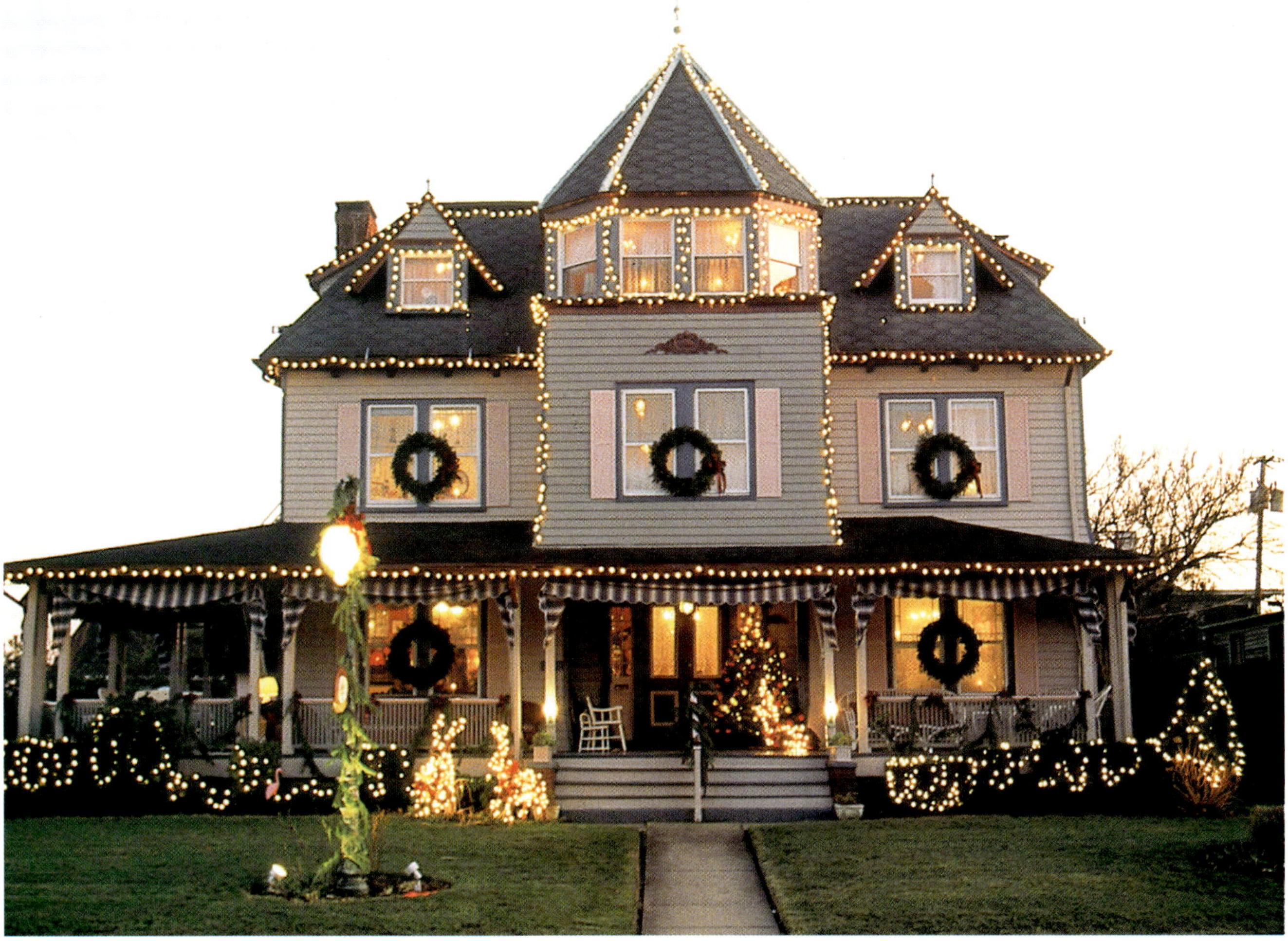

Sea Crest By The Sea

19 TUTTLE AVENUE, SPRING LAKE, NEW JERSEY 07762
TEL: 1 732 449 9031 FAX: 1 732 974 0403 E-MAIL: jk@seacrestbythesea.com

The owners of this charming inn – a perfect retreat from the hustle and bustle of modern life – describe it as "a fantasy for grown-ups". Guests, greeted on arrival by soft classical music and the aroma of fresh flowers, will quickly appreciate the efforts made to marry today's comforts with yesterday's elegance. In this romantic inn, every bedroom has a queen-sized bed, fitted with linens of fine Egyptian cotton, French damask and Belgium lace. Each is also equipped with a private bath, television/video and air-conditioning. A candlelit gourmet breakfast begins at the civilised hour of 9am, with the antique French sideboards laden with fresh fruit, home-made yogurt and granola, warm scones and breads and freshly-squeezed orange juice. Although there is no restaurant, menus from the 20 best restaurants in the area are made available. The Sea Crest is a stone's throw from the quiet beach. A stable of bicycles is provided for guests' use, while back at the inn there are opportunities to play croquet on the lawn or to simply enjoy the soft sea breezes while relaxing on the verandah. **Directions**: From New York and North: Garden State Parkway to exit 98. Route 34 south to the first traffic circle and proceed round to Route 524 east to ocean. Turn right, go on one block and turn right into Tuttle Avenue. Price guide: Room $145–$265.

Connecticut, Massachusetts and Rhode Island

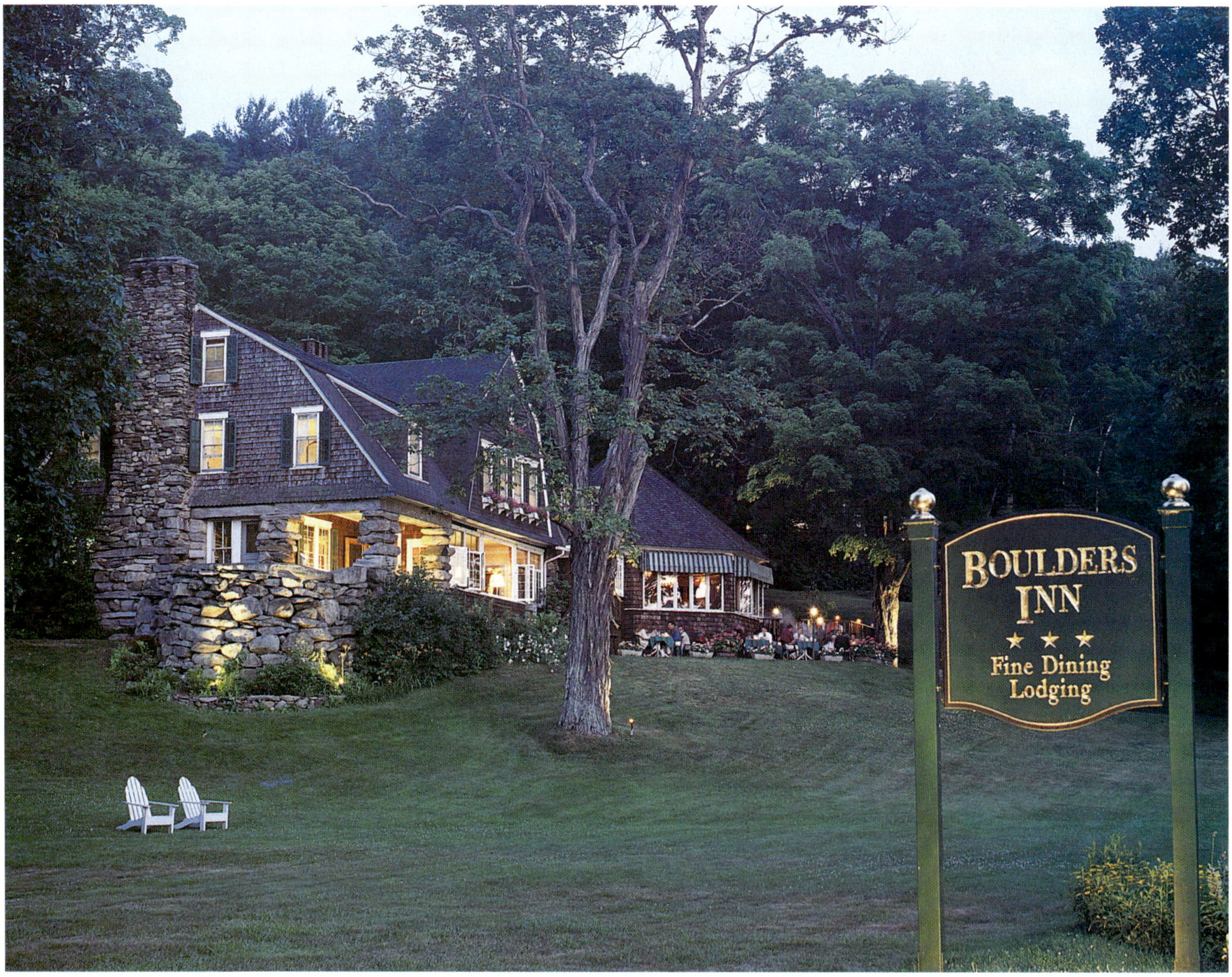

THE BOULDERS INN

EAST SHORE ROAD (ROUTE 45), NEW PRESTON, CONNECTICUT 06777
TEL: 1 860 868 0541 FAX: 1 860 868 1925

This enchanting Inn is in the Berkshire Hills with spectacular views of Lake Waramaug. The sound of water lapping on the shore and the sight of this lovely Victorian house will add to guests' anticipation of a perfect stay. The hotel has just seventeen guest rooms, all filled with a melange of antiques and country furniture, patchwork quilts and cushions adding colour. Six rooms in the main inn, three are in the Carriage House and others are in four guest cottages behind the Inn with their own decks overlooking the Lake. Several of the cottages have double whirlpool baths. The lounge at the foot of the elegant staircase is the focal point of The Boulders, where guests gather for apéritifs. The big sofas are in joyous floral chintz, the polished floors gleam and charming ornaments add a personal touch. Residents change for dinner as it is a memorable occasion, for not only has the restaurant won much acclaim for its imaginative interpretation of New England dishes, but the wine list has also won many awards. The Inn has its own beach, a private trail to Pinnacle Mountain, its own boats and canoes, tennis, bikes, a games room and skating on the lake in winter. Golf, riding, antique hunting and exploring nearby villages are alternative activities. **Directions:** From New Milford, Rt. 202 to New Preston, turning left onto Route 45 to Boulders Inn. Price guide: Rooms and suites $175–$395.

Homestead Inn

420 FIELDPOINT ROAD, GREENWICH, CONNECTICUT 06830
TEL: 1 203 869 7500 FAX: 1 203 869 7502

The Homestead was built as a private home. Sixty years later, after extensive architectural renovation, it became an inn, but it was not until 1978 that it became the outstandingly handsome property that it is today, perfectly sited in the Belle Haven area. The restaurant Thomas Henkelmann has a reputation for excellence that reaches far beyond the affluent and pleasant environment in which it is situated. Wine connoisseurs will be delighted with the sensational selection of clarets and burgundies on the wine list. The food too is of a similar, classic style. The temptations of the wonderful entrées should not distract diners from leaving room for the final pièce de resistance – Henkelmann's desserts and cheese dishes. The bedrooms, all of the highest quality, are in the old mansion and also in the annexes. The inn is particularly suitable for top quality meetings in secluded conducive surroundings. Places to visit locally include the Bruce Museum in Greenwich, New York City, Yale University at New Haven, the Whitney Museum in Stamford and the Cavalier Art Gallery. Golf and tennis are practised nearby. **Directions:** From New York City leave Route 1–95 at exit 3. Turn left at foot of ramp. Continue to 2nd light, then turn left into Horseneck Lane. At the end of the road turn left into Field Point Road. The inn is on your right. Price guide: Rooms $160–$185; suite $250–$300.

RIVERWIND INN

209 MAIN STREET, DEEP RIVER, CONNECTICUT 06417
TEL: 1 860 526 2014

Conveniently placed in the Connecticut River Valley, the Riverwind Inn is a fascinating place in which to stay. The old mid-nineteenth century mansion, authentically refurbished just over ten years ago, offers a delightful blend of modern facilities and authentic works of art. Every modern comfort and convenience is offered whilst the venerable architecture, both interior and exterior, is complemented by the inn's eclectic array of collectors' items. These comprise antique animal mounts, books, ornaments, quilts and other pieces of American folk art. The bedrooms are beautiful; individually decorated with antique furnishings and providing guests with the latest amenities. A nourishing complimentary breakfast is served according to the Southern buffet tradition and includes a variety of delectable specialities such as Smithfield ham and home-baked biscuits. There are several restaurants nearby which offer exquisite dishes, made with fresh regional produce and the famous local seafood. Places to visit within close proximity are Mystic Seaport, Hammonasset Beach, Gillette Castle, the Goodspeed Opera House, the Ivoryton Playhouse and the Essex steam train/riverboat. **Directions:** From New York City follow I95 Northward to Route 9, leave Route 9 at exit 4. Go left on to Route 154. The inn is on the right. Price guide: Rooms $95–$175.

A Cambridge House

2218 MASSACHUSETTS AVENUE, CAMBRIDGE, MASSACHUSETTS 02140–1836
TEL: 1 617 491 6300 FAX: 1 617 868 2848 E-MAIL: InnACH@AOL.com

A Cambridge House is a most prestigious Inn offering impeccable service. The house is glorious, Colonial revival built in 1892 and its fin de siècle grace has been meticulously restored. This is a most superior bed and breakfast establishment, nothing but the best clearly being the rule (also no smoking) The guest rooms are exquisite, delicately patterned papers and fragile toiles, lots of cushions and bolsters, period furniture, porcelain ornaments and fresh flowers all creating a romantic ambience. Breakfast is a nourishing experience served early for professional guests and later for those on vacation – fresh fruits and/or seductive pastries, and also waffles/omelettes cooked to order for those who want it. Every evening, distinguished guests gather in the parlour, an elegant room filled with burnished antiques and gleaming silver, relaxing over delicious fresh hors d'oeuvres, with jazz playing quietly in the background. Both Boston and Cambridge have excellent restaurants, famous universities, a busy waterfront, harbour cruises, galleries, theatres, bookstores, museums and diverse sporting facilities not too far away. **Directions:** The hotel has a parking lot – Boston's airport is 20 minutes away. The rapid transit subway is recommended for visitors heading for campuses or financial and high technology districts. Price guide: Rooms $99–$275.

15 rms MasterCard VISA AMERICAN EXPRESS other 6

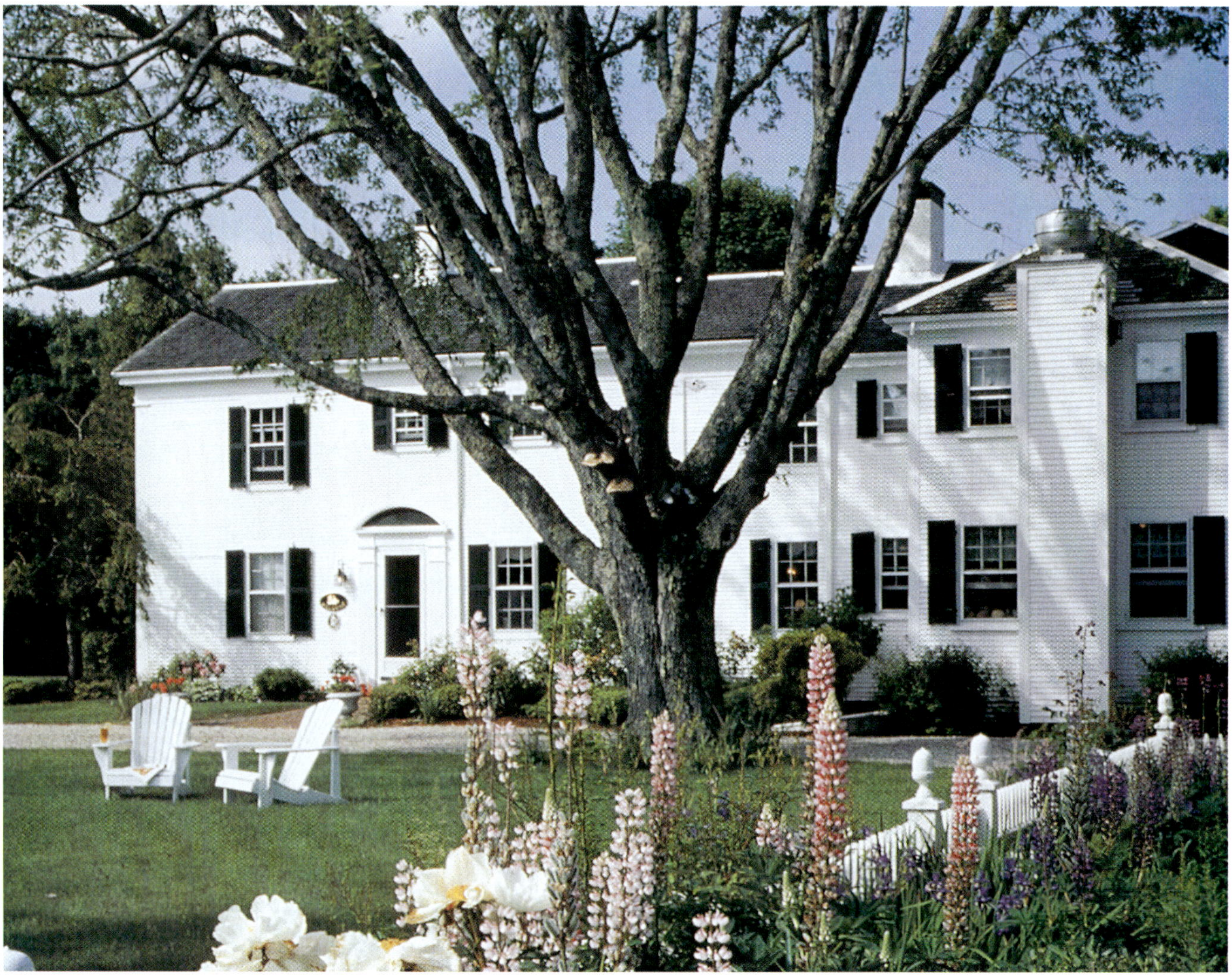

THE CAPTAIN'S HOUSE INN

369–377 OLD HARBOR ROAD, CHATHAM, CAPE COD, MASSACHUSETTS 02633
TEL: 1 508 945 0127 FAX: 1 508 945 0866

What better name for a fine hotel in Chatham, still a busy port today with yachtsmen, private craft and its fishing fleet. Captain Harding, a famous sailor in the 1800s, built this graceful white neo-classic home and some guest rooms are named after the ships he skippered. The inn, surrounded by splendid old trees, is peaceful and secluded. The interior has period wallpapers, Queen Anne chairs, Williamsburg antiques and Oriental rugs on polished floors – a grand country house ambience with a no smoking rule. The guest quarters are extremely comfortable and wonderfully different, each with its own elegant Colonial style. Luxurious suites are in the Carriage House beyond the English Garden, The Stables, or the romantic Captain's Cottage. Disabled travellers have not been forgotten. The dining room is exquisite with floor length windows, hanging plants and pristine linen. A delicious breakfast starts the day; a full English afternoon tea appears at 4 o'clock. The friendly hosts have a list of recommended restaurants for dinner. The Inn has a croquet lawn and bikes to borrow. Chatham has its fascinating harbour, a Friday night band, sailing, fishing, galleries, golf and glorious sunsets. **Directions:** Route 28 to Chatham Centre, continuing towards Orleans. After ½ mile the Inn is on the left. Price guide: Rooms \$135–\$275; suite \$200–\$325.

DEERFIELD INN

108 OLD MAIN STREET, DEERFIELD, MASSACHUSETTS 01342
TEL: 1 413 774 5587 FAX: 1 413 773 8712

Step back in time and stay in this select country inn in the centre of Deerfield, a three hundred years old New England village, nominated a National Historic Landmark. The Inn is an enchanting, classical building with its tall pillars and balcony over the entrance. The drawing rooms are elegant, with lovely curtains draped round the tall sash windows, yielding sofas and chairs and old rugs. The guest rooms are gorgeous – decorated in soft colours, with antique wooden bedsteads. Some are in the South Wing, reached by a covered walkway. All are wondrously peaceful and inviting. The host, Karl Sabo, trained as a chef, also has a great interest in wines, which is displayed in the renowned restaurant, an exquisite room with graceful chandeliers and authentic period furniture. Breakfast is generous, country-style and dinner is by candlelight. The menu is cosmopolitan New American and the cellar houses some great vintages. Non-smoking prevails throughout the Inn. Deerfield is ideal for discreet strategy meetings and magical for special celebrations. The fourteen 'museum' dwellings in the village should be visited. Nearby golf, tennis, hiking, cycling, and white water rafting occupy athletic residents; others may go antique hunting. **Directions:** Exits 24/25/26 from Interstate 91, then routes 5 and 10, marked to Historic Deerfield. Price guide: Rooms $128–$241.

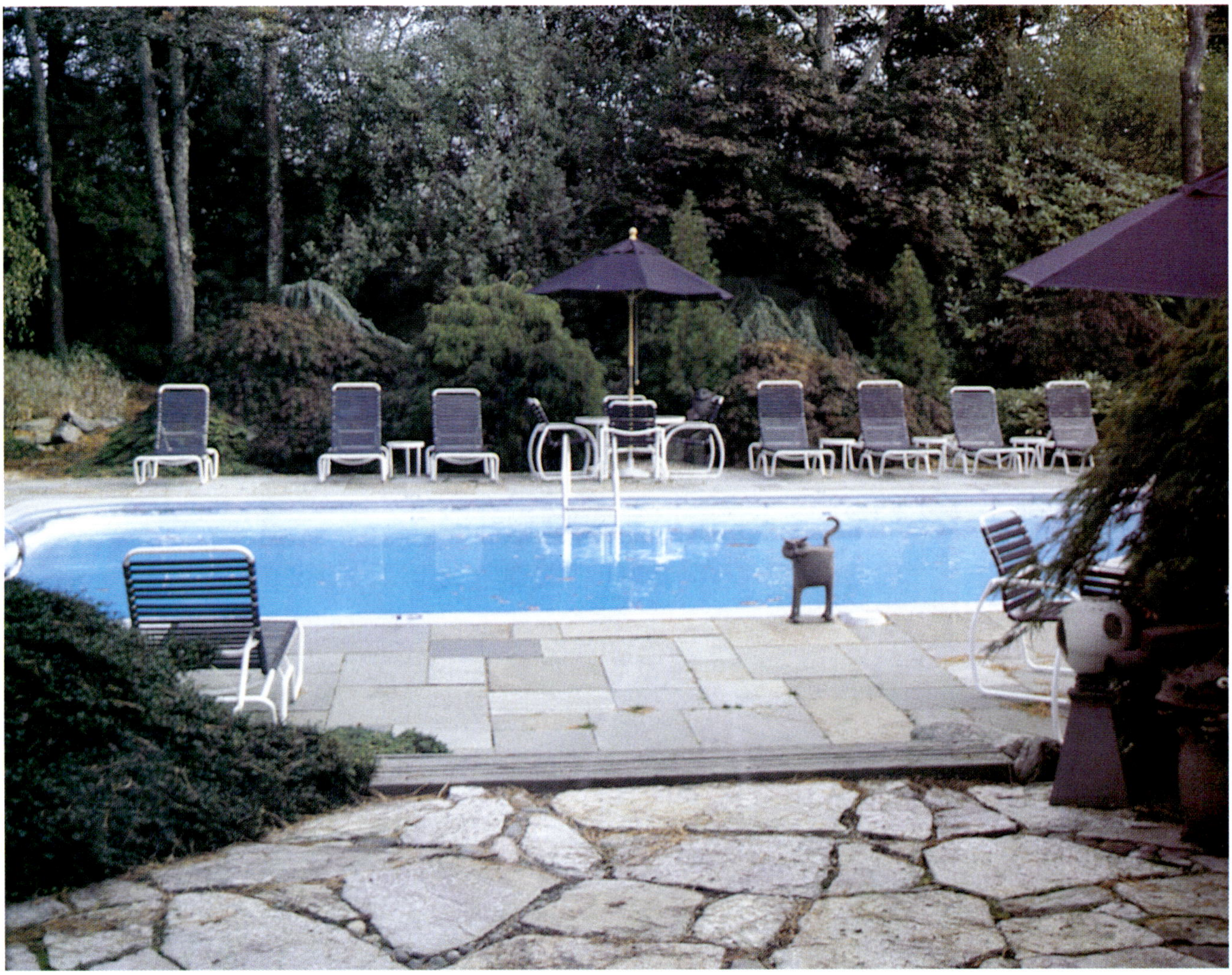

Pleasant Bay Village Resort Motel

ROUTE 28, CHATHAM, MASSACHUSETTS 02633
TEL: 1 508 945 1133 FAX: 1 508 945 9701

Chatham is a delightful seaside town on Cape Cod Peninsula and Pleasant Bay Village is an appropriate name for this superb motel resort complex. Pleasant Bay has easy access to thirteen coves and sandy beaches. Guests mostly maintain an independent lifestyle, but meet in the restaurant or round the pool. The residential buildings are well spaced out, with playgrounds close by. Six acres of landscaped gardens have a dramatic waterfall as the central feature. Families may prefer to stay in the 'Efficiencies', which have a kitchen and dining alcove, or the bedroom suites, which also have outdoor tables, chairs, chaise longues and barbecues. The rooms vary in size, some having patios. All are pristine, with comfortable modern furniture. Breakfast is served in the handsome dining room. A light lunch is available poolside. The motel has a beer and wine licence for dinner. Evening meals in Chatham are great, most restaurants having Cape Cod lobster on the menu. Exploring Martha's Vineyard, playing golf, swimming, enjoying the beaches, browsing in galleries, biking, whale-watching and summer concerts fill the day. **Directions:** On Cape Cod take Route 6 to Exit 11, left after extra ramp, then left onto Pleasant Bay Road, and right onto Route 28. The Resort is 1 mile further on the right. Price guide: Rooms $135–$415.

WEDGEWOOD INN

83 MAIN STREET, ROUTE 6A, YARMOUTH PORT, MASSACHUSETTS 02675
TEL: 1 508 362 5157 FAX: 1 508 362 5851

Yarmouth Port flourished in Cape Cod in the 19th century, and Main Street, the most fashionable street in this historic town, is the address of the Wedgewood Inn, a fine colonial house built in 1812. The mansion is lovely, with its white facade, green shutters and graceful lines, and stands in formal gardens, ablaze with chrysanthemums in the Autumn. The interior is faultless – polished floors, attractive wall coverings, colourful rugs, nautical prints, comfortable chairs, flowers and intriguing bibelots. The lounges have a warm elegance. The guest rooms, three in the Carriage Barn, are romantic with traditional quilts, wooden bedsteads and luxurious bathrooms. Some have garden patios and others a private, sheltered terrace. In winter the aroma of burning wood fires adds to the joy of staying here. Breakfast and afternoon tea are served in the sunny dining room, but the Inn does not have a licence – residents should 'bring their own', and hosts, Milt & Gerrie Graham, will suggest where to dine in the evenings. Guests enjoy the beaches, swim, fish, sail, play golf and tennnis, explore the Cape on bikes and hunt for antiques. Nantucket and Martha's Vineyard are close by. **Directions:** Interstate 3, over Sagamore Bridge on Route 6, exit 7, turning right, at halt sign right onto Route 6A, finding Inn 75yds on right. Price guide: Rooms $125–$145; suite $125–$185

THE WHALEWALK INN

220 BRIDGE ROAD, EASTHAM (CAPE COD), MASSACHUSETTS 02642
TEL: 1 508 255 0617 FAX: 1 508 240 0017 E-MAIL: whalewalk@capecod.net

Whales have always had an important role in Cape Cod, and this prestigious 1830's mansion was built by one of the famous Whaling Masters. It is in the unspoiled Outer Cape, near the forty mile long National Seashore. Dick and Carolyn Smith have enjoyed restoring their distinguished house, collecting authentic 19th century antiques and giving meticulous attention to the minutest detail. The romantic guest rooms are immaculate and inviting, with delicate drapes in soft colours. All are light and airy and the luxurious suites have charming sitting rooms. Guests relax on the colourful patio or in the pleasant sitting room, which has original contemporary paintings hung on the walls. Breakfast is an inspired feast – "put your diet on vacation" is one of the inn's maxims, although the light repast is equally delicious. The inn is unlicensed, but hors d'oeuvres are served each evening. Good places to dine are nearby. Residents are able to watch whales, follow the nature trails, explore the sandy beaches and salt marshes,swim, sail, bike through the lovely countryside, play golf and tennis, hunt antiques or visit Martha's Vineyard, a nearby island. **Directions:** Having crossed Sagamore Bridge, follow Route 6 past exit 12 to the Orleans rotary. Take third exit onto Rock Harbour Road, find Bridge Road on right and watch for Whalewalk Inn sign, also on right. Price guide: Rooms $135–$250; suite $175–$200.

WHEATLEIGH

HAWTHORNE ROAD, LENOX, MASSACHUSETTS 01240
TEL: 1 413 637 0610 FAX: 1 413 637 4507

Wheatleigh, an enchanting Florentine palazzo in the elite Berkshires, between New York and Boston, is today a country house hotel. Built as a wedding present from a wealthy father to his beautiful daughter in 1893, its romantic ambience is rivalled only by its perfection. Surrounded by 22 acres of well manicured gardens, parkland and tall trees, it also offers peace and privacy – ideal for an important summit meeting. The Tiffany lanterns at the gate, a fountain in front of the elaborate canopied entrance leading into the impressive Great Hall, with its graceful archways, stately columns, carved balustrades, a fine grand piano, sparkling chandelier and beautiful flowers confirm that Wheatleigh is both unique and cherished. The guestrooms, mostly overlooking the lake, are delightfully eccletic, 20th century comforts and necessities merging easily with fine period furniture and luxurious fabrics. The splendour of the dining room – Chippendale chairs, Waterford crystal and exquisite china – is matched by the inspired French dishes with American overtones and magnificent wines served by the impeccable staff. Guests can enjoy the fitness room, play tennis, swim, ski in winter, stroll in the gardens, enjoy golf nearby, hunt for antiques and in the evenings appreciate concerts at Tanglewood, home of the Boston Symphony Orchestra. **Directions:** Route 183 leads to Lenox. Price guide: Rooms $175–$565

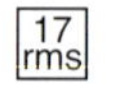

       30  9    

CLIFFSIDE INN

2 SEAVIEW AVENUE, NEWPORT, RHODE ISLAND 02840
TEL: 1 401 847 1811 FAX: 1 401 848 5850 US TOLL FREE: 1 800 845 1811

In the 19th century East Coast tycoons built magnificent weekend retreats in fashionable Rhode Island. Today Newport is a major yachting centre. Cliffside Inn is the epitome of the style and grace of the late 19th century, standing on a tree lined avenue, close to the famous Cliff Walk and the Gilded Age mansions. The interior is sumptuous Victoriana – the spectacular carved stairway, the elaborate (and comfortable) sofas, the lamps and chandeliers, self portraits of the esteemed previous owner, painter Beatric Turner, adorning the walls, grand antique sideboards, even the plants in the patios and decks are evocative of that era. Past residents might not approve of the no-smoking regime, however. The guest rooms are glorious, wonderfully peaceful, romantic floral fabrics at the windows and covering the generous-sized beds. The opulent bathrooms are a joy! Two of the luxurious suites are in the adjoining delightful Seaview Cottage. A lavish breakfast is served and a fabulous Victorian tea is offered later in the day. There is no bar, but guests may bring their own. Guests stroll along the cliffs, go to the beach, sail,play tennis, golf or fish nearby and explore Newport's fascinating old buildings and shops. **Directions:** Seaview Avenue is off Memorial Boulevard (Route 138). Abundant parking. Price guide: Rooms $195–$295; suite $295–$500.

15 rms · MasterCard · VISA · AMERICAN EXPRESS · other · 13

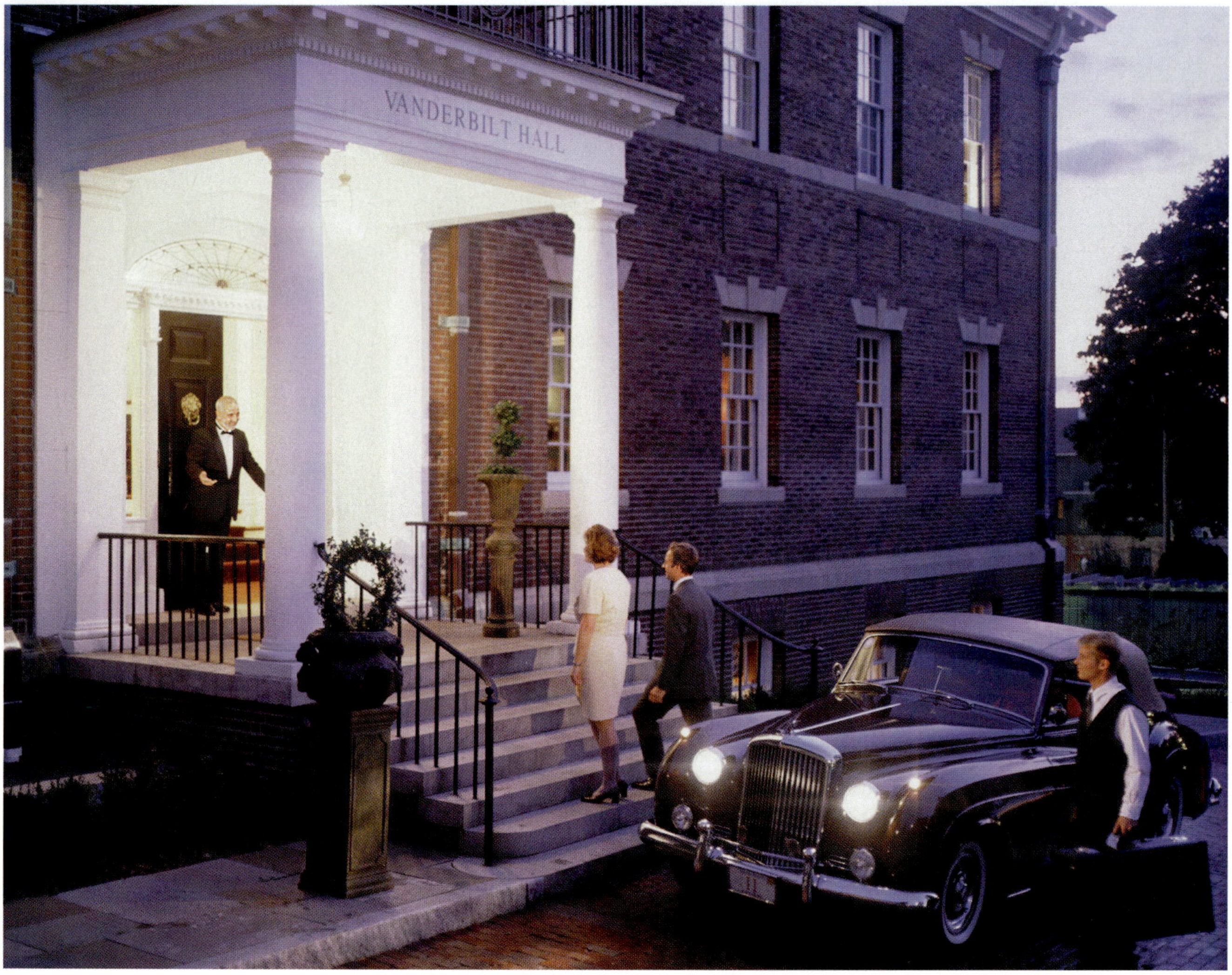

VANDERBILT HALL

41 MARY STREET, NEWPORT, RHODE ISLAND 02840
TEL: 1 401 846 6200 FAX: 1 401 846 0701

This imposing building with its white pillared façade was presented by the Vanderbilt family to the people of Newport in 1909. Vanderbilt Hall has maintained the refined atmosphere and elegance of its early years yet has undergone a careful refurbishment and the addition of many of the latest amenities. The result is a mansion house hotel with the grandeur and ambience of a grand home. The public rooms are the essence of comfort. There are several open areas, such as the roof deck, where guests can gather, relax or simply admire the panoramic views. Each of the 50 rooms is individually styled with beautiful fabrics and décor. Vanderbilt Hall is renowned for fine dining and the talented chef serves a varied and intersting menu accompanied by some excellent wines in the exquisute dining room. After dinner, guests can relax beside the fire with a cigar or a glass of brandy in the charming billiards room. Fitness facilities include a sauna, steam room and massage whilst sailing may also be practised nearby. Other pastimes include walking along the beach and harbour, shopping or exploring the historic city of Newport. **Directions:** Boston- From I-93, Rt24S for 70 miles, this becomes Rt114 (Broadway). Continue to Washington Square, bear left, at the light turn left onto Thames St. Continue 50 yards, turn left onto Mary Street. Price guide: Rooms from $95; suite $720.

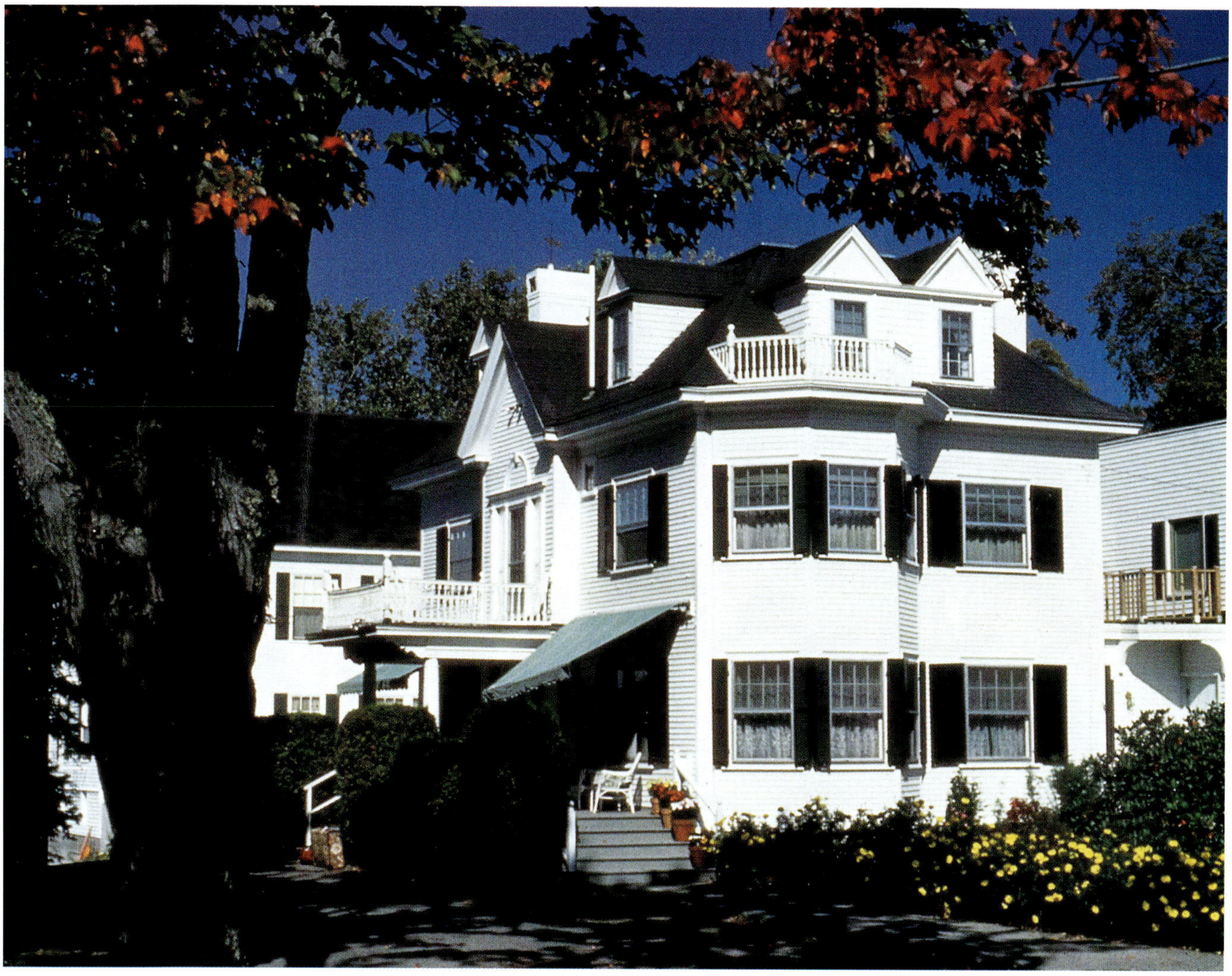

KENNEBUNKPORT INN

DOCK SQUARE, KENNEBUNKPORT, MAINE 04046
TEL: 1 207 967 2621 FAX: 1 207 967 3705

Built in 1899 by a sea captain, the Kennebunkport Inn is an attractive federal-style property, located in the centre of the village. The 19th century mansion affords beautiful views across the estuary and the surrounding New England landscape. Situated in either the mansion itself or the attached River House, the 34 bedrooms are individually appointed with antiques and fine furnishings. All offer en suite facilities and modern amenities including televisions. Guests may relax in the convivial bar, enhanced by a grand piano bar, and indulge in a pre-dinner drink. A refined ambience envelopes the exquisite dining room where the attentive staff serve regional specialities. The very best of fresh local produce such as Maine lobster is used to create the imaginative dishes. A variety of sports is available nearby and these include golf, tennis, deep sea fishing and riding. More leisurely pursuits such as rambling along the sandy beaches or exploring the rocky coastline may also be enjoyed. The Old Port at Portland, LL Bean store and other discount outlets are within easy driving distance. A fine array of boutiques, galleries and craft shops are only footsteps away. **Directions:** Leave I-95 at exit 3. Then turn left onto Route 35. Left at Route 9, over the bridge into Dock Square. Price guide: Rooms $69.50–$259; all inclusive plan from $99 per person.

The Lodge At Moosehead Lake

UPON LILY BAY ROAD, BOX 1167, GREENVILLE, MAINE 04441
TEL: 1 207 695 4400 FAX: 1 207 695 2281 E-MAIL: Lodge@Moosehead.Net

The North Woods of Maine have a rugged beauty, dense forests, and more moose than anywhere else in New England. The Lodge is typical Cape Cod colonial, in brown shingle. The façade may be rustic, the interior is not. Roger and Jennifer Cauchi have great style – their imaginative use of colour, light, raw materials and local folklore has created a friendly ambience with sophisticated overtones. The spectacular views over the lake are focus points. The guest rooms have handcarved Queen-sized beds, with individual themes. They are all luxuriously appointed and every bathroom has a Jacuzzi. Attention to detail includes concealed television and full ice-buckets! Guests recount their day over hors d'oeuvres and drinks in the charismatic Great Room, adjacent to the charming dining room which has a wall of windows overlooking the shimmering water. There is also a minute Library, the snug Toby Room and colourful Moosehead Games Room. Breakfast is a small feast, dinner (only off season when the Greenville restaurants are closed) a candlelit gastronomic experience. Activities – moose safaris, fly fishing, canoeing, seaplane expeditions, exploring national parks, boating on the lake; winter sports when the snows come. **Directions:** Interstate 95N to Newport then Route 7 North, then Route 23 North to Route 15 North. Price guide: Rooms $175–$295; suites $250–$395.

Colby Hill Inn

3 THE OAKS, PO BOX 779, HENNIKER, NEW HAMPSHIRE 03242
TEL: 1 603 428 3281 FAX: 1 603 428 9218 US TOLL FREE: 1 800 531 0330

Nestling in the hills of New Hampshire and surrounded by classic New England scenery, Colby Hill Inn is located just half a mile from the small college town of Henniker. The 18th century house is the centrepiece of a five-acre farm and comprises traditional barns, a restored carriage house, rolling fields, lush perennial gardens, and a swimming pool. While each of its 16 individually-decorated guest rooms offers a range of modern amenities to guarantee a comfortable stay, some feature the added attraction of a working fireplace. The friendly hosts have created an informal and very relaxed atmosphere; the only written rule refers to the resident dog, "please don't feed Delilah, she's had too many cookies". Guests are invited to enjoy the solitude provided by the inn's many nooks and crannies or gather by the parlour fire or over a puzzle in the games room. The popular restaurant's menu features over a dozen entrées and a choice of desserts including sumptuous home-made treats and evening drinks. The inn is only a 90 minutes' drive from Boston and Manchester airports, ideal for those touring New England. Leisure activities include downhill and cross-country skiing, hiking, bicycling, kayaking, visiting the many beaches and exploring the small shops and old book stores. **Directions:** 17 miles west of Concord off routes 202/9. Go ½ mile south on route 114 to blinking light and village centre. Turn right. The inn is ½ mile on right. Price guide: Rooms $85–$185; suites $275–$315.

16 rms MasterCard VISA AMERICAN EXPRESS other M 30 7

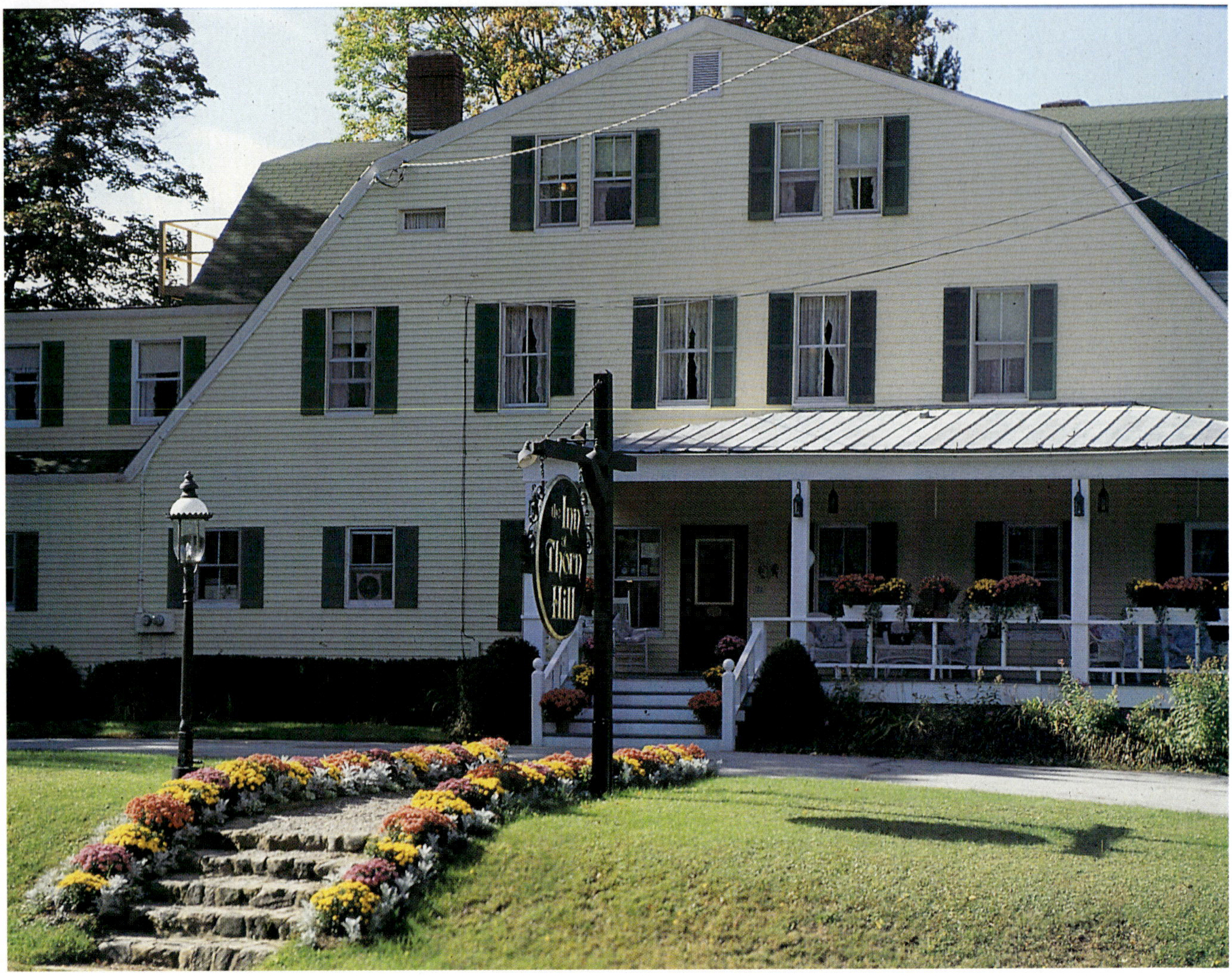

INN AT THORN HILL

THORN HILL ROAD, JACKSON, NEW HAMPSHIRE 03846
TEL: 1 603 383 4242 FAX: 1 603 383 8602

Jackson can only be reached through the 'Honeymoon Covered Bridge' – a delightful introduction to this enchanting village and the inn stands high above it, looking across to the dramatic Presidential Mountain Range. This idyllic retreat was built in 1895 and Victoriana is the theme throughout the Main Inn, with its lace curtains and fine antiques. The Parlour has a grand piano and the only television in the inn – board games, cards and books await guests' pleasure. The romantic guest rooms have old world charm. Other accommodation is country style in The Carriage House while three recently renovated cottages offer more privacy. The cosy Bar resembles a small pub, alternatively residents relax in the charming lounges or settle in the wicker chairs on the porch overlooking the gardens and mountains. The restaurant is joyous, the aroma of marvellous home cooking pervading the air. Hungry diners appreciate the rich seasonal dishes, fabulous soups and glorious pastries, accompanied by fine wines. In summer the inn has a pool; tennis, golf and riding are nearby. The Appalachian Mountain Club gives hikers and climbers good routes. In winter Jackson offers cross country and downhill skiing, skating and sleigh rides. **Directions:** From Montreal, Can-10 to Can-55, I-91 to I-93, Exit 40, take Route 302 to Route 16 North to Jackson. Price guide: Rooms $150–$300.

NESTLENOOK FARM

DINSMORE ROAD, JACKSON VILLAGE, NEW HAMPSHIRE 03846
TEL: 1 603 383 8071/9443 FAX: 1 603 383 9823

Beautifully situated in an charming little village, Nestlenook is an idyllic retreat with stunning views over the dramatic Presidential Mountain Range. Built in the Victorian gingerbread style, it is surrounded by picturesque lakeside gardens. Nestlenook Farm is a wonderfully romantic escape from the daily routine. The Victorian Village on the farm has romantic villa-style accommodation featuring large, screened-in porches with rocking chairs, queen-size beds, two-person Jacuzzis and fabulous mountain views. Every guest room is a delight. They are cosy, intimate, stylishly furnished and have every home-from-home comfort, including a Jacuzzi. Residents can relax during the evenings over a game of billiards or darts in the games rooms, which also have televisions and an extensive video collection. Outdoor activities include rowing and fishing on the lake, hiking, canoeing and mountain biking. During the colder months when the area is a scenic winter wonderland, guests can enjoy carriage and sleigh riding, ice skating, snowshoeing, cross-country skiing, or just sipping hot chocolate in the peace and quiet of the lakeside gazebo. All these activities are complimentary! **Directions:** From Montreal, Can-10 to Can-55, I-91 to I-93, Exit 40. Take Route 302 to Route 16 North to Jackson. Price guide: Rooms $125–$320.

1811 House

PO BOX 39, ROUTE 7A, MANCHESTER VILLAGE, VERMONT 05254
TEL: 1 802 362 1811 FAX: 1 802 362 2443 US TOLL FREE: 800 432 1811 E-MAIL: info@1811house.com

Pretty Manchester Village is proud of its enchanting inn, the 1811 House which has extensive gardens filled with daffodils in Spring and its own Scottish pub appreciated as much by the locals as by the hotel guests! Loving restoration work has resulted in the joyous interior of this Federal house – a fine collection of American and English antiques sits well on rich Persian carpets, handsome paintings adorn the walls while silver photograph frames and other memorabilia add a personal touch. Discreet air conditioning controls the atmosphere. It is a non-smoking house. The attractive guest rooms are filled with gracious period furniture, and many have spectacular views of the Green Mountains. A few bedrooms are in the adjacent cottage. Marnie and Bruce Duff, good Scottish names, have their individual skills. Marnie is a superb cook and her breakfasts are fabulous. Bruce is a great gardner. He is also 'mine host' of the traditional 'snug' which offers good company, well-kept ale and 63 malt whiskies. The parlour is an elegant rendezvous, the library peaceful and residents relax over a game of snooker in the games room. Restaurants abound for dinner, and in the day antique shops, boutiques, galleries, museums fishing, cycling, boating, good golf, tennis are but a selection of local activities. **Directions:** On the historic Route 7A. Price guide: Rooms $120–$230; suite $230.

14 rms MasterCard VISA AMERICAN EXPRESS other M 10 16

BASIN HARBOR CLUB

ON LAKE CHAMPLAIN, VERGENNES, VERMONT 05491
TEL: 1 802 475 2311 FAX: 1 802 475 6545 US TOLL FREE: 1 800 622 4000 E-MAIL: info@basinharbor.com

Upon arriving at this delightful New England resort, set on a cove on Lake Champlain, guests abandon the pressures of a modern existence and relax in this haven of seclusion. Basin Harbor has been in the hands of the Beach family for four generations and the warmth and hospitality of a past era is still offered here today. Three guest houses and 77 cottages lie in the 700 acres of beautiful grounds. Log fires, wooden floors and soft rugs featured throughout the property. All of the cottages are individually decorated with simple floral patterns and comfortable furnishings; many offer a view of either the lake or the waterfront. After a day of golf or other outdoor pursuits, hearty appetites are truly satisfied in the attractive Main Dining Room. Traditional American cuisine fuses with more unusual flavours, creating dishes such as Dijon-garlic marinated grilled shrimp with thyme beurre blanc and pan-roasted breast of duck with raspberry bordelaise. The excellent wine list has been thoughtfully compiled. Sporting activities include canoeing, kayaking, sailing, water-skiing and hiking. Trips to the Ben and Jerry factory, Burlington's Church Street and Lake Champlain Maritime Museum are popular excursions. **Directions:** Take Interstate 89 to exit 1 at Woodstock. Take route 4 to Rutland, then North onto route 7 to Vergennes. Take 22A through Vergennes, turn right onto Basin Harbor Road for six miles. Price guide: Rooms $119–$210; suite $200–$425.

CHURCHILL HOUSE INN

ROUTE 73 EAST RR3 BOX 3265, BRANDON, VERMONT 05733
TEL: 1 802 247 3078 E-MAIL: innkeeper@churchillhouseinn.com

Nestling on the edge of the National Forest, the Churchill House Inn is a charming property retaining the gracious hospitality and fine service of its past years. Built in 1872 by the Churchill family, this old farmhouse has been frequented by travellers for over a century and its popularity with visitors to New England remains today. The interior is decorated in a country-house style and features a delightful blend of antique and modern furnishings. Comfort is an important criterion in the nine bedrooms. Each offers en suite bathrooms, large beds and attractive décor. Guests recline and enjoy a book or converse with others in the inviting sitting rooms whilst jigsaw puzzles, solitaire and other games may be played in the games room. The Inn has a licence for wine and beer and guests mix their own drinks at the bar on the porch before savouring the country-style dinner. The sumptuous cuisine features home-made soups, freshly baked breads and desserts and is served by candlelight on a grand oak table. A hearty breakfast prepares guests for the active day ahead. The Green Mountain National Forest is adjacent to the inn and provides excellent opportunities for hiking, skiing, fishing and biking. **Directions:** Take Route 7 to Brandon. The Inn is 4 miles east on Route 73. Price guide: Rooms \$110–\$120; suite \$140–\$200.

CORNUCOPIA OF DORSET

ROUTE 30, DORSET, VERMONT 05251

TEL: 1 802 867 5751 FAX: 1 802 867 5753 E-MAIL: innkeeper@cornucopiaofdorset.com

Cornucopia of Dorset is set in a picturesque New England village, situated in the hills of the breathtaking Green Mountains and lying only footsteps away from the local church. A champagne greeting is just one of the delightful surprises that await guests to this romantic getaway, which prides itself on offering the elegance, amenities and personal service found in the finest properties. The main house has four de luxe and spacious bedrooms, each named after local mountain peaks. There is also an attractive cottage suite with a loft bedroom and full range of modern amenities. Guests relax in front of the fire in the comfortable study and living room or enjoy the beautiful views afforded from the marble patio. Exotic and local seasonal fruits feature on the first course of the candlelit breakfast, followed by delicious entrées, freshly-squeezed fruit juice and superior blends of tea and coffee. Many fine dining establishments and a convivial pub are within walking distance. Dorset is the site of the first marble quarry in North America and features on the National Register of Historic Places. A huge range of cultural, leisure and outdoor activities lie within easy reach. The area is a haven for enthusiasts of the dramatic arts with Southern Vermont Art Center and the Dorset Theatre Festival among the many nearby attractions. **Directions:** The inn is 6 miles north of Manchester on Route 30, south of the Dorset Village Green. Price guide: Rooms $125–$175; cottage $210–$255.

The Inn At Shelburne Farms

1611 HARBOR ROAD, SHELBURNE, VERMONT 05482
TEL: 1 802 985 8498 FAX: 1 802 985 8123

Shelburne Farms is a magnificent estate extending to the shore of Lake Champlain (the 6th largest lake in the United States). It is still a working farm. The Inn was built by a member of the Vanderbilt family in 1887, an impressive mansion overlooking the sparkling water, standing in formal gardens and set against a background of the Adirondack and Green Mountains. It is incredibly beautiful. The salons are evocative of an era of gracious living – graceful archways, handsome paintings, rich rugs on polished floors and exceptional antiques. The guest rooms (a few in adjacent cottages) are also reminiscent of times past – washbasins with a patina of 100 years of use – not all are en suite. The splendid comfortable brass bedsteads, lovely views and tranquility are timeless. The day starts with a traditional breakfast – brunch on Sundays! Delicious picnic hampers can be arranged. Reservations should be made for dinner, a gourmet meal accompanied by fine wines. The Inn offers tennis, canoeing, croquet, fishing, swimming and recommends walking trails through the estate. Golf and sailing are nearby, also the Shelburne Museum. Tours of the farm and concerts are shared with non-residents. Boat trips on the lake are entertaining. **Directions:** The estate is at the intersection of Bay and Harbor Roads, off Route 7 in Shelburne. Price guide: Rooms $95–$350.

24 rms MasterCard VISA AMERICAN EXPRESS other M 20

THE MOUNTAIN ROAD RESORT

STOWE, VERMONT 05672

TEL: 1 802 253 4566 FAX: 1 802 253 7397 UK FREEPHONE 0800 894 581 E-MAIL: stowevt@aol.com

The Mountain Road Resort is a vibrant, cosmopolitan and stylish hotel surrounded by seven acres of landscaped gardens. The complex is pristine and the accommodation includes commodious bedrooms with comfortable country-style furnishings, air conditioning, modern bathrooms and many gas-powered fireplaces. There are also luxurious studios and split level suites with full kitchens, large windows and Jacuzzis. No smoking is the rule. A lavish continental breakfast is served in The Library. There is no restaurant but afternoon refreshments are served. Children have a Games Room. Billy's Wine Bar has excellent vintages, several beers, 'munchable' snacks and Ben & Jerry's ice cream. The Mountain Road has a 'Dine Around' option and the Stowe Trolley transports guests into town – babysitters available. The Resort has a splendid outdoor pool, tennis and boules – indoors a marvellous Aqua-Centre with fitness facilities. The sun terraces are great for doing nothing! Special green fees have been organised at local golf clubs and other summer sports are tennis, canoeing, fishing, hiking and riding. Winter sports include downhill and cross-country skiing. Boat trips on Lake Champlain and gondola rides up the mountain are leisure activities. Internet: www.stowevtusa.com **Directions:** Interstate 89 to Junction 10, then Route 100 to Stowe. Price guide: Rooms \$95–\$205; suites \$215–\$395.

MOUNTAIN TOP INN & RESORT

MOUNTAIN TOP ROAD, CHITTENDEN, VERMONT 05737
TEL: 1 802 483 2311 FAX: 1 802 483 6373 E-MAIL: info@mountaintopinn.com

Mountain Top, known as 'Vermont's best kept secret' is a marvellous resort, famous for its cross country ski-ing but also delightful in summer – and the Inn plays an important role in its success. This is an enchanting small hotel – as it name suggests, at the top of a mountain, so the views are spectacular all the year round. Purpose built, it has every modern comfort. The spacious guest rooms are charming, decorated in soft colours, with country style furniture, and the bathrooms are efficient. Some are in the adjacent cottages and chalets. The lounges are also simplistic and attractive, looking out onto the mountains and the games room is the social centre. The elegant restaurant has big picture windows, and offers New England cooking at its best. Good wines are listed. The Inn is no smoking throughout. Mountain Top has its own ski instructors and shop. Skating and sleighrides are other popular winter diversions. In summer the Golf School is active, with tuition for all handicaps. The enormous estate has excellent facilities for shooting, riding, fishing, tennis, swimming, while the lake has a sandy beach and opportunities for windsurfing and other water sports. Also Vermont must be explored. **Directions:** Route 7, then Route 4, left onto Meadowlake Drive and follow road to the very top. Price guide: Rooms $168–$226; suite $226–$268.

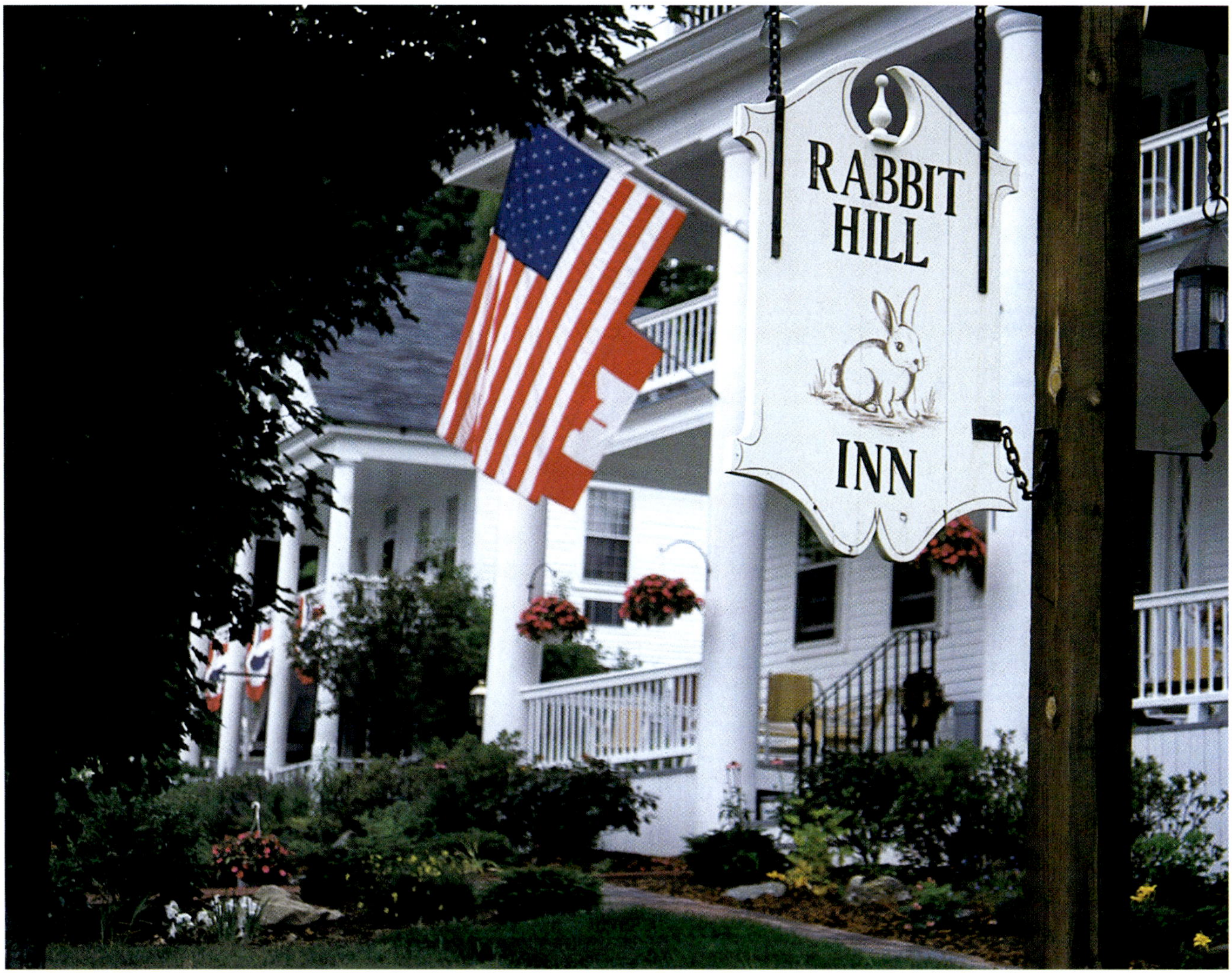

RABBIT HILL INN

1 PUCKER STREET, LOWER WATERFORD, VERMONT 05848
TEL: 1 802 748 5168 FAX: 1 802 748 8342

Rabbit Hill Inn is a luxurious and historical escape from the pressures of today's busy world. The property is truly romantic: from the soft strains of music welcoming visitors as they step across the entrance porch to the restful glow of candles pervading the bedrooms as they retire for the night. Innkeepers Brian and Leslie Mulcahy are dedicated to pampering guests in a stylish and comfortable environment. Overlooking the beautiful White Mountains and the Connecticut River Valley, the Inn was built in 1795 to serve the needs of travellers journeying between Canada and the New England harbours. The property has been completely restored and modernised but has retained many of its classic features, antique furnishings and its historical atmosphere. The stylish bedrooms are enhanced by original artworks, whirlpool baths and magnificent King and Queen-sized canopy beds. The whimsical use of rabbits is delightful: from bunny-shaped butter to sculpted rabbits tucked into the beams, these animals are scattered throughout. Guests relax in the parlours or the Snooty Fox Pub before indulging in the superb cuisine offered in the candlelit dining room. The exquisite dishes are made with fresh ingredients and include produce from the Inn's own greenhouse and garden. On site activities include canoeing, hiking and sledding. **Directions:** From I93 north, exit 44, onto Rt18 north, 2 miles to the inn. Price guide (incl. breakfast, tea, dinner & all service charges): Rooms $210–$295; suites $275–$370.

Red Clover Inn

WOODWARD ROAD, MENDON, VERMONT 05701
TEL: 1 802 775 2290 US TOLL FREE: 1 800 752 0571

Red Clover Inn was built in 1840 by General John Woodward who used it as a private retreat. The qualities that made it perfect for that purpose nearly 160 years ago are still evident today. The inn lies on a quiet road in the shadow of the Green Mountains and guests invariably comment that they feel like guests in a private home. There are 14 charmingly appointed bedrooms, most offering splendid views . While all are equipped with private baths, some also boast fireplaces, whirlpools and air conditioning. Home-cooked delights such as cinnamon swirl French toast are among the specialities served in the sun-lit breakfast room. The dinner menu is exceptional – savour the boneless Vermont trout, stuffed with garlic rosemary potato soufflé surrounded by assorted baby squashes or treat your palate to grilled Portabello Mushroom Cap Napoleon, layered with spinach, eggplant and Vermont goat cheese on a red and yellow pepper coulis. An excellent range of leisure and recreational activities in the area include cross-country skiing, hiking, biking and riding. In the summer months, guests are invited to make use of the inn' s knoll-top pool. **Directions:** I–87N to route 149E to route 4 into and through Rutland. Then take route 4E. Go 5.2m and turn right onto Woodward Road. I–91N to I-89N to exit 1 in Vermont. Take route 4W to Mendon and turn left onto Woodward Road. Price guide: Rooms $140–$275 (low season); $165–$365 (high season).

Canada

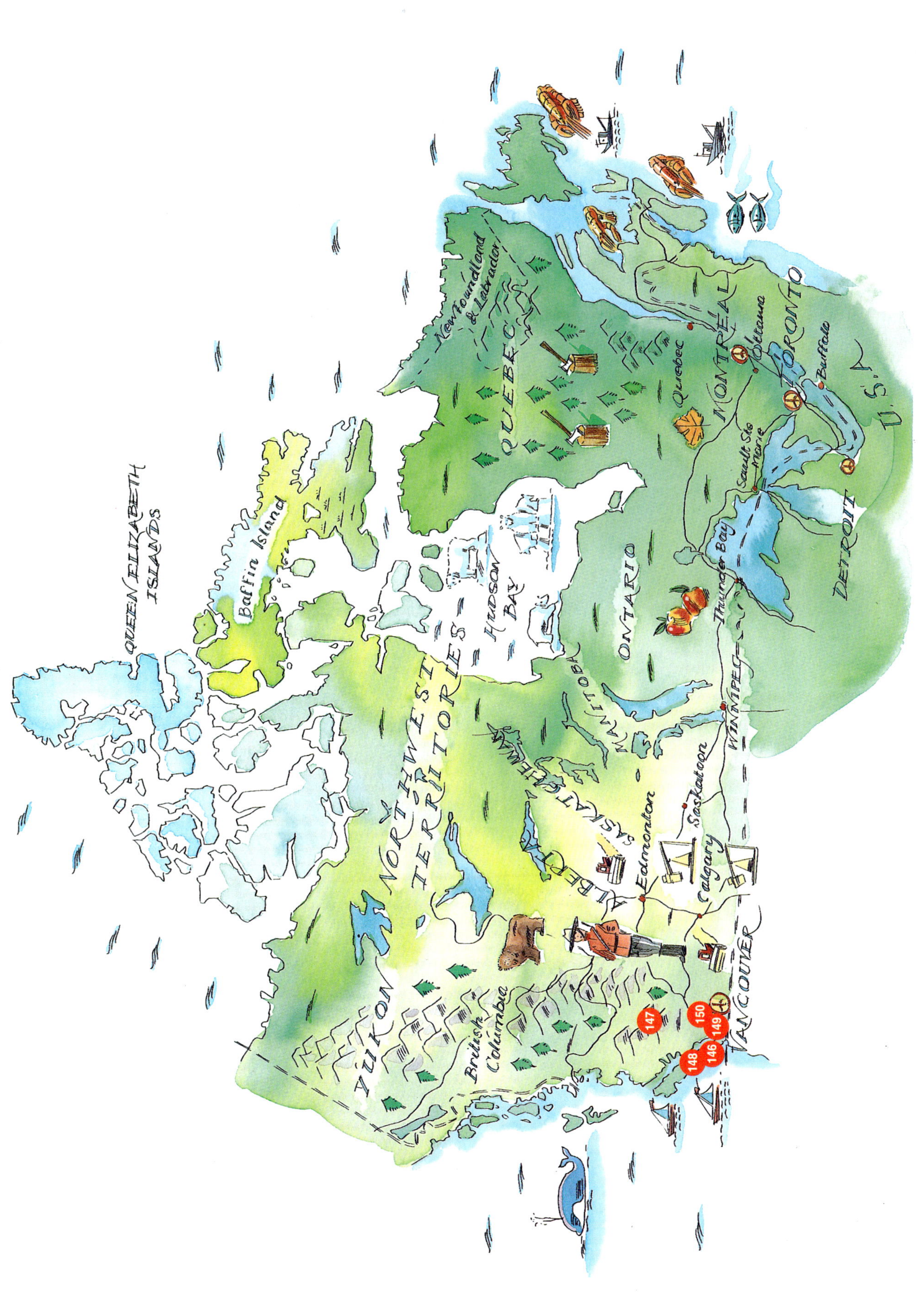
QUEEN ELIZABETH ISLANDS
Baffin Island
HUDSON BAY
NORTHWEST TERRITORIES
YUKON
British Columbia
ALBERTA
SASKATCHEWAN
MANITOBA
ONTARIO
QUEBEC
Newfoundland & Labrador
Edmonton
Calgary
Saskatoon
WINNIPEG
VANCOUVER
Thunder Bay
Sault Ste Marie
MONTREAL
Ottawa
Quebec
TORONTO
Buffalo
DETROIT
U.S.A.
146
147
148
149
150

Dashwood Manor

1 COOK STREET, VICTORIA, BRITISH COLUMBIA V8V 3W6

TEL: 1 250 385 5517 FAX: 1 250 383 1760 TOLL FREE: 1 800 667 5517 E-MAIL: reservations@dashwoodmanor.com

This grand Edwardian house, its half timbering and large gables reflecting the Tudor revival period of the early 20th century has been imaginatively transformed into a unique bed and breakfast residence. Dashwood Manor, named after its owner Derek Dashwood, is in a magnificent position, right across the road from the shore of lovely Vancouver Island, with spectacular views over the Strait of Juan de Fuca, yet only minutes walk through verdant Beacon Hill Park to the centre of Victoria. All the accommodation is in self-contained suites, each equipped with a small kitchen offering a simple yet satisfying breakfast. Guests appreciate the privacy offered and the elegance of the rooms, some having chandeliers, fireplaces, balcony or Jacuzzi, others hideaway beds in the attractive living rooms. All have Queen beds with traditional floral quilts and period piece furniture. Budget suites do not look over the Ocean, however the grandest suites do. Early risers may see whales, seals and sea otters close to the beach while eagles soar in the sky and birdsong fills the air. The waterfront is fascinating with big ships, yachts and windsurfers all on the move. Downtown Victoria has excellent restaurants, fine museums and traditional buildings, harbour trips and good sports facilities. **Directions:** The Manor is on the corner of Cook Street and Dallas Road, right on the coast. Price guide: Rooms $175 Cdn–$385 Cdn.

15 rms

DURLACHER HOF

BOX 1125-7055 NESTERS ROAD, WHISTLER, BRITISH COLUMBIA VON IBO
TEL: 1 604 932 1924 FAX: 1 604 938 1980 E-MAIL: durlacher.hof@bc.sympalico.ca

Seventy-five miles north of Vancouver, in the province of British Columbia, is the internationally famed Canadian ski-resort and summer playground of Whistler. There, amidst the breathtaking landscape, lies this wonderful alpine country inn run by the Durlacher family whose roots are in Austria. It is a holiday resort par excellence, offering superb sporting facilities for the energetic and a relaxing ambience for those seeking tranquillity. The timber building has been constructed in a traditional style and conserves warmth during the winter season. Indoors, the lounge and bar are charmingly comfortable and friendly. Slippers are de rigueur, thus adding to the homely atmosphere. Breakfasts are a banquet, packed lunches are available and special dinners are often arranged. The guest rooms are well-appointed – all have baths, showers or Jacuzzis – the beds are adorned with goose-down duvets. In addition to the excellent customary winter sports facilities there is, in the warmer seasons, a variety of activities for all visitors: golf at three championship courses, riding on either horses or mountain bikes, canoeing, walking and para-gliding. Entertainment includes jazz festivals, bluegrass music and the celebrated Oktoberfest. **Directions:** The Durlachers will be delighted to arrange for you to be collected from Vancouver Airport, or to have you greeted at the local rail or bus station. Drivers must take Highway 99. Price guide: Price on application.

SEASIDE LUXURY RESORT

8355 LOCKSIDE DRIVE, SIDNEY, BRITISH COLUMBIA, CANADA
TEL: 1 250 544 1000 FAX: 1 250 544 1001

Created to provide its guests with unsurpassed warmth, luxury and privacy, this exclusive property enjoys a superb location. Situated in 3 acres of the finest ocean front on Vancouver Island and surrounded by magnificent beaches, the Seaside Luxury Resort is ideal for those seeking complete seclusion and privacy. The interior is furnished in a stylish manner and no detail has been overlooked. Each of the luxurious suites offers glorious views of the ocean, private bathrooms, satellite televisions and patio doors opening out onto the sundeck. The Diamond Suite and the Emerald Suite feature a Jacuzzi hot tub. Gourmet breakfasts are served in the privacy of the guests' own rooms or, for the more sociable, in the dining room. Fitness enthusiasts may use the Swedish designed indoor heated ozonated pool, hot tub and the fitness area. Outdoor activities are also provided and these include crabbing, fishing charters, whale-watching, sea kayaking and canoeing. For the less energetic, the beach front is perfect for strolling and admiring the spectacular sunrises whilst bird-watchers will be fascinated with the resident bald eagle, nesting beside the house. Weddings, reunions and other private functions can be held at the Resort. Whether they seek a private hideaway or wish to join other friends; all guests are promised a most memorable stay. **Directions:** Turn off HWY 17 onto Mt Newton Cross Road, then right on Lochside Drive, 15 mins from Victoria. Price guide: Rooms $150– $295.

6 rms

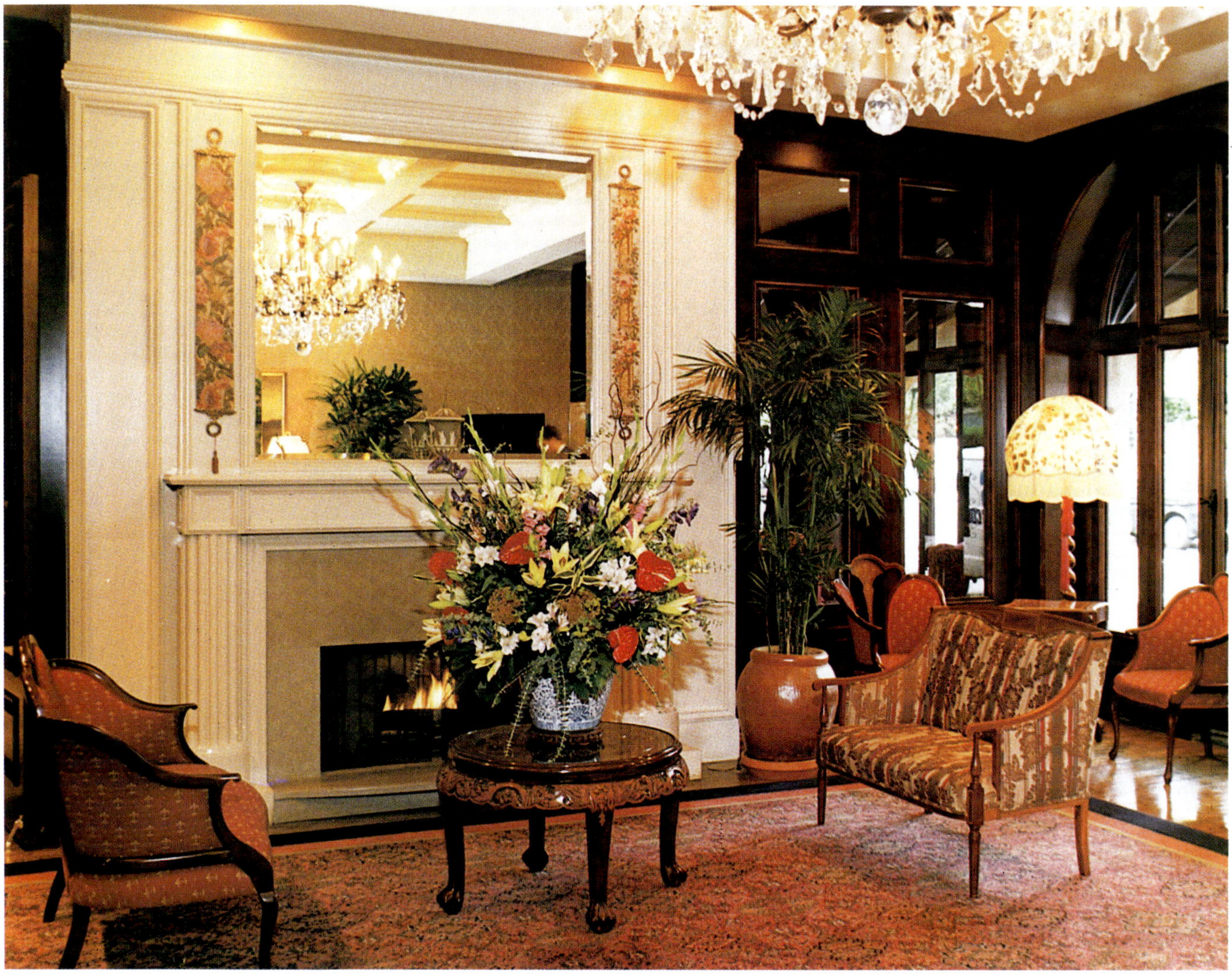

The Wedgewood Hotel

845 HORNBY STREET, VANCOUVER, BRITISH COLUMBIA, V6Z 1V1

TEL: 1 604 689 7777 FAX: 1 604 608 5348 US/CDA TOLL FREE 1 800 663 0666 E-MAIL: info@wedgewoodhotel.com

The Wedgewood, situated on Vancouver's stylish Robson Square, is a charming boutique-style hotel offering the latest modern amenities and excellent service. The refined interior is the height of European elegance. The hotel offers an interesting selection of individually appointed bedrooms which feature floral arrangements, original antiques, fine tapestries and other pieces of art. All rooms feature balconies, while the penthouse suites offer fireplaces, wet-bars, Jacuzzis and scenic garden terraces. The Wedgewood offers extraordinary dining in its popular restaurant, Bacchus. Its adaptation of Northern Italian cuisine, prepared with the freshest of local ingredients, creates a surprisingly light and pleasing version of the old country's original recipes. The extensive wine list will please the most particular of connoisseurs while the richly furnished cigar room with its rare selection of cigars, ports, double malt whiskies and cognacs is a perfect accompaniment. Advance reservations are highly recommended! The Piano Lounge offers an exciting and well-attended cocktail hour and after-theatre "Rendez-vous". Other delights include traditional afternoon tea and weekend brunch. The hotel's central location offers every leisure activity within walking distance from shopping, fine dining to entertainment, sightseeing and markets. **Directions**: The hotel is situated downtown, 30 minutes from Vancouver International Aiport. Price guide: Rooms Cdn$200–$340; suites Cdn$420– $540.

M 65

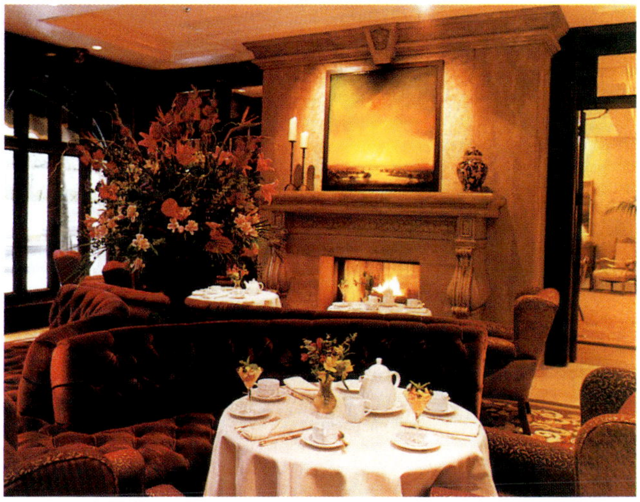

THE WEST END GUEST HOUSE

1362 HARO STREET, VANCOUVER, BRITISH COLUMBIA V6E 1G2
TEL: 1 604 681 2889 FAX: 1 604 688 8812

Those wishing to explore the exciting city of Vancouver will be pleased with location of the West End Guest House. This delightful property offers warmth and character whilst exuding old world charm. Following a careful refurbishment, the interior of the house has been updated and offers many modern amenities alongside old Victorian furnishings. The bedrooms, varying in size, are all individually decorated with diverse colour schemes. A beautiful fireplace forms the centrepiece of the Parlour and the sun deck, verandah and small garden, are ideal places to recline and enjoy the relaxing atmosphere. Gourmet breakfasts comprising freshly baked pastries, cereals, fruit and daily entrées are served in the main floor salons whilst home-made cookies or tarts await the guests at turndown. Activities include visiting art galleries and museums, shopping and dining in the many restaurants within the area. The interesting cities of Granville Island, Chinatown, Gastown and Yaletown are worth a visit. **Directions:** From Vancouver International Airport, take Grant McConachie Way following signs to Vancouver over Arthur Lang Bridge. Take the Granville Street exit, follow Granville to bridge and exit at Seymour Street and then left to Robson Street. Exit left at Broughton Street, the hotel is one block on the left. Price guide: Rooms $150 Cdn–$225 Cdn.

8 rms MasterCard VISA AMERICAN EXPRESS

Bermuda & Caribbean

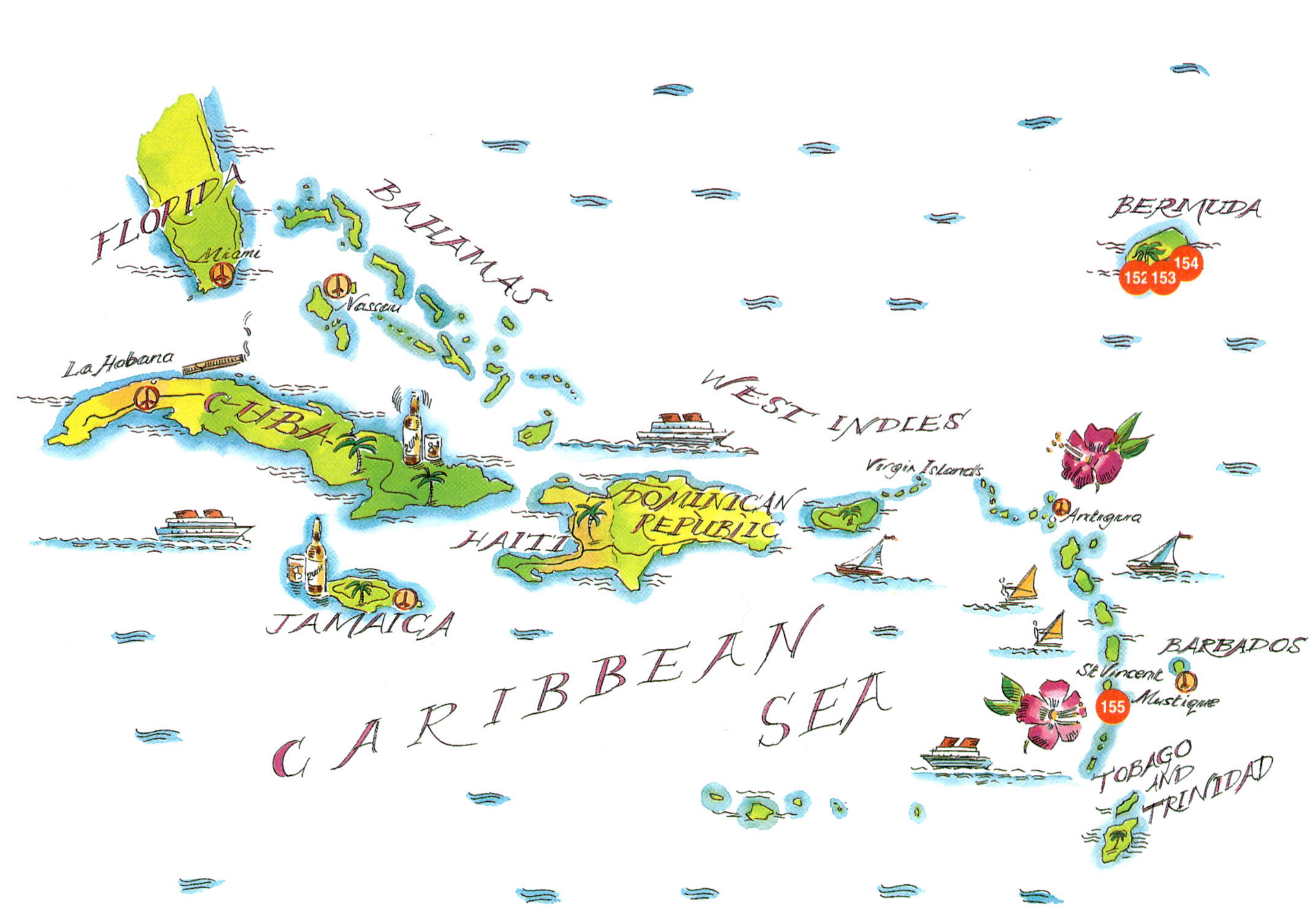

HARMONY CLUB

PO BOX 299, PAGET, BERMUDA PG BX
TEL: 1 441 236 3500 FAX: 1 441 236 2624

Surrounded by gorgeous colours under a cloudless blue sky, Bermuda's first all-inclusive resort is a glorious hideaway nestling in the heart of this sunshine island. Harmony Club combines privacy, casual elegance and gracious warmth with convenience, quality and excellent value for money. It can be as lively or as restful as you want it to be and guests can pursue their favourite pastimes at their leisure. Every guest can feel pampered by the facilities, which include tennis, swimming, a sauna and a whirlpool. Two-seater scooters are provided for those wishing to explore the island. Scattered among the brightly coloured hibiscus blossoms, tropical flowers, tall palms and manicured lawns are 68 intimate, pink and white guest rooms built in traditional British cottage-style. They are delightfully appointed and have every amenity from air conditioning, bathrooms, radio and television to de luxe toiletries and tea/coffee making facilities. Superb food, generous drinks, complimentary evening cocktails and nightcaps can be enjoyed in the enchanting gardens. The attractions of Bermuda are close at hand and special packages, including green fees and transportation, can be arranged for golfing enthusiasts. **Directions:** The resort is nine miles from the airport and two miles from Hamilton city centre. Harmony Club provides airport transfers for all their guests. Price guide: De luxe double rooms $311–$431.

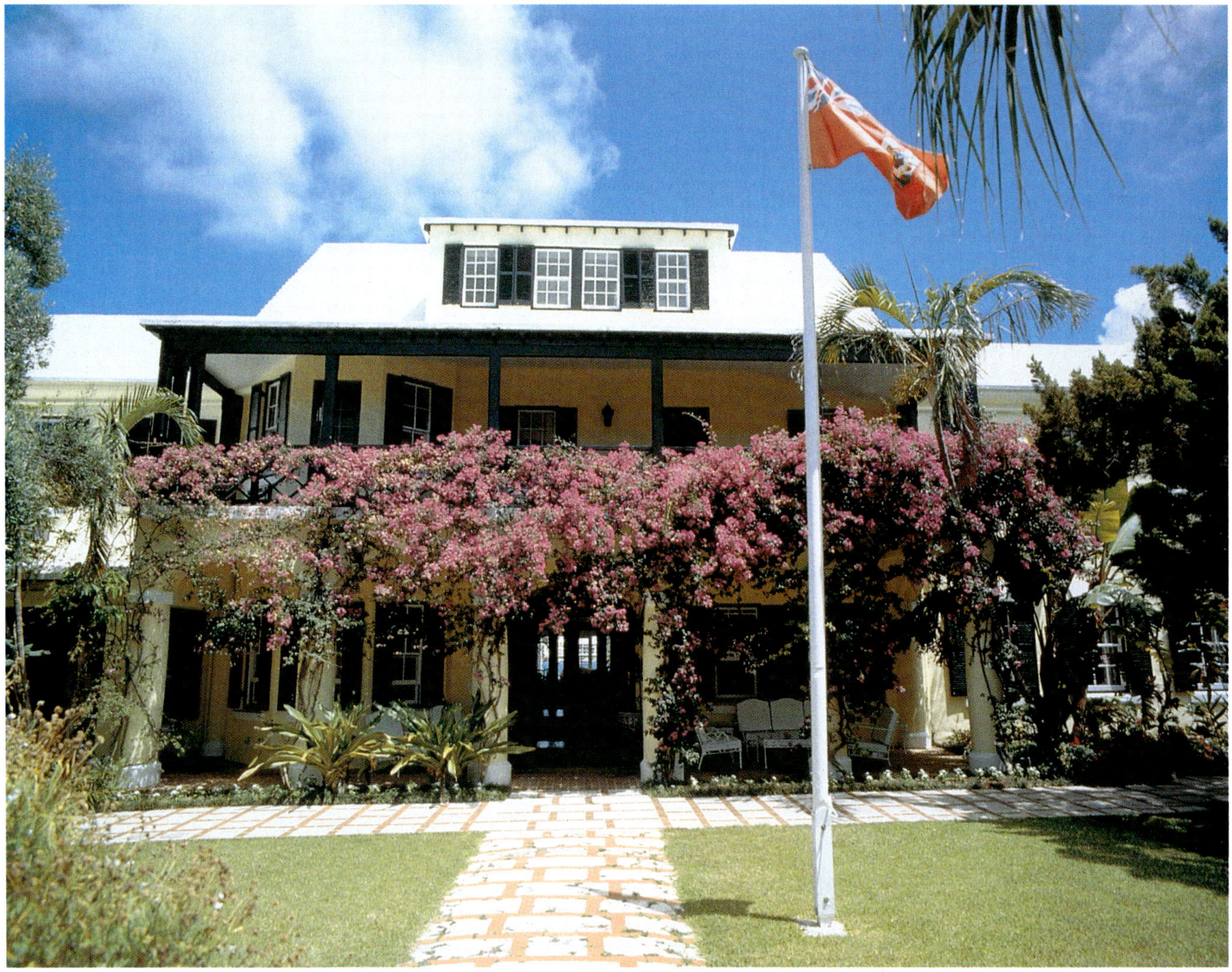

THE NEWSTEAD HOTEL

27 HARBOUR ROAD, PAGET PG02, BERMUDA
TEL: 1 441 236 6060 FAX: 1 441 236 7454

Sunshine yellow under a sparkling white roof the gracious, classical colonial style Newstead Hotel stands regally on a gently terraced hillside overlooking Hamilton Harbour and the beautiful outer islands of Bermuda. It is an enchanting manor house incorporating the traditional and modern in an exquisitely manicured garden setting of quiet tranquillity. Most of the bedrooms have been recently refurbished with cheerful prints and the finest fabrics and furniture. All have private terraces and enjoy panoramic views over the harbour, the garden or the superb freshwater swimming pool surrounded by lounges and sun umbrellas. The hotel's kitchens produce the best of American and European cuisine which diners can enjoy on the Harbour Terrace after leisurely sunset cocktails prior to dancing under the stars. There are two clay tennis courts and a putting green. Guests can also enjoy the privileges of the hotel's sister property, the exclusive Coral Beach and Tennis Club, taking advantage of the most spectacular beach on the island, tennis on championship courts, croquet, squash, bowls and the fitness centre with an in-house personal trainer. Windsailing, waterskiing and scuba diving amenities and major golf courses are within easy reach. **Directions:** Overlooking Hamilton Harbour a short ferry ride from the town centre. Price guide: Rooms from $275; suites from $375.

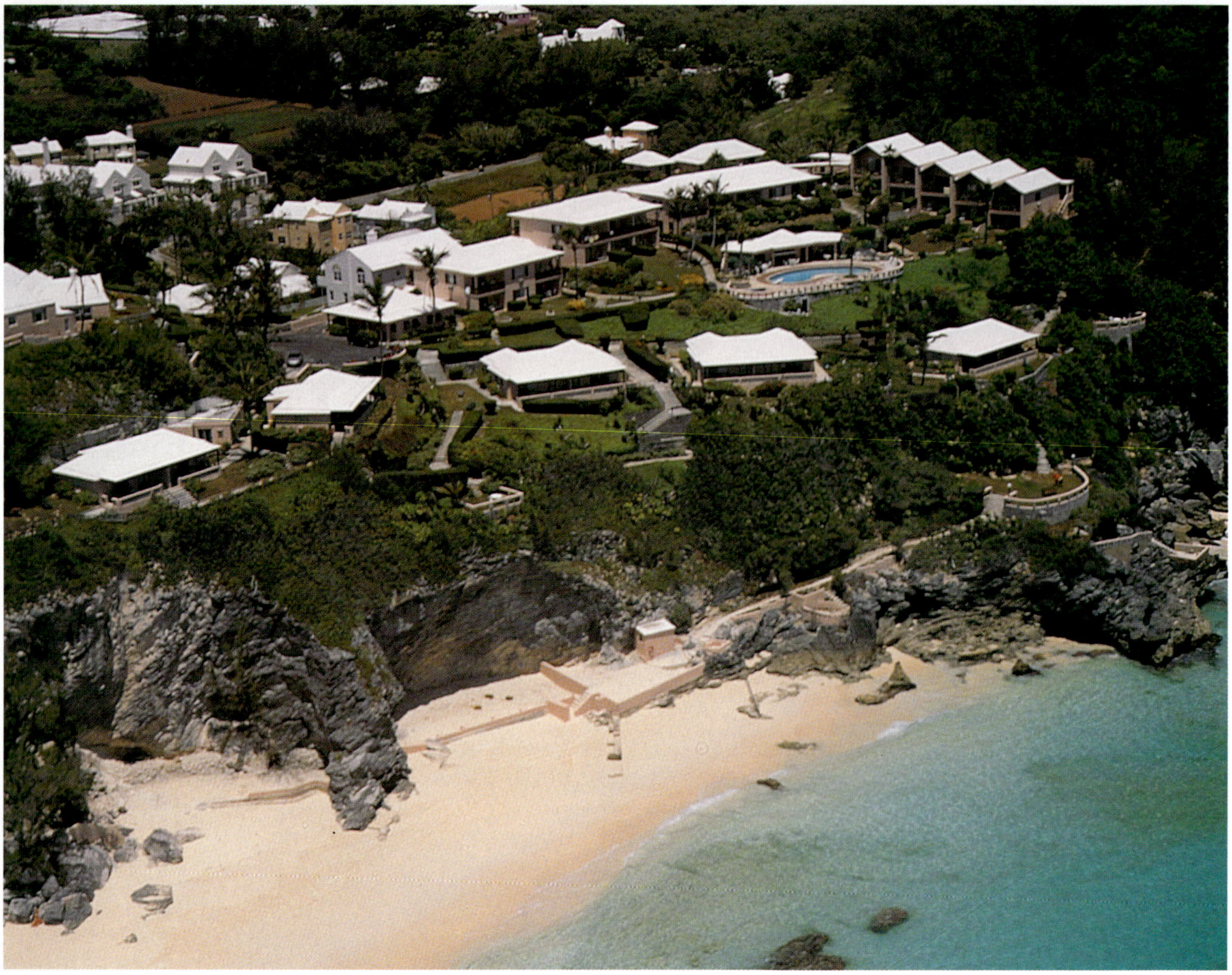

Surf Side Beach Club

90 SOUTH SHORE ROAD, WARWICK, BERMUDA
TEL: 1 441 236 7100 FAX: 1 441 236 9765

Surf Side is a sunny hideaway overlooking Bermuda's unique South Shore, surrounded by five acres of landscaped hillside terraces and walkways above beautiful, white-sanded beaches and coves. Scattered among the colourful hibiscus blossoms, tall palms and manicured lawns are 37 cottages, apartment-style units and penthouses. Each has its own sea view and is designed for privacy. Guests are provided with every home comfort, from tastefully furnished bedrooms and lounges to fully-fitted kitchens and either a secluded garden patio or a wide, plant-bedecked balcony where the only sound is that of breaking waves. With a natural ambience created by the moon, stars, soft tropical breezes and delicate scent of flowers, the Palms Restaurant and Bar serves outstanding cuisine and island cocktails beside the pool. Views from the pool's sun lounges are magnificent. The same family have owned Surf Side for more than 20 years and guarantee a relaxed and unpretentious atmosphere which is ideal for those who love to be self-sufficient and free to discover the delights of the island. For the energetic visitor Surf Side has a fully equipped fitness centre, complete with sauna, Jacuzzi and a personal fitness trainer. Golf and riding are nearby. **Directions:** 3 miles west of of Hamilton. Price guide (until March 1998): Studio units $185; family unit from $215; Penthouse West/East $325.

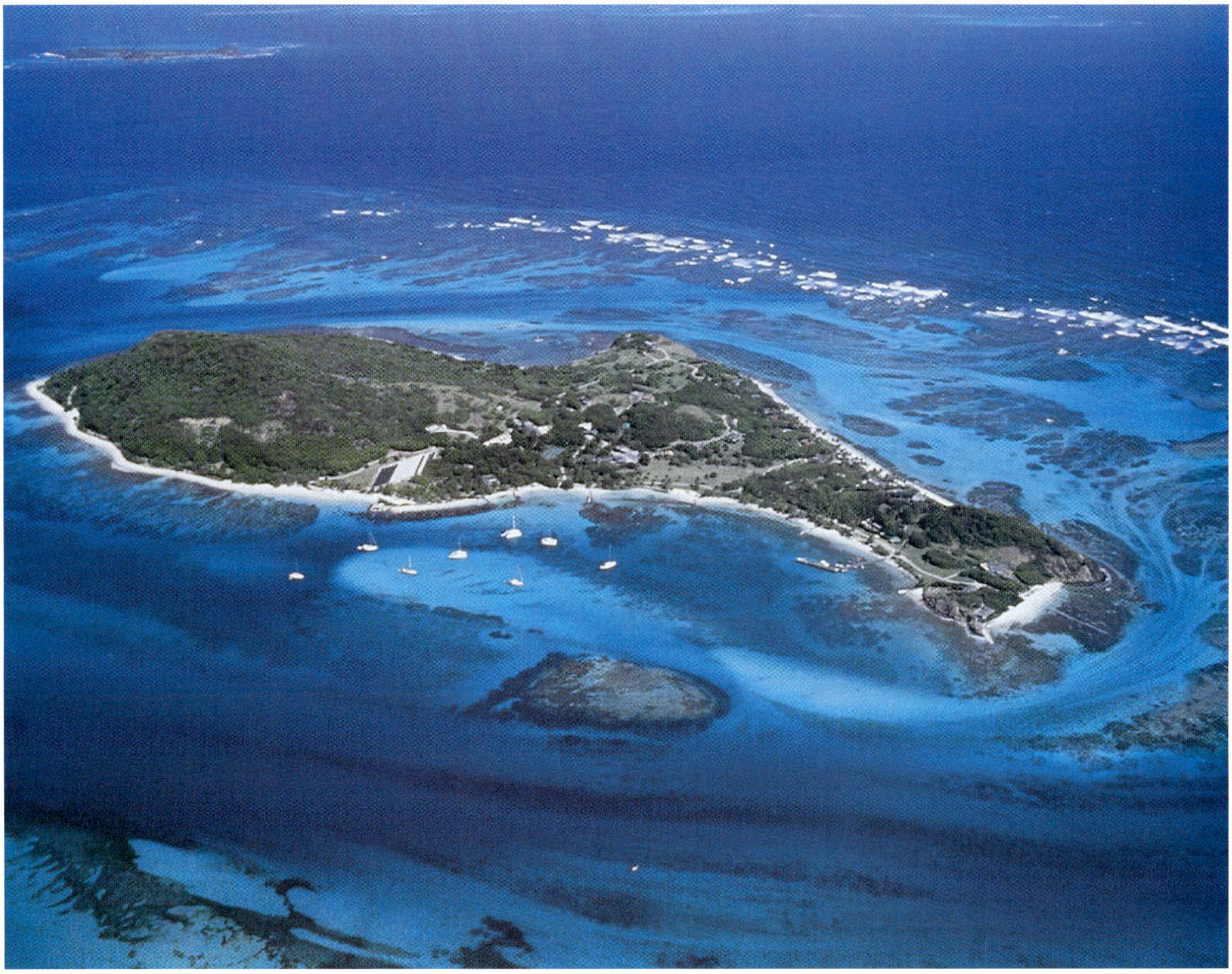

Petit St Vincent Resort

THE GRENADINES, ST VINCENT, WEST INDIES
TEL: 1 787 458 8801 FAX: 1 787 458 8428

Petit St Vincent is one of 200 small islands in the Grenadines, discovered by Christopher Columbus in 1498. One seldom thinks of paradise as an island, but here it is – just 113 privately owned acres surrounded by white sand beaches. This resort is magical, accessible only by boat, a sophisticated yet wonderfully casual lifestyle prevailing. There is the Main House and, set well apart, 22 gorgeous cottages built in the local bluebitch stone and purpleheart hardwood. Each has a flagpole – for refreshments fly the yellow flag and a room service patrol driver collects your order; for 'do not disturb' fly the red one. There are no distracting telephones nor televisions. The patios and decks look out over the Caribbean; gently rock in a hammock to the sound of the sea lapping against the shore. Guests mingle in the bars, some tables in the shade, others for sun-worshippers, before enjoying the colourful buffet lunch or fabulous dinners served in the cool pavilion, with attractive cane furniture, overlooking the harbour – local fish (including lobsters) and West Indian specialities featuring on the menu. A string band plays at the weekly barbecues Active guests sail, snorkel, go deep sea fishing, play tennis, windsurf, ride Hobie Cats or swim. Others have a wonderful time doing nothing! **Directions:** Fly to Union Island – the hotel launch collects you. Prices guide: Rooms $510–$800

1999 Johansens Recommended Hotels in North America listed alphabetically by Country and State

Hotels accepting the Johansens Privilege Card

10% discount, room upgrade where available, VIP service at participating establishments. Full Terms & Conditions available on request.

Alphabetical lists of Johansens recommendations in Great Britain and Ireland, and also Europe, published in full in other Johansens guides. See the back cover and p163 for more details and how to order all these publications.

Hotels

London

Chelsea ... Draycott House Apartments ... 0171 584 4659
Chelsea ... Park Consul Hotel ... 0171 225 7500
Covent Garden ... One Aldwych ... 0171 300 1000
Holland Park ... The Halcyon ... 0171 727 7288
Kensington ... The Cranley ... 0171 373 0123
Kensington ... Harrington Hall ... 0171 396 9696
Kensington ... The Milestone ... 0171 917 1000
Kensington ... Pembridge Court Hotel ... 0171 229 9977
Knightsbridge ... Basil Street Hotel ... 0171 581 3311
Knightsbridge ... The Beaufort ... 0171 584 5252
Knightsbridge ... Beaufort House Apartments ... 0171 584 2600
Knightsbridge ... The Cadogan ... 0171 235 7141
Knightsbridge ... The Cliveden Town House ... 0171 730 6466
Knightsbridge ... The London Outpost of the Carnegie Club ... 0171 589 7333
Knightsbridge ... Number Eleven Cadogan Gardens ... 0171 730 7000
Lancaster Gate ... The Hempel ... 0171 298 9000
Mayfair ... The Ascott Mayfair ... 0171 499 6868
Mayfair ... The Dorchester ... 0171 629 8888
Portman Square ... The Leonard ... 0171 935 2010
South Kensington ... Blakes Hotel ... 0171 370 6701
South Kensington ... Number Sixteen ... 0171 589 5232
Whitehall ... The Royal Horseguards ... 0171 839 3400
Wimbledon Common ... Cannizaro House ... 0181 879 1464

England

Abberley ... The Elms ... 01299 896666
Aldeburgh ... Wentworth Hotel ... 01728 452312
Alderley Edge ... The Alderley Edge Hotel ... 01625 583033
Alfriston ... White Lodge Country House Hotel ... 01323 870265
Alston ... Lovelady Shield Country House Hotel ... 01434 381203
Amberley ... Amberley Castle ... 01798 831992
Ambleside ... Holbeck Ghyll Country House Hotel ... 015394 32375
Ambleside ... Langdale Hotel & Country Club ... 015394 37302
Ambleside ... Nanny Brow Country House Hotel ... 015394 32036
Ambleside ... Rothay Manor ... 015394 33605
Andover ... Esseborne Manor ... 01264 736444
Appleby-in-Westmorland ... Appleby Manor Country House Hotel ... 017683 51571
Appleby-In-Westmorland ... Tufton Arms Hotel ... 017683 51593
Arundel ... Bailiffscourt ... 01903 723511
Ascot ... Royal Berkshire ... 01344 623322
Ashbourne ... Callow Hall ... 01335 343403
Ashbourne ... The Izaak Walton Hotel ... 01335 350555
Ashburton ... Holne Chase Hotel ... 01364 631471
Ashford ... Eastwell Manor ... 01233 219955
Ashford-In-The-Water ... Riverside House Hotel ... 01629 814275
Aylesbury ... Hartwell House ... 01296 747444
Aylesbury ... The Priory Hotel ... 01296 641239
Bakewell ... Hassop Hall ... 01629 640488
Banbury ... Wroxton House Hotel ... 01295 730777
Basingstoke ... Tylney Hall ... 01256 764881
Baslow ... The Cavendish Hotel ... 01246 582311
Baslow ... Fischer's ... 01246 583259
Bath ... The Bath Priory Hotel and Restaurant ... 01225 331922
Bath ... Combe Grove Manor & Country Club ... 01225 834644
Bath ... Homewood Park ... 01225 723731
Bath ... Hunstrete House ... 01761 490490
Bath ... Lucknam Park ... 01225 742777
Bath ... The Queensberry ... 01225 447928
Bath ... The Royal Crescent ... 01225 823333
Bath ... Ston Easton Park ... 01761 241631
Battle ... Netherfield Place ... 01424 774455
Battle ... PowderMills Hotel ... 01424 775511
Beaminster ... Bridge House Hotel ... 01308 862200
Beaulieu ... The Master Builder's House ... 01590 616253
Beaulieu ... The Montagu Arms Hotel ... 01590 612324
Bedford ... Woodlands Manor ... 01234 363281
Berwick-Upon-Tweed ... Marshall Meadow Country House Hotel ... 01289 331133
Berwick-Upon-Tweed ... Tillmouth Park ... 01890 882255
Bibury ... The Swan Hotel At Bibury ... 01285 740695
Birmingham ... The Burlington Hotel ... 0121 643 9191
Birmingham ... The Mill House Hotel & Lombard Room Restaurant ... 0121 459 5800
Birmingham ... New Hall ... 0121 378 2442
Birmingham ... The Swallow Hotel ... 0121 452 1144
Bishop's Stortford ... Down Hall Country House Hotel ... 01279 731441
Bolton Abbey ... The Devonshire Arms Country House Hotel ... 01756 710441
Bournemouth ... The Dormy ... 01202 872121
Bournemouth ... The Norfolk Royale Hotel ... 01202 551521
Bovey Tracey ... The Edgemoor ... 01626 832466
Bradford-On-Avon ... Woolley Grange ... 01225 864705
Brampton ... Farlam Hall Hotel ... 016977 46234
Bray-on-Thames ... Chauntry House Hotel & Restaurant ... 01628 73991
Bray-on-Thames ... Monkey Island Hotel ... 01628 623400
Brighton ... Topps Hotel ... 01273 729334
Bristol ... Swallow Royal Hotel ... 0117 9255200
Bristol South ... Daneswood House Hotel ... 01934 843145
Broadway ... Dormy House ... 01386 852711
Broadway ... The Lygon Arms ... 01386 852255
Brockenhurst ... Careys Manor Hotel ... 01590 623551
Brockenhurst ... New Park Manor ... 01590 623467
Brockenhurst ... Rhinefield House Hotel ... 01590 622922
Bromsgrove ... Grafton Manor Country House Hotel ... 01527 579007
Burford ... The Bay Tree Hotel & Restaurant ... 01993 822791
Burrington ... Northcote Manor ... 01769 560501
Burton upon Trent ... The Brookhouse ... 01283 814188
Bury St Edmunds ... The Angel Hotel ... 01284 753926
Bury St Edmunds ... Ravenwood Hall ... 01359 270345
Buxted, Near Uckfield ... Buxted Park Country House Hotel ... 01825 732711
Buxton ... The Palace Hotel ... 01298 22001
Canterbury ... Howfield Manor ... 01227 738294
Castle Combe ... The Manor House ... 01249 782206
Chaddesley Corbett ... Brockencote Hall ... 01562 777876
Chagford ... Gidleigh Park ... 01647 432367
Chelmsford ... Pontlands Park Country Hotel ... 01245 476444
Cheltenham ... The Greenway ... 01242 862352
Cheltenham ... Hotel On The Park ... 01242 518898
Chester ... Broxton Hall Country House Hotel ... 01829 782321
Chester ... Carden Park ... 01829 731000
Chester ... The Chester Grosvenor ... 01244 324024
Chester ... Crabwall Manor ... 01244 851666
Chester ... Mollington Banastre ... 01244 851471
Chester ... Nunsmere Hall ... 01606 889100
Chester ... Rowton Hall Hotel ... 01244 335262
Chichester ... The Millstream Hotel ... 01243 573234
Chipping Campden ... Charingworth Manor ... 01386 593555
Chipping Campden ... The Cotswold House ... 01386 840330
Clanfield ... The Plough at Clanfield ... 01367 810222
Cobham ... Woodlands Park Hotel ... 01372 843933
Colchester ... Five Lakes Hotel Golf & Country Club ... 01621 868888
Colchester ... The White Hart Hotel & Restaurant ... 01376 561654
Coventry ... Coombe Abbey ... 01203 450450
Coventry ... Nailcote Hall ... 01203 466174
Crathorne ... Crathorne Hall Hotel ... 01642 700398
Cuckfield ... Ockenden Manor ... 01444 416111
Darlington ... Headlam Hall ... 01325 730238
Dartford ... Rowhill Grange ... 01322 615136
Dartmoor ... Bel Alp House ... 01364 661217
Daventry ... Fawsley Hall Hotel ... 01327 892000
Dedham ... Maison Talbooth ... 01206 322367
Derby ... Makeney Hall Country House Hotel ... 01332 842999
Derby ... Mickleover Court ... 01332 521234
Derby ... The Priest House On the River ... 01332 810649
Derby ... Risley Hall Country House Hotel ... 0115 939 9000
Diss ... Cornwallis Arms ... 01379 870326
Durham ... Lumley Castle Hotel ... 0191 389 1111
Easington ... Grinkle Park Hotel ... 01287 640515
Eastbourne ... The Grand Hotel ... 01323 412345
Egham ... Great Fosters ... 01784 433822
Evershot ... Summer Lodge ... 01935 83424
Evesham ... The Evesham Hotel ... 01386 765566
Evesham ... Wood Norton Hall ... 01386 420007
Exeter ... St Olaves Court Hotel ... 01392 217736
Falmouth ... Budock Vean Golf & Country Club ... 01326 250288
Falmouth ... Meudon Hotel ... 01326 250541
Falmouth ... Nansidwell Country House ... 01326 250340
Falmouth ... Penmere Manor ... 01326 211411
Fawkham ... Brandshatch Place Hotel ... 01474 872239
Forest Row ... Ashdown Park Hotel ... 01342 824988
Fowey ... Fowey Hall Hotel & Restaurant ... 01726 833866
Gatwick ... Alexander House ... 01342 714914
Gatwick ... Langshott Manor ... 01293 786680
Glossop ... The Wind In The Willows ... 01457 868001
Grange-Over-Sands ... Graythwaite Manor ... 015395 32001
Grantham ... Belton Woods ... 01476 593200
Grasmere ... Michaels Nook ... 015394 35496
Grasmere ... The Wordsworth Hotel ... 015394 35592
Grayshott ... Grayshott Hall Health Fitness Retreat ... 01428 604331
Guildford ... The Angel Posting House And Livery ... 01483 564555
Hadley Wood ... West Lodge Park ... 0181 440 8311
Halifax ... Holdsworth House ... 01422 240024
Hampton Court ... The Carlton Mitre Hotel ... 0181 979 9988
Harrogate ... The Balmoral Hotel ... 01423 508208
Harrogate ... The Boar's Head Hotel ... 01423 771888
Harrogate ... Grants Hotel ... 01423 560666
Harrogate ... Hob Green Hotel & Restaurant ... 01423 770031
Harrogate ... Rudding Park House & Hotel ... 01423 871350
Haslemere ... Lythe Hill Hotel ... 01428 651251
Hathersage ... George Hotel ... 01433 650436
Hawes ... Simonstone Hall ... 01969 667255
Hazlewood ... Hazlewood Castle Hotel ... 01937 535353
Helmsley ... The Pheasant ... 01439 771241 /770416
Hemel Hempstead ... Stocks ... 01442 851341
Henley-On-Thames ... Phyllis Court Club ... 01491 570500
Hockley Heath ... Nuthurst Grange ... 01564 783972
Honiton ... Combe House Hotel ... 01404 540400
Horsham ... South Lodge Hotel ... 01403 891711
Hovingham ... The Worsley Arms Hotel ... 01653 628234
Huddersfield ... Bagden Hall Hotel & Golf Course ... 01484 865330
Hull ... Willerby Manor Hotel ... 01482 652616
Huntingdon ... The Old Bridge Hotel ... 01480 452681
Ilkley ... Rombalds Hotel ... 01943 603201
Ilsington ... Ilsington Country Hotel ... 01364 661452
Ipswich ... Hintlesham Hall ... 01473 652268
Ipswich ... Swallow Belstead Brook Hotel ... 01473 684241
Keswick ... The Borrowdale Gates Country House ... 017687 77204
King's Lynn ... Congham Hall ... 01485 600250
Kingham ... Mill House Hotel ... 01608 658188
Kingsbridge Estuary ... Buckland-Tout-Saints ... 01548 853055
Lacock ... Beechfield House ... 01225 703700
Lake Ullswater ... Rampsbeck Country House Hotel ... 017684 86442
Lake Ullswater ... Sharrow Bay Country House Hotel ... 017684 86301
Launceston ... Percy's at Coombeshead ... 01409 211236
Leeds ... 42 The Calls ... 0113 244 0099
Leeds ... Haley's Hotel and Restaurant ... 0113 278 4446
Leeds ... Oulton Hall ... 0113 282 1000
Leicester ... Quorn Country Hotel ... 01509 415050
Lewdown ... Lewtrenchard Manor ... 01566 783 256
Lewes ... Newick Park ... 01825 723633
Lichfield ... Hoar Cross Hall Health Spa Resort ... 01283 575671
Lichfield ... Swinfen Hall ... 01543 481494
Lifton ... The Arundell Arms ... 01566 784666
Liphook ... Old Thorns ... 01428 724555
Lower Slaughter ... Washbourne Court Hotel ... 01451 822143
Ludlow ... Dinham Hall ... 01584 876464
Lymington ... Passford House Hotel ... 01590 682398
Lymington ... Stanwell House ... 01590 677123
Lyndhurst ... Parkhill Hotel ... 01703 282944
Macclesfield ... Shrigley Hall Hotel Golf & Country Club ... 01625 575757
Maidencombe ... Orestone Manor Hotel & Restaurant ... 01803 328098
Maidenhead ... Cliveden ... 01628 668561
Maidenhead ... Fredrick's Hotel & Restaurant ... 01628 635934
Maidstone ... Chilston Park ... 01622 859803
Malmesbury ... Crudwell Court Hotel ... 01666 577194
Malmesbury ... The Old Bell ... 01666 822344
Malmesbury ... Whatley Manor ... 01666 822888
Malvern ... The Colwall Park Hotel ... 01684 540206
Malvern Wells ... The Cottage In The Wood ... 01684 575859
Manchester ... The Stanneylands Hotel ... 01625 525225
Manchester Airport ... Etrop Grange ... 0161 499 0500
Marlborough ... Ivy House Hotel ... 01672 515333
Marlow-On-Thames ... Danesfield House ... 01628 891010
Matlock ... Riber Hall ... 01629 582795
Middle Wallop ... Fifehead Manor ... 01264 781565
Middlecombe ... Periton Park Hotel ... 01643 706885
Midhurst ... The Angel Hotel ... 01730 812421
Midhurst ... The Spread Eagle Hotel & Health Spa ... 01730 816911
Milton Keynes ... Moore Place Hotel ... 01908 282000
Monk Fryston ... Monk Fryston Hall ... 01977 682369
Moreton-In-Marsh ... The Manor House Hotel ... 01608 650501
Nantwich ... Rookery Hall ... 01270 610016
Newbury ... Donnington Valley Hotel & Golf Course ... 01635 551199
Newbury ... Elcot Park Hotel & Country Club ... 01488 658100
Newbury ... Hollington House Hotel ... 01635 255100
Newbury ... The Vineyard At Stockcross ... 01635 528770
Newcastle-Upon-Tyne ... Linden Hall Hotel ... 01670 516611
Newcastle-Upon-Tyne ... Slaley Hall Hotel ... 01434 673350
Newmarket ... Swynford Paddocks Hotel & Restaurant ... 01638 570234
Newton Aycliffe ... Redworth Hall Hotel & Country Club ... 01388 772442
North Huish ... Brookdale House Restaurant & Hotel ... 01548 821661
Norwich ... Park Farm Hotel & Leisure ... 01603 810264
Norwich ... Petersfield House Hotel ... 01692 630741

Norwich	Sprowston Manor Hotel	01603 410871
Nottingham	Langar Hall	01949 860559
Oakham	Hambleton Hall	01572 756991
Otley	Chevin Lodge Country Park Hotel	01943 467818
Ottershaw	Foxhills	01932 872050
Oxford	Le Manoir Aux Quat' Saisons	01844 278881
Oxford	Studley Priory	01865 351203
Oxford	Weston Manor	01869 350621
Padstow	Treglos Hotel	01841 520727
Painswick	The Painswick Hotel	01452 812160
Peterborough	The Haycock	01780 782223
Poole	The Mansion House Hotel and Dining Club	01202 685666
Portloe	The Lugger Hotel	01872 501322
Prestbury	The Bridge Hotel	01625 829326
Preston	The Gibbon Bridge Country House Hotel	01995 61456
Redhill	Nutfield Priory	01737 822066
Richmond-Upon-Thames	The Richmond Gate Hotel And Restaurant	0181 940 0061
Ross-On-Wye	The Chase Hotel	01989 763161
Ross-On-Wye	Pengethley Manor	01989 730211
Rusper	Ghyll Manor Country Hotel	01293 871571
Rutland Water	Barnsdale Lodge	01572 724678
Rye	Broomhill Lodge	01797 280421
Salcombe	Bolt Head Hotel	01548 843751
Salcombe	Soar Mill Cove Hotel	01548 561566
Scarborough	Hackness Grange	01723 882345
Scarborough	Wrea Head Country Hotel	01723 378211
Sheffield	Charnwood Hotel	0114 258 9411
Sheffield	Whitley Hall Hotel	0114 245 4444
Shepton Mallet	Charlton House and The Mulberry Restaurant	01749 342008
Shrewsbury	Albrighton Hall Hotel & Restaurant	01939 291000
Shrewsbury	Hawkstone Park Hotel	01939 200611
Sidmouth	Hotel Riviera	01395 515201
Slough	Stoke Park	01753 717171
Sonning-On-Thames	The French Horn	01189 692204
South Molton	Whitechapel Manor	01769 573377
Southwold	The Swan Hotel	01502 722186
St Agnes	Rose-in-Vale Country House Hotel	01872 552202
St Albans	Sopwell House Hotel & Country Club	01727 864477
St. Ives	The Garrack Hotel	01736 796199
St Keyne	The Well House	01579 342001
St Mawes	Hotel Tresanton	01326 270055
Stamford	The George Of Stamford	01780 755171
Stansted	Whitehall	01279 850603
Stapleford	Stapleford Park, An Outpost of The Carnegie Club	01572 787522
Stonehouse	Stonehouse Court	01453 825155
Storrington	Little Thakeham	01903 744416
Stow-On-The-Wold	The Grapevine Hotel	01451 830344
Stow-On-The-Wold	Wyck Hill House	01451 831936
Stratford-Upon-Avon	Billesley Manor	01789 279955
Stratford-Upon-Avon	Ettington Park Hotel	01789 450123
Stratford-Upon-Avon	Salford Hall Hotel	01386 871300
Stratford-Upon-Avon	Welcombe Hotel & Golf Course	01789 295252
Streatley-On-Thames	Swan Diplomat	01491 873737
Sturminster Newton	Plumber Manor	01258 472507
Swindon	The Pear Tree at Purton	01793 772100
Talland-By-Looe	Talland Bay Hotel	01503 272667
Taunton	Bindon Country House Hotel & Restaurant	01823 400070
Taunton	The Castle At Taunton	01823 272671
Taunton	The Mount Somerset Country House Hotel	01823 442500
Telford	Madeley Court	01952 680068
Tetbury	Calcot Manor	01666 890391
Tewkesbury	Corse Lawn House Hotel	01452 780479 / 771
Ticehurst	Dale Hill	01580 200112
Torquay	The Osborne Hotel & Langtry's Restaurant	01803 213311
Torquay	The Palace Hotel	01803 200200
Tring	Pendley Manor Hotel & Conference Centre	01442 891891
Tunbridge Wells	Hotel Du Vin & Bistro	01892 526455
Tunbridge Wells	The Spa Hotel	01892 520331
Uckfield	Horsted Place Hotel	01825 750581
Upper Slaughter	Lords Of The Manor Hotel	01451 820243
Uppingham	The Lake Isle	01572 822951
Veryan	The Nare Hotel	01872 501279
Wallingford	The Springs Hotel & Golf Club	01491 836687
Ware	Hanbury Manor	01920 487722
Wareham	The Priory	01929 551666
Warminster	Bishopstrow House	01985 212312
Warwick	The Glebe At Barford	01926 624218
Wetherby	Linton Springs	01937 585353
Wetherby	Wood Hall	01937 587271
Weybridge	Oatlands Park Hotel	01932 847242
Weymouth	Moonfleet Manor	01305 786948
Willington	Willington Hall Hotel	01829 752321
Winchester	Hotel Du Vin & Bistro	01962 841414
Winchester	Lainston House Hotel	01962 863588
Windermere	Gilpin Lodge	015394 88818
Windermere	Lakeside Hotel On Lake Windermere	0541 541586
Windermere	Langdale Chase	015394 32201
Windermere	Linthwaite House Hotel	015394 88600
Windermere	Miller Howe	015394 42536
Windsor	Oakley Court	01753 609988
Windsor	Sir Christopher Wren's Hotel	01753 861354
Woburn	Flitwick Manor	01525 712242
Wolverhampton	The Old Vicarage Hotel	01746 716497
Woodbridge	Seckford Hall	01394 385678
Woodstock	The Feathers Hotel	01993 812291
Woolacombe	Watersmeet Hotel	01271 870333
Woolacombe	Woolacombe Bay Hotel	01271 870388
Yarmouth	The George Hotel	01983 760331
York	The Grange Hotel	01904 644744
York	Middlethorpe Hall	01904 641241
York	Mount Royale Hotel	01904 628856
York	York Pavilion Hotel	01904 622099

Wales

Abergavenny	Allt-Yr-Ynys Hotel	01873 890307
Abergavenny	Llansantffraed Court Hotel	01873 840678
Abersoch	Porth Tocyn Country House Hotel	01758 713303
Aberystwyth	Conrah Country House Hotel	01970 617941
Anglesey	Trearddur Bay Hotel	01407 860301
Bala	Palé Hall	01678 530285
Barmouth	Bontddu Hall	01341 430661
Beaumaris	Ye Olde Bull's Head	01248 810329
Brecon	Llangoed Hall	01874 754525
Bridgend	Coed-Y-Mwstwr Hotel	01656 860621
Caernarfon	Gwesty Seiont Manor Hotel	01286 673366
Cardiff	Egerton Grey Country House Hotel	01446 711666
Cardiff	Miskin Manor	01443 224204
Cardiff	St. David's Spa	01222 454045
Chester	Soughton Hall	01352 840811
Chester	St. David's Park Hotel	01244 520800
Corwen	Tyddyn Llan Country House Hotel	01490 440264
Criccieth	Bron Eifion Country House Hotel	01766 522385
Crickhowell	Gliffaes Country House Hotel	01874 730371
Dolgellau	Penmaenuchaf Hall	01341 422129
Harlech	Hotel Maes-Y-Neuadd	01766 780200
Lake Vyrnwy	Lake Vyrnwy Hotel	01691 870 692
Llandegla	Bodidris Hall	01978 790434
Llandudno	Bodysgallen Hall	01492 584466
Llandudno	St Tudno Hotel	01492 874411
Llangammarch Wells	The Lake Country House	01591 620202
Llangollen	Bryn Howel Hotel & Restaurant	01978 860331
Machynlleth	Ynyshir Hall	01654 781209
Pembroke	The Court Hotel & Restaurant	01646 672273
Portmeirion Village	The Hotel Portmeirion	01766 770228
St David's	Warpool Court Hotel	01437 720300
Swansea	Norton House Hotel & Restaurant	01792 404891
Tenby	Penally Abbey	01834 843033
Tywyn	Tynycornel Hotel	01654 782282
Usk	The Cwrt Bleddyn Hotel	01633 450521

Scotland

Aberdeen	Ardoe House Hotel & Restaurant	01224 867355
Aberdeen	Thainstone House Hotel & Country Club	01467 621643
Angus	Letham Grange Hotel & Golf Course	01241 890373
Auchencairn	Balcary Bay Hotel	01556 640217
Auchterarder	Auchterarder House	01764 663646 / 7
Ballater	Darroch Learg Hotel	013397 55443
Banchory	Raemoir House Hotel	01330 824884
Banchory	Tor-na-coille Hotel	01330 822242
Beasdale By Arisaig	Arisaig House	01687 450622
Biggar	Shieldhill	01899 220035
Blairgowrie	Kinloch House Hotel	01250 884237
Callander	Roman Camp Hotel	01877 330003
Craigellachie	Craigellachie Hotel	01340 881204
Dunoon	Enmore Hotel	01369 702230
Edinburgh	The Bonhams	0131 226 6050
Edinburgh	Borthwick Castle	01875 820514
Edinburgh	Channings	0131 315 2226
Edinburgh	Dalhousie Castle Hotel & Restaurant	01875 820153
Edinburgh	The Howard	0131 557 3500
Edinburgh	The Norton House Hotel	0131 333 1275
Edinburgh	Prestonfield House	0131 668 3346
Elgin	Mansion House Hotel & Country Club	01343 548811
Elgin	Rothes Glen	01340 831254
Falkirk	Airth Castle Hotel	01324 831411
Fort Augustus	Knockie Lodge Hotel	01456 486276
Fort William	Glenspean Lodge Hotel	01397 712223
Gatehouse Of Fleet	Cally Palace Hotel	01557 814341
Glasgow	Gleddoch House	01475 540711
Glenshee	Dalmunzie House	01250 885224
Gullane	Greywalls	01620 842144
Inverness	Culloden House Hotel	01463 790461
Inverness	Kingsmills Hotel	01463 237166
Inverurie	Pittodrie House	01467 681444
Irvine	Montgreenan Mansion House Hotel	01294 557733
Isle Of Eriska, by Oban	Isle Of Eriska	01631 720371
Isle Of Mull	Western Isles Hotel	01688 302012
Kelso	Ednam House Hotel	01573 224168
Kelso	Sunlaws House Hotel & Golf Course	01573 450331
Kilchrenan by Taynuilt	Ardanaiseig	01866 833333
Kildrummy	Kildrummy Castle Hotel	019755 71288
Kinbuck Nr Stirling	Cromlix House	01786 822125
Loch Lomond	Cameron House	01389 755565
Lochinver	Inver Lodge Hotel	01571 844496
Newton Stewart	Kirroughtree House	01671 402141
Oban	Knipoch Hotel	01852 316251
Peebles	Cringletie House Hotel	01721 730233
Perth	Ballathie House Hotel	01250 883268
Perth	Huntingtower Hotel	01738 583771
Perth	Kinfauns Castle	01738 620777
Pitlochry	Pine Trees Hotel	01796 472121
Selkirk	Philipburn Country House Hotel	01750 720747
St. Andrews	St. Andrews Golf Hotel	01334 472611
St Boswells	Dryburgh Abbey Hotel	01835 822261
Stranraer	Corsewall Lighthouse Hotel	01776 853220
Strathpeffer	Coul House Hotel	01997 421487
Tain	Mansfield House Hotel	01862 892052
Tarbert	Stonefield Castle Hotel	01880 820836
Torridon	Loch Torridon Hotel	01445 791242
Troon	Piersland House Hotel	01292 314747
Uphall	Houstoun House	01506 853831

Ireland

Adare	Adare Manor	00 353 61 396566
Ballymena	Galgorm Manor	01266 881001
Belfast	Culloden Hotel	01232 425223
Belfast	The McCausland Hotel	01232 220200
Carrickmacross	Nuremore Hotel & Country Club	00 353 42 61438
Clonakilty	The Lodge & Spa at Inchydoney Island	00 353 23 33143
Cong	Ashford Castle	00353 92 46003
Connemara	Renvyle House Hotel	00 353 95 43511
Dublin	Barberstown Castle	00 353 1 6288157
Dublin	Brooks Hotel	00 353 1 670 4000
Dublin	The Hibernian	00 353 1 668 7666
Dublin	Kildare Hotel & Country Club	00 353 1 601 7200
Dublin	The Merrion Hotel	00 353 1 603 0600
Dublin	Portmarnock Hotel & Golf Links	00 353 1 846 0611
Furbo	Connemara Coast Hotel	00 353 91 592108
Gorey	Marlfield House	00 353 55 21124
Kenmare	The Park Hotel Kenmare	00 353 64 41200
Kenmare	Sheen Falls Lodge	00 353 64 41600
Killarney	Aghadoe Heights Hotel	00 353 64 31766
Killarney	Dunloe Castle	00 353 64 44111
Killarney	Muckross Park Hotel	00 353 64 31938
Killarney	Randles Court Hotel	00 353 64 35333
Kiltegan	Humewood Castle	00 353 508 73215
Mallow	Longueville House & Presidents' Restaurant	00 353 22 47156
Newcastle	Slieve Donard Hotel	013967 23681
Newmarket-On-Fergus	Dromoland Castle	00 353 61 368144
Parknasilla	Parknasilla Hotel	00 353 64 45122
Rathnew	Hunter's Hotel	00 353 404 40106
Rosslare	Kelly's Resort Hotel	00 353 53 32114
Wicklow	Tinakilly Country House Hotel	00 353 40469274

Channel Islands

Guernsey	St Pierre Park Hotel	01481 728282
Jersey	The Atlantic Hotel	01534 44101
Jersey	Château La Chaire	01534 863354
Jersey	Hotel L'Horizon	01534 43101
Jersey	Longueville Manor	01534 725501

Traditional Inns, Hotels & Restaurants

England

Acton Trussell	The Moat House	01785 712217
Adderbury	The Red Lion Inn	01295 810269
Aldbury	The Greyhound Inn	01442 851228
Amberley, Near Arundel	The Boathouse Brasserie	01798 831059
Ambleside	The New Dungeon Ghyll Hotel	015394 37213
Andoversford	The Frogmill Hotel	01242 820547
Appleby-In-Westmorland	The Royal Oak Inn	017683 51463
Ashbourne	Old Beams Restaurant with Rooms	01538 308254
Ashbourne	Red Lion Inn	01335 370396
Askrigg	The Kings Arms Hotel And Restaurant	01969 650258
Axminster	Tytherleigh Cot Hotel	01460 221170
Badby Nr Daventry	The Windmill At Badby	01327 702363
Bassenthwaite Lake	The Pheasant	017687 76234
Beckington Nr Bath	The Woolpack Inn	01373 831244

Belford	The Blue Bell Hotel	01668 213543
Bibury	The Catherine Wheel	01285 740250
Bickleigh	The Fisherman's Cot	01884 855237 / 855289
Binfield	Stag & Hounds	01344 483553
Blakeney	White Horse Hotel	01263 740574
Bourton-On-The-Water	Dial House Hotel	01451 822244
Bridport	The Manor Hotel	01308 897616
Bristol	The Boars Head	01454 632581
Bristol	The New Inn	01454 773161
Broadway	The Broadway Hotel & Restaurant	01386 852401
Brockenhurst	The Snakecatcher	01590 624155
Buckden	The George Coaching Inn	01480 810307
Buckfastleigh	The Dartbridge Inn	01364 642214
Burford	Cotswold Gateway Hotel	01993 822695
Burford	The Golden Pheasant Hotel & Restaurant	01993 823417
Burford	The Lamb Inn	01993 823155
Burnham Market	The Hoste Arms Hotel	01328 738777
Burnley	Fence Gate Inn	01282 618101
Burnsall	The Red Lion	01756 720204
Burton Upon Trent	Boar's Head Hotel	01283 820344
Calver	The Chequers Inn	01433 630231
Camborne	Tyacks Hotel	01209 612424
Cambridge	Panos Hotel & Restaurant	01223 212958
Carlisle	The Tarn End House Hotel	016977 2340
Castle Ashby	The Falcon Hotel	01604 696200
Castle Cary	The George Hotel	01963 350761
Cheltenham	Kingshead House Restaurant	01452 862299
Chester	The Pheasant Inn	01829 770434
Chippenham	The Crown Inn	01249 782229
Chipping Campden	The Noel Arms Hotel & Restaurant	01386 840317
Chipping Sodbury	The Codrington Arms	01454 313145
Cirencester	The New Inn at Coln	01285 750651
Clare	The Plough Inn	01440 786789
Clavering	The Cricketers	01799 550442
Cleobury Mortimer	Crown At Hopton	01299 270372
Cleobury Mortimer	The Redfern Hotel	01299 270 395
Colchester	The White Hart Hotel & Restaurant	01376 561654
Coleford	The New Inn	01363 84242
Congleton	The Plough Inn & Old Barn Restaurant	01260 280207
Crowborough	Winston Manor	01892 652772
Dartmouth	The Victoria Hotel	01803 832572
Dorchester-On-Thames	The George Hotel	01865 340404
Dronfield	Manor House Hotel & Restaurant	01246 413971
Duns Tew	The White Horse Inn	01869 340272
East Witton	The Blue Lion	01969 624273
Eccleshall	The George Hotel	01785 850300
Edenbridge	Ye Old Crown	01732 867896
Egton	The Wheatsheaf Inn	01947 895271
Eton	The Christopher Hotel	01753 811677 / 852359
Evershot	The Acorn Inn Hotel	01935 83228
Evesham	Riverside Restaurant And Hotel	01386 446200
Exmoor	The Royal Oak Inn	01643 831506/7
Exmoor	The Royal Oak of Luxborough	01984 640319
Falmouth	Trengilly Wartha Country Inn & Restaurant	01326 340332
Ford, Nr Bath	The White Hart	01249 782213
Fordingbridge	The Woodfalls Inn	01725 513222
Goathland	Mallyan Spout Hotel	01947 896486
Goring-On-Thames	The Leatherne Bottel Riverside Inn	01491 872667
Grimsthorpe	The Black Horse Inn	01778 591247
Grindleford	The Maynard Arms	01433 630321
Halifax/Huddersfield	The Rock Inn Hotel	01422 379721
Handcross	The Chequers At Slaugham	01444 400239/400996
Harrogate	The Boar's Head Hotel	01423 771888
Harrogate	The Dower House	01423 863302
Harrogate	The Low Hall Hotel	01423 508598
Hartley Wintney	The Hatchgate	01189 32666
Hathersage	The Plough Inn	01433 650319
Haverhill	The White Horse Inn	01440 706081
Haworth	Old White Lion Hotel	01535 642313
Hay-On-Wye	Rhydspence Inn	01497 831262
Hayfield	The Waltzing Weasel	01663 743402
Helmsley	The Feathers Hotel	01439 770275
Helmsley	The Feversham Arms Hotel	01439 770766
Hindon, Nr Salisbury	The Lamb at Hindon	01747 820573
Honiton	Home Farm Hotel	01404 831278
King's Lynn	The Rose & Crown	01485 541382
Kingsbridge	The Kings Arms Hotel	01548 852071
Kingskerswell	The Barn Owl Inn	01803 872130
Knutsford	Longview Hotel And Restaurant	01565 632119
Ledbury	Feathers Hotel	01531 635266
Leek	The Three Horseshoes Inn & Restaurant	01538 300296
Lincoln	Hare & Hounds	01400 272090
Long Melford	The Countrymen	01787 312356
Long Sutton	The Devonshire Arms Hotel	01458 241271
Ludlow	Mr Underhill's	01584 874431
Lymington	Hotel Gordleton Mill	01590 682219
Lynmouth	The Rising Sun	01598 753223
Maidstone	The Harrow At Warren Street	01622 858727
Maidstone	Ringlestone Inn	01622 859900
Malmesbury	The Horse And Groom Inn	01666 823904
Market Weighton	The Londesborough	01430 872214
Mells	The Talbot Inn at Mells	01373 812254
Milton Keynes	The Different Drummer	01908 564733
Montacute	The King's Arms Inn & Restaurant	01935 822513
Newbury	The Swan Inn	01488 648271
Newby Bridge	The Swan Hotel	015395 31681
North Walsham	Elderton Lodge Hotel & Restaurant	01263 833547
Norwich	The Stower Grange	01603 860210
Nottingham	Hotel Des Clos	01159 866566
Onneley	The Wheatsheaf Inn At Onneley	01782 751581
Oundle	The Talbot	01832 273621
Oxford	Holcombe Hotel	01869 338274
Oxford	The Jersey Arms	01869 343234
Oxford	The Mill & Old Swan	01993 774441
Padstow	The Old Custom House Hotel	01841 532359
Pelynt, Nr Looe	Jubilee Inn	01503 220312
Penistone	The Fountain Inn & Rooms	01226 763125
Petworth	Badgers	01798 342651
Petworth	The Stonemason's Inn	01798 342510
Petworth	White Horse Inn	01798 869 221
Port Gaverne	The Port Gaverne Hotel	01208 880244
Preston	Ye Horn's Inn	01772 865230
Reading	The Bull at Streatley	01491 875231
Romsey	Dukes Head	01794 514450
Ross-on-Wye	Cottage of Content	01432 840242
Rothley	The Rothley Court	0116 237 4141
Rugby	The Golden Lion Inn of Easenhall	01788 832265
Rutland Water	Normanton Park Hotel	01780 720315
Rye	The George Hotel	01797 222144
Saddleworth	The Old Bell Inn Hotel	01457 870130
Salisbury	The Old Mill Hotel & Restaurant	01722 327517
Salisbury	The White Horse	01725 510408
Sevenoaks	The Royal Oak	01732 451109
Sheffield	The Old Vicarage	0114 247 5814
Sherborne	The Walnut Tree	01935 851292
Shifnal	Naughty Nell's	01952 411412
Shipton Under Wychwood	The Shaven Crown Hotel	01993 830330
Shipton-Under-Wychwood	The Lamb Inn	01993 830465
Southport	Tree Tops Country House Restaurant & Hotel	01704 879651
St. Ives	Olivers Lodge Hotel & Restaurant	01480 463252
Stafford	The Dower House	01889 270707
Stow-on-the-Wold	The Horse and Groom Inn & Restaurant	01451 830584
Stow-On-The-Wold	The Kings Head Inn & Restaurant	01608 658365
Stow-on-the-Wold	The Unicorn Hotel & Restaurant	01451 830257
Stratford-upon-Avon	The Coach House Hotel & Cellar Restaurant	01789 204109
Stroud	The Bear of Rodborough Hotel & Restaurant	01453 878522
Sudbury	The Bull Hotel	01787 378494
Telford	The Hundred House Hotel	01952 730353
Tenterden	The White Lion Hotel	01580 765077
Tetbury	The Close Hotel	01666 502272
Thelbridge	Thelbridge Cross Inn	01884 860316
Thornham	The Lifeboat Inn	01485 512236
Thornham Magna	Four Horseshoes	01379 678777
Thorpe Market	Green Farm Restaurant And Hotel	01263 833602
Tintagel	The Port William	01840 770230
Totnes	The Sea Trout Inn	01803 762274
Totnes	The Watermans Arms	01803 732214
Troutbeck	The Mortal Man Hotel	015394 33193
Upton-Upon-Severn	The White Lion Hotel	01684 592551
Walberswick	The Bell Inn	01502 723109
Weobley	Ye Olde Salutation Inn	01544 318443
West Witton	The Wensleydale Heifer Inn	01969 622322
Whitewell	The Inn At Whitewell	01200 448222
Wooler	The Tankerville Arms Hotel	01668 281581
Worcester	The Old Schoolhouse	01905 371368
Worthing	The Old Tollgate Restaurant And Hotel	01903 879494
Wroxham	The Barton Angler Country Inn	01692 630740
York	The George at Easingwold	01347 821698

Wales

Chepstow	The Castle View Hotel	01291 620349
Llanarmon Dyffryn Ceiriog	The West Arms Hotel	01691 600665
Llandeilo	The Plough Inn	01558 823431
Welshpool	The Lion Hotel And Restaurant	01686 640452

Scotland

Aboyne	Birse Lodge Hotel	01339 886253
Blair Atholl	The Loft Restaurant	01796 481377
Blairgowrie	The Glenisla Hotel	01575 582223
Cullen	The Seafield Arms Hotel	01542 840791
Inverness	Grouse & Trout	01808 521314
Isle Of Skye	Hotel Eilean Iarmain or Isle Ornsay Hotel	01471 833332
Isle Of Skye	Uig Hotel	01470 542205
Kenmore	The Kenmore Hotel	01887 830205
Killearn	The Black Bull	01360 550215
Loch Ness	The Foyers Hotel	01456 486216
Moffatt	Annandale Arms Hotel	01683 220013
Pitlochry	The Moulin Hotel	01796 472196
Plockton	The Plockton Hotel & Garden Restaurant	01599 544274
Poolewe	Pool House Hotel	01445 781272
Powmill	The Gartwhinzean	01577 840595
St Andrews	The Grange Inn	01334 472670

Channel Islands

Jersey	Sea Crest Hotel And Restaurant	01534 46353

Country Houses & Small Hotels

England

Alcester	Arrow Mill Hotel And Restaurant	01789 762419
Appleton-Le-Moors	Appleton Hall	01751 417227
Arundel	Burpham Country House Hotel	01903 882160
Ashbourne	The Beeches Farmhouse	01889 590288
Atherstone	Chapel House	01827 718949
Badminton	Petty France	01454 238361
Bakewell	East Lodge Country House Hotel	01629 734474
Bakewell	The Peacock Hotel at Rowsley	01629 733518
Bamburgh	Waren House Hotel	01668 214581
Bath	Apsley House	01225 336966
Bath	Bath Lodge Hotel	01225 723040
Bath	Bloomfield House	01225 420105
Bath	Duke's Hotel	01225 463512
Bath	Eagle House	01225 859946
Bath	Oldfields	01225 317984
Bath	Paradise House	01225 317723
Bath	Widbrook Grange	01225 864750 / 863173
Bath	Woolverton House	01373 830415
Belper	Dannah Farm Country Guest House	01773 550273 / 630
Beverley	The Manor House	01482 881645
Bibury	Bibury Court	01285 740337
Bideford	Yeoldon House Hotel	01237 474400
Biggin-By-Hartington	Biggin Hall	01298 84451
Blockley	Lower Brook House	01386 700286
Bolton	Quarlton Manor Farm	01204 852277
Bridgnorth	Cross Lane House Hotel	01746 764887
Brighton	The Granville	01273 326302
Broadway	Collin House Hotel	01386 858354
Broadway	The Old Rectory	01386 853729
Brockenhurst	Thatched Cottage Hotel & Restaurant	01590 623090
Brockenhurst	Whitley Ridge & Country House Hotel	01590 622354
Bury St. Edmunds	The Priory	01284 766181
Cambridge	Melbourn Bury	01763 261151
Carlisle	Crosby Lodge Country House Hotel	01228 573618
Cartmel	Aynsome Manor Hotel	015395 36653
Chagford	Easton Court Hotel	01647 433469
Cheltenham	Charlton Kings Hotel	01242 231061
Cheltenham	Halewell	01242 890238
Chichester	Crouchers Bottom Country Hotel	01243 784995
Chichester	Woodstock House Hotel	01243 811666
Chipping Campden	The Malt House	01386 840295
Church Stretton	Mynd House Hotel & Restaurant	01694 722212
Clearwell	Tudor Farmhouse Hotel & Restaurant	01594 833046
Clovelly	Foxdown Manor	01237 451325
Coalville	Abbots Oak	01530 832 328
Combe Martin	Ashelford	01271 850469
Crediton	Coombe House Country Hotel	01363 84487
Crewe	Pear Tree Lake Farms	01270 820307
Dartmoor	Bel Alp House	01364 661217
Dartmoor	Prince Hall Hotel	01822 890403
Dartmouth	Broome Court	01803 834275
Dartmouth	Nonsuch House	01803 752829
Diss	Chippenhall Hall	01379 588180 / 586733
Dorchester	Yalbury Cottage Hotel	01305 262382
Dover	Wallett's Court	01304 852424
Dover	The Woodville Hall	01304 825256
Dulverton	Ashwick Country House Hotel	01398 323868
Enfield	Oak Lodge Hotel	0181 360 7082
Epsom	Chalk Lane Hotel	01372 721179
Evershot	Rectory House	0193583 273
Evesham	The Mill At Harvington	01386 870688
Exeter	The Lord Haldon Hotel	01392 832483
Exford	The Crown Hotel	01643 831554/5
Exmoor	The Beacon Country House Hotel	01643 703476
Fakenham	Vere Lodge	01328 838261
Falmouth	Trelawne Hotel-The Hutches Restaurant	01326 250226
Fenny Drayton	White Wings	01827 716100
Gatwick	Stanhill Court Hotel	01293 862166
Golant by Fowey	The Cormorant Hotel	01726 833426
Grasmere	White Moss House	015394 35295

Great Snoring	The Old Rectory	01328 820597
Hampstead Village	Sandringham Hotel	0171 435 1569
Hampton Court	Chase Lodge	0181 943 1862
Hamsterley Forest	Grove House	01388 488203
Harrogate	The White House	01423 501388
Hawes	Rookhurst Georgian Country House Hotel	01969 667454
Helmsley	Ryedale Country Lodge	01439 748246
Helston	Nansloe Manor	01326 574691
Hereford	The Bowens Country House	01432 860430
Hereford	The Steppes	01432 820424
Holt	Felbrigg Lodge	01263 837588
Hope	Underleigh House	01433 621372
Ilminster	The Old Rectory	01460 54364
Isle of Wight	Rylstone Manor	01983 862806
Keswick	Dale Head Hall Lakeside Hotel	017687 72478
Keswick	Swinside Lodge Hotel	017687 72948
Kingsbridge	The White House	01548 580580
Kirkby Lonsdale	Hipping Hall	015242 71187
Lavenham	Lavenham Priory	01787 247404
Leominster	Lower Bache House	01568 750304
Lifton	The Thatched Cottage Country Hotel	01566 784224
Lincoln	Washingborough Hall	01522 790340
Looe	Allhays Country House	01503 272434
Looe	Coombe Farm	01503 240223
Loughborough	The Old Manor Hotel	01509 211228
Ludlow	Delbury Hall	01584 841267
Ludlow	Overton Grange Hotel	01584 873500
Luton	Little Offley	01462 768243
Lydford	Moor View House	01822 820220
Lyme Regis	Thatch Lodge Hotel	01297 560407
Lynton	Hewitt's Hotel	01598 752293
Maidstone	Tanyard	01622 744705
Malton	Newstead Grange	01653 692502
Matlock	The Manor Farmhouse	01629 534246
Matlock	Sheriff Lodge Hotel	01629 760760
Middlecombe	Periton Park Hotel	01643 706885
Middleham	Millers House Hotel	01969 622630
Minchinhampton	Burleigh Court	01453 883804
Minehead	Channel House Hotel	01643 703229
Morchard Bishop	Wigham	01363 877350
Morpeth	Eshott Hall	01670 787777
New Polzeath	The Cornish Cottage Hotel	01208 862213
New Romney	Romney Bay House	01797 364747
North Walsham	Beechwood Hotel	01692 403231
Norwich	The Beeches Hotel & Victorian Gardens	01603 621167
Norwich	Catton Old Hall	01603 419379
Norwich	Norfolk Mead Hotel	01603 737531
Norwich	The Old Rectory	01603 700772
Nottingham	The Cottage Country House Hotel	01159 846882
Nottingham	Langar Hall	01949 860559
Oswestry	Pen-y-Dyffryn Country Hotel	01691 653700
Ottery St. Mary	Venn Ottery Barton	01404 812733
Owlpen	Owlpen Manor	01453 860261
Oxford	Fallowfields	01865 820416
Padstow	Cross House Hotel	01841 532391
Penrith	Temple Sowerby House Hotel	017683 61578
Petersfield	Langrish House	01730 266941
Porlock Weir	The Cottage Hotel	01643 863300
Porthleven	Tye Rock Hotel	01326 572695
Portsmouth	The Beaufort Hotel	01705 823707
Pulborough	Chequers Hotel	01798 872486
Redditch	The Old Rectory	01527 523000
Ringwood	Moortown Lodge	01425 471404
Rock	The St Enodoc Hotel	01208 863394
Ross-On-Wye	Glewstone Court	01989 770367
Rye	White Vine House	01797 224748
Saham Toney	Broom Hall	01953 882125
Salcombe	The Lyndhurst Hotel	01548 842481
Saunton	Preston House Hotel	01271 890472
Seavington St Mary	The Pheasant Hotel	01460 240502
Sheffield	Staindrop Hotel & Restaurant	0114 284 6727
Sherborne	The Eastbury Hotel	01935 813131
Shipton-Under-Wychwood	The Shaven Crown Hotel	01993 830330
Simonsbath	Simonsbath House Hotel	01643 831259
South Molton	Marsh Hall Country House Hotel	01769 572666
St. Ives	Boskerris Hotel	01736 795295
St Ives	The Countryman At Trink Hotel	01736 797571
St Mawes	The Hundred House Hotel	01872 501336
Staverton	Kingston House	01803 762 235
Stevenage	Redcoats Farmhouse Hotel & Restaurant	01438 729500
Stonor	The Stonor Arms	01491 638866
Stow-On-The-Wold	Conygree Gate Hotel	01608 658389
Stratford-upon-Avon	Glebe Farm House	01789 842501
Tewkesbury	Upper Court	01386 725351
Tintagel	Trebrea Lodge	01840 770410
Truro	The Royal Hotel	01872 270345
Uckfield	Hooke Hall	01825 761578
Wadebridge	Trehellas House & Memories of Malaya Restaurant	01208 72700
Wareham	Kemps Country House Hotel & Restaurant	01929 462563
Warwick	The Ardencote Manor Hotel	01926 843111
Wells	Beryl	01749 678738
Wells	Coxley Vineyard	01749 670285
Wells	Glencot House	01749 677160
Whitby	Dunsley Hall	01947 893437
Wimborne Minster	Beechleas	01202 841684
Wincanton	Holbrook House Hotel	01963 32377
Windermere	Fayrer Garden House Hotel	015394 88195
Windermere	Quarry Garth Country House Hotel	015394 88282
Windermere	Storrs Hall	015394 47111
Witherslack	The Old Vicarage Country House Hotel	015395 52381
Woodbridge	Wood Hall Hotel & Country Club	01394 411283
Worthing	Findon Manor	01903 872733
York	The Parsonage Country House Hotel	01904 728111
Yoxford	Hope House	01728 668281

Wales

Aberdovey	Plas Penhelig Country House Hotel	01654 767676
Abergavenny	Glangrwyney Court	01873 811288
Abergavenny	Llanwenarth House	01873 830289
Abergavenny	Penyclawdd Court	01873 890719
Betws-y-Coed	Tan-y-Foel	01690 710507
Brecon	Old Gwernyfed Country Manor	01497 847376
Caernarfon	Ty'n Rhos Country House	01248 670489
Cardigan	The Pembrokeshire Retreat	01239 841387
Conwy	Berthlwyd Hall Hotel	01492 592409
Conwy	The Old Rectory	01492 580611
Dolgellau	Plas Dolmelynllyn	01341 440273
Monmouth	The Crown At Whitebrook	01600 860254
Pwllheli	Plas Bodegroes	01758 612363
Tenby	Waterwynch House Hotel	01834 842464
Tintern	Parva Farmhouse and Restaurant	01291 689411
Welshpool	Buttington House	01938 553351

Scotland

Ballater,Royal Deeside	Balgonie Country House	013397 55482
By Huntly	The Old Manse of Marnoch	01466 780873
Castle Douglas	Longacre Manor	01556 503576
Comrie	The Royal Hotel	01764 679200
Drumnadrochit	Polmaily House Hotel	01456 450343
Dunfries	Trigony House Hotel	01848 331211
Dunkeld	The Pend	01350 727586
Edinburgh	No 22 Murrayfield Gardens	0131 337 3569
Fintry	Culcreuch Castle Hotel & Country Park	01360 860555
Helmsdale	Navidale House Hotel	01431 821 258
Inverness	Culduthel Lodge	01463 240089
Isle Of Harris	Ardvourlie Castle	01859 502307
Isle of Mull	Highland Cottage	01688 302030
Isle Of Mull	Killiechronan	01680 300403
Isle of Skye	Bosville Hotel & Chandlery Seafood Restaurant	01478 612846
Kentallen Of Appin	Ardsheal House	01631 740227
Killiecrankie,By Pitlochry	The Killiecrankie Hotel	01796 473220
Kinlochbervie	The Kinlochbervie Hotel	01971 521275
Kinross	Nivingston Country House	01577 850216
Lockerbie	The Dryfesdale Hotel	01576 202427
Moffat	Well View Hotel	01683 220184
Nairn	Boath House	01667 454896
Oban	Dungallen House Hotel	01631 563799
Oban	The Manor House Hotel	01631 562087
Perth	Newmiln Country House	01738 552364
Pitlochry	Dunfallandy House	01796 472648
Port Appin	Druimneil	01631 730228
Port Of Menteith	The Lake Hotel	01877 385258
Rhu	Aldonaig	01436 820863
St. Boswell By Melrose	Clint Lodge	01835 822027
Strathtummel	Queen's View Hotel	01796 473291

Ireland

Bantry	Ballylickey Manor House	00 353 27 50071
Caragh Lake Co Kerry	Ard-na-Sidhe	00 353 66 69105
Caragh Lake Co Kerry	Caragh Lodge	00 353 66 69115
Cashel Co Tipperary	Cashel Palace Hotel	00 353 62 62707
Connemara	Ross Lake House Hotel	00 353 91 550109
Dublin	Aberdeen Lodge	00 353 1 2838155
Dublin	Fitzwilliam Park	00 353 1 6628 280
Killadeas	The Inishclare Restaurant	013656 28550
Kilkee Co Clare	Halpins Hotel & Vittles Restaurant	00 353 65 56032
Killarney Co Kerry	Earls Court House	00 353 64 34009
Kilmeaden	The Old Rectory - Kilmeaden House	00 353 51 384254
Letterkenny	Castle Grove Country House	00 353 745 1118
Riverstown,Co Sligo	Coopershill House	00 353 71 65108
Skibbereen Co.Cork	Liss Ard Lake Lodge	00 353 28 22365
Sligo,Co Sligo	Markree Castle	00 353 71 67800
Wicklow,Co Wicklow	The Old Rectory	00 353 404 67048

Channel Islands

Guernsey	Bella Luce Hotel & Restaurant	01481 38764
Guernsey	La Favorita Hotel	01481 35666
Herm Island	The White House	01481 722159
Jersey	Hotel La Tour	01534 43770

Hotels – Europe & The Mediterranean

Austria

Austria

Altaussee	Landhaus Hubertushof	+43 36 22 71 280
Bad Gastein	Hotel & Spa Haus Hirt	+43 64 34 27 97
Bad Hofgastein	Kur-Sport & Gourmethotel Moser	+43 6432 6209
Baden bei Wien	Grand Hotel Sauerhof	+43 2252 41251 0
Dürnstein	Hotel Schloss Dürnstein	+43 2711 212
Graz	Schlossberg Hotel	+43 316 80700
Igls	Schlosshotel Igls	+43 512 37 72 17
Igls	Sporthotel Igls	+43 512 37 72 41
Innsbruck	Romantik Hotel Schwarzer Adler	+43 512 587109
Kitzbühel	Romantik Hotel Tennerhof	+43 53566 3181
Klagenfurt	Hotel Palais Porcia	+43 463 51 1590
Kösthach-Mauthen	Landhaus Kellerwand	+43 47 15 269
Lech	Sporthotel Kristiania	+43 55 83 25 610
Pörtschach Am Wörther See	Hotel Schloss Leonstein	+43 4272 28160
Salzburg	Hotel Altstadt Radisson SAS	+43 662 8485710
Salzburg	Hotel Auersperg	+43 662 88944
Salzburg	Hotel Schloss Mönchstein	+43 662 84 85 55 0
Salzburg	Schloss Haunsperg	+43 62 45 80 662
Schwarzenberg im Bregenzerwald	Romantik-Hotel Gasthof Hirschen	+43 55 12/29 44 0
Seefeld	Hotel Viktoria	+43 52 12 44 41
Seefeld in Tyrol	Hotel Klosterbräu	+43 5212 26210
St Wolfgang am See	Romantik Hotel im Weissen Rössl	+43 61 38 23 060
Velden	Seeschlössl Velden	+43 4274 2824
Vienna	Hotel im Palais Schwarzenberg	+43 1 798 4515
Zürs	Thurnhers Alpenhof	+43 5583 2191

Belgium

Antwerp	Firean Hotel	+32 3237 02 60
Antwerp	Hotel Rubens	+32 32 22 48 48
Bruges	Die Swaene	+32 50 34 27 98
Bruges	Hotel Acacia	+32 50 34 44 11
Bruges	Hotel de Orangerie	+32 50 34 16 49
Bruges	Hotel Hansa	+32 50 33 84 44
Bruges	Hotel Jan Brito	+32 50 33 06 01
Bruges	Hotel Montanus	+32 50 33 11 76
Bruges	Hotel Prinsenhof	+32-50- 34 26 90
Brussels	Art Hotel Siru	+32 2 203 35 80
Brussels	L'Amigo	+32 2 547 47 47
Brussels	The Stanhope	+32 2 506 91 11
Florenville	Hostellerie Le Prieuré De Conques	+32 61 41 14 17
Knokke-Heist	Hotel Manoir Du Dragon	+32 50 63 05 80
Lanaken	La Butte Aux Bois	+32 89 72 12 86
Malmedy	Hostellerie Trôs Marets	+32-80- 33 79 17
Marche-en-Famenne	Château d'Hassonville	+32 84 31 10 25
Vieuxville	Chateau de Palogne	+32 86 21 38 74

Cyprus

Limassol	The Four Seasons Hotel	+35 75 310 222

Czech Republic

Prague	Hotel Hoffmeister	+420 2 5731 0942
Prague	Sieber Hotel & Apartments	+420 224 25 00 25

Denmark

Faaborg	Steensgaard Herregårdspension	+45 62 61 94 90
Nyborg	Hotel Hesselet	+45 65 31 30 29

British Isles

Amberley	Amberley Castle	+44 1798 831992
Ashford	Eastwell Manor	+44 233 219955
Battle	Powdermills	+44 1424 775511
Berwick-Upon-Tweed	Tillmouth Park	+44 1890 882255
Chester	The Chester Grosvenor	+44 1244 324024
Clanfield	The Plough At Clanfield	+44 1367 810222
Gatwick	Langshott Manor	+44 1293 786680
Haslemere	Lythe Hill Hotel	+44 1428 651251
Jersey	The Atlantic Hotel	+44 1534 44101
Lake Ullswater	Sharrow Bay Country House Hotel	+44 17684 86301
London	The Dorchester	+44 171 629 8888
London	The Hempel	+44 171 298 9000
London	The Leonard	+44 171 935 2010
London	The Milestone	+44 171 917 1000
London	Number Eleven Cadogan Gardens	+44 171 730 7000
London	The London Outpost of the Carnegie Club	+44 171 589 7333

London .... Draycott House Apartments .... +44 171 584 4659
London .... Pembridge Court Hotel .... +44 171 229 9977
London .... Basil Street Hotel .... +44 171 581 3311
London .... The Beaufort .... +44 171 584 5252
London .... Beaufort House Apartments .... +44 171 584 2600
London .... The Cliveden Town House .... +44 171 730 6466
London .... The Ascott Mayfair .... +44 171 499 6868
London .... Blakes Hotel .... +44 171 370 6701
London .... Number Sixteen .... +44 171 589 5232
London .... Cannizaro House .... +44 181 879 1464
Stapleford .... Stapleford Park .... +44 1572 787522
Streatley-On-Thames .... Swan Diplomat .... +44 1491 873737
Wallingford, North Stoke .... The Springs Hotel .... +44 1491 836687
Windermere .... Miller Howe .... +44 15394 42536

Estonia

Tallinn .... Park Consul Schlössle .... +372 699 7700

France

Avallon .... Château de Vault de Lugny .... +33 3 86 34 07 86
Beaulieu-sur-Mer .... La Réserve de Beaulieu .... +33 4 93 01 00 01
Beaune .... Ermitage de Corton .... +33 3 80 22 05 28
Biarritz .... Hôtel du Palais .... +33 5 59 41 64 00
Billiers .... La Domaine de Rochevilaine .... +33 2 97 41 61 61
Cannes .... Hôtel Savoy .... +33 4 92 99 72 00
Chambéry-le-Vieux .... Château de Candie .... +33 4 79 96 63 00
Champigné .... Château des Briottières .... +33 2 41 42 00 02
Chinon .... Château de Danzay .... +33 2 47 58 46 86
Connelles .... Le Moulin de Connelles .... +33 2 32 59 53 33
Courchevel .... Hôtel Annapurna .... +33 4 79 08 04 60
Courchevel .... Le Byblos des Neiges .... +33 4 79 00 98 00
Divonne-les-Bains .... Grand Hôtel du Domaine de Divonne .... +33 4 50 40 3434
Épernay .... Hostellerie La Briqueterie .... +33 3 26 59 99 99
Eze Village .... Château Eza .... +33 4 93 41 12 24
Gérardmer .... Hostellerie les Bas Rupts et son Chalet Fleuri .... +33 3 29 63 09 25
Gressy-en-France .... Le Manoir de Gressy .... +33 1 60 26 68 00
Honfleur .... La Chaumière .... +33 2 31 81 63 20
Honfleur .... La Ferme Saint Siméon .... +33 2 31 89 23 61
Honfleur .... Le Manoir du Butin .... +33 2 31 81 63 00
Les Issambres .... Villa Saint Elme .... +33 4 94 49 52 52
Lyon .... La Tour Rose .... +33 4 78 37 25 90
Megève .... Hôtel Mont-Blanc .... +33 4 50 21 20 02
Megève .... Lodge Park Hôtel .... +33 4 50 93 05 03
Meribel .... L'Antarès .... +33 4 79 23 28 23
Monestier .... Château des Vigiers .... +33 5 53 61 50 00
Montlouis-sur-Loire .... Château de la Bourdaisière .... +33 2 47 45 16 31
Mougins .... Hôtel de Mougins .... +33 4 92 92 17 07
Paris .... Hôtel Buci Latin .... +33 1 43 29 07 20
Paris .... Hôtel de Crillon .... +33 1 44 71 15 00
Paris .... Hôtel de L'Arcade .... +33 1 53 30 60 00
Paris .... Hôtel du Louvre .... +33 1 44 58 38 38
Paris .... Hôtel le Saint-Grégoire .... +33 1 45 48 23 23
Paris .... Hôtel Le Tourville .... +33 1 47 05 62 62
Paris .... Hôtel Square .... +33 1 44 14 91 90
Paris .... Hôtel Westminster .... +33 1 42 61 57 46
Paris .... L'Hôtel .... +33 1 43 25 27 22
Paris .... L'Hôtel Pergolese .... +33 1 53 64 04 04
Paris .... Le Relais Saint-Germain .... +33 1 43 29 12 05
Pleven .... Le Manoir de Vaumadeuc .... +33 2 96 84 46 17
Roquebrune Cap-Martin/Monaco .... Grand Hôtel Vista Palace .... +33 4 92 10 40 00
Saint Paul .... Mas d'Artigny .... +33 4 93 32 84 54
Saint Tropez .... Hôtel Byblos .... +33 4 94 56 68 00
Saint Tropez .... Hôtel Sube .... +33 4 94 97 30 04
Saint Tropez .... Hôtel Villa Belrose .... +33 4 94 55 97 97
Saint Tropez .... La Résidence de la Pinède .... +33 4 94 55 91 00
Saint-Rémy-de-Provence .... Château des Alpilles .... +33 4 90 92 03 33
Sarlat-Vitrac .... Domaine de Rochebois .... +33 5 53 31 52 52
Sciez sur Leman .... Château de Coudrée .... +33 4 50 7262 33
Serre-Chevalier .... L'Auberge du Choucas .... +33 4 92 24 42 73
Strasbourg .... Hôtel Regent Petite France .... +33 3 88 76 43 43

Germany

Bad Herrenalb .... Mönchs Posthotel .... +49 70 83 74 40
Coburg .... Romantik Hotel Goldene Traube .... +49 9561 8760
Cologne .... Hotel Cristall .... +49 221 163 00
Garmisch Partenkirchen .... Reindl's Partenkirchner Hof .... +49 8821 58025
Munich .... Hotel Königshof .... +49 89 551 360
Niederstotzingen .... Schlosshotel Oberstotzingen .... +49 7325 1030
Oberwesel/Rhein .... Burghotel Auf Schönburg .... +49 67 44 93 93 0
Rothenburg Ob der Tauber Hôtel Eisenhut .... +49 9861 70 50
Schlangenbad .... Parkhotel Schlangenbad .... +49 61 29 420
Speyer .... RR Binshof Resort .... +49 6232 6470
Waldeck .... Hotel Schloss Waldeck .... +49 5623 5890
Wassenberg .... Hotel Burg Wassenberg .... +49 2432 9490
Wernberg-Köblitz .... Hotel Burg Wernberg .... +49 9604 9390
Wertheim-Bettingen .... Schweizer Stuben .... +49 9342 3070

Greece

Athens .... Hotel Pentelikon .... +30 1 62 30 650 6
Crete .... Elounda Bay Palace .... +30 841 41502
Crete .... Elounda Beach .... +30 841 41 412/3
Hydra .... Hotel Bratsera .... +30 298 53971

Hungary

Budapest .... Danubius Hotel Gellért .... +36 1 185 2200

Italy

Assisi .... Le Silve di Armenzano .... +39 075 801 90 00
Breuil-Cervinia .... Hotel Bucaneve .... +39 0166 949119/948386
Capri .... Europa Palace Hotel .... +39 081 837 3800
Castellina In Chianti .... Romantik Hotel Tenuta Di Ricavo .... +39 0577 740221
Cogne .... Romantik Hotel Miramonti .... +39 0165 74030
Como .... Albergo Terminus .... +39 031 329111
Como .... Hotel Villa Flori .... +39 031 573105
Etna .... Hotel Villa Paradiso Dell' Etna .... +39 751 2409
Ferrara .... Albergo Annunziata .... +39 0532 20 11 11
Ferrara .... Ripagrande Hotel .... +39 0532 765250
Florence .... Grand Hotel Villa Cora .... +39 055 22 98 451
Florence .... Hotel J &J .... +39 55 2345005
Forte Dei Marmi-Lucca .... Hotel Il Negresco .... +39 0584 787133
Giardini Naxos .... Hellenia Yachting Hotel .... +39 942 51737
Ischia .... Hotel Miramare E Castello .... +39 081 991333
Isla d'Ischia .... La Villarosa Albergo E Terme .... +39 081 99 13 16
Lake Garda .... Grand Hotel Fasano .... +39 0365 290 220
Lido .... Albergo Quattro Fontane .... +39 041 5260227
Madonna Di Campiglio .... Hotel Lorenzetti .... +39 0 465 44 1404
Mantova .... Albergo San Lorenzo .... +39 0376 220500
Maratea .... Romantik Hotel Villa Cheta Elite .... +39 0 973 878 134
Marling-Meran .... Romantic Hotel Oberwirt .... +39 0473 22 20 20
Mauls .... Romantik Hotel Stafler .... +39 0472 771136
Messina, Sicily .... Museo Albergo Atelier Sul Mare .... +39 0921 334 295
Milan .... Hotel Auriga .... +39 02 66 98 58 51
Milan .... Regency Hotel .... +39 02 39216021
Nova Levante .... Posthotel Weisses Rössl .... +39 0 471 613113
Novi Ligure .... Relais Villa Pomela .... +39 0143 329910
Pietrasanta .... Albergo Pietrasanta-Palazzo Bonetti-Barsanti .... +39 0584 793727
Pievescola .... Hotel Relais La Suvera .... +39 0577 960 300
Porto Ercole .... Il Pellicano .... +39 0564 858111
Portobuffolé-Treviso .... Romantik Hotel Villa Giustinian .... +39 0422 850244
Positano .... Romantik Hotel Poseidon .... +39 089 81 11 11
Rimini .... Il Grand Hotel Di Rimini .... +39 0541 56000
Rome .... Hotel Farnese .... +39 06 321 25 53
Rome .... Hotel Giulio Cesare .... +39 06 321 0751
Rome .... Romantik Hotel Barocco .... +39 0 6 4872001
Rome-Palo Laziale .... La Posta Vecchia .... +39 06 9949 501
Salerno-Santa Maria di Castellabate Hotel Villa Sirio .... +39 0974 960 162
San Candino .... Parkhotel Sole Paradiso .... +39 0474 913120
San Floriano Del Collio-Gorizia .... Romantik Golf Hotel-Castello Formentini +39 0481 884051
Saturnia .... Hotel Terme Di Saturnia .... +39 0 564 601061
Sestri Levante .... Grand Hotel Villa Balbi .... +39 0185 42941
Sorrento .... Grand Hotel Cocumella .... +39 081 878 2933
Sorrento .... Grand Hotel Excelsior Vittoria .... +39 081 80 71 044
Südtirol-Völs am Schlern .... Romantik Hotel Turm .... +39 0471 725014
Taormina .... Hotel Villa Diodoro .... +39 0942 23312
Taormina .... Romantik Hotel Villa Ducale .... +39 0942 28153
Taormina Mare .... Hotel Villa Sant' Andrea .... +39 0942 23125
Torino .... Hotel Victoria .... +39 011 56 11 909
Tremezzo - Lake Como .... Grand Hotel Tremezzo .... +39 0344 40446
Varese Lake - Malpensa .... Romantik Hotel Locanda Dei Mai Intees .... +39 0332 457223
Venice .... Hotel Metropole .... +39 041 52 05 044
Venice .... Villa Condulmer .... +39 041 45 71 00
Vicenza-Arcugnano .... Hotel Villa Michelangelo .... +39 0444 550300

Latvia

Riga .... Hotel de Rome .... +37 1 708 7600
Riga .... Hotel Konventa Seta .... +371 708 7501

Liechtenstein

Vaduz .... Parkhotel Sonnenhof .... +41 75 232 1192

Luxembourg

Berdorf .... Parc Hotel .... +352 790195
Remich .... Hotel Saint Nicolas .... +352 69 8888

Netherlands

Amsterdam .... Ambassade Hotel .... +31 20 626 2333
Bergambacht .... Hotel De Arendshoeve .... +31 182 35 1000
Drunen .... Hotel De Duinrand .... +31 416 372 498
Kruiningen .... Manoir Restaurant Inter Scaldes .... +31 11338 1753
Oisterwijk .... Hotel Restaurant de Swaen .... +31 135 23 3233
Ootmarsum .... Hotel de Wiemsel .... +31 541 292 155
Voorburg .... Restaurant-Hotel Savelberg .... +31 70 387 2081

Norway

Balestrand .... Kvikne's Hotel .... +47 57 69 11 01
Bergen .... Grand Hotel Terminus .... +47 55 31 16 55
Dalen .... Dalen Hotel .... +47 35 07 70 00
Honefoss .... Grand Hotel Honefoss .... +47 32 12 27 22
Norangsfjorden .... Hotel Union Oye .... +47 70 06 21 00
Oslo .... First Hotel Bastion .... +47 22 47 77 00
Sandane .... Gloppen Hotel .... +47 57 86 53 33
Sandnes/Stavanger .... Kronen Gaard Hotel .... +47 51 62 14 00
Solvorn .... Walaker Hotell .... +47 576 84 207
Voss .... Fleischers Hotel .... +47 56 51 11 55

Portugal

Carvoeiro .... Casa Domilu .... +351 82 358 409
Coimbra .... Hotel Quinta das Lagrimas .... +351 39 44 16 15
Faro .... La Réserve .... +351 89 999474
Faro .... Monte do Casal .... +351 89 91503
Lagos .... Romantik Hotel Vivenda Miranda .... +351 82 763 222
Lisbon .... As Janelas Verdes .... +351 1 39 68 143
Lisbon .... Hotel Tivoli Lisboa .... +351 1 319 89 00
Madeira .... Quinta Da Bela Vista .... +351 91 764144
Pinhao .... Vintage House Hotel .... +351 54 730 230
Sintra .... Hotel Palacio de Seteais .... +351 1 923 32 00
Sintra .... Quinta de Sao Thiago .... +351 1 923 29 23

Slovenia

Bled .... Hotel Vila Bled .... +386 64 7915

Spain

Arcos De La Frontera .... Hacienda El Santiscal .... +34 9 56 70 83 13
Barcelona .... Hotel Claris .... +34 93 487 62 62
Cazalla De La Sierra .... Trasierra .... +34 95 488 43 24
Ibiza .... Pikes .... +34 971 34 22 22
Lloret de Mar .... Hotel Rigat Park .... +34 972 36 52 00
Madrid .... Villa Real .... +34 91420 37 67
Malaga .... La Posada Del Torcal .... +34 9 5 203 11 77
Mallorca .... Hotel Vistamar De Valldemosa .... +34 971 61 23 00
Mallorca .... La Reserva Rotana .... +34 9 71 84 56 85
Mallorca .... Read's .... +34 9 971 140 262
Marbella .... Hotel Puente Romano .... +34 9 52 82 09 00
Marbella .... Hotel Rincon Andaluz .... +34 9 5 281 1517
Marbella .... Marbella Club Hotel .... +34 95 282 22 11
Marbella/Estepona .... Las Dunas Suites .... +34 95 279 43 45
Mijas-Costa .... Hotel Byblos Andalus .... +34 95 246 0250
Oviedo .... Hotel de la Reconquista .... +34 98524 1100
Pals .... Hotel La Costa .... +34 972 66 77 40
Puerto de Santa Maria-Cádiz .... Monasterio de San Miguel .... +34 956 54 04 40
Salamanca .... Residencia Rector .... +34 923 21 84 82
Seville .... Casa De Carmona .... +34 954 19 10 00
Seville .... Hacienda Benazuza .... +34 95 570 33 44
Sotogrande/San Roque .... The San Roque Club .... +34 956 613 030
Tarragona .... Hotel Termes Montbrío Resort, Spa & Park .... +34 9 77 81 40 00
Tenerife .... Gran Hotel Bahia Del Duque .... +34 922 74 69 00
Tenerife .... Hotel Botánico .... +34 922 38 14 00
Tenerife .... Hotel Jardin Tropical .... +34 922 746 000

Sweden

Åre .... Hotell Åregården .... +46 647 178 00
Aspa Bruk .... Aspa Herrgård .... +46 583 50210
Bastad .... Buena Vista .... +46 431 760 00
Borgholm .... Halltorps Gästgiveri .... +46 485 85000
Eskilstuna .... Sundbyholms Slott .... +46 16 96500
Gothenburg .... Hotel Eggers .... +46 31 80 60 70
Lagan .... Toftaholm Herrgård .... +46 370 44055
Söderköping .... Romantik Hotel Söderköpings Brunn .... +46 121 109 00
Stockholm .... Hotell Diplomat .... +46 8 459 68 00
Svartå .... Svartå Herrgård .... +46 585 500 03
Tällberg .... Romantik Hotel Åkerblads .... +46 247 50800
Tanndalen .... Hotel Tanndalen .... +46 684 22020
Tanumshede .... Tanums Gestgifveri .... +46 525 29010

Switzerland

Chateau d'Oex .... Hostellerie Bon Accueil .... +41 26 924 6320
Kandersteg .... Royal Hotel Bellevue .... +41 33 675 88 88
Lucerne/ Luzern .... Romantik Hotel Wilden Mann .... +41 41 210 16 66
Lugano .... Villa Principe Leopoldo & Residence .... +41 91 985 8855
Zouz .... Posthotel Engiadina .... +41 81 85 41 021

Turkey

Alanya .... Hotel Grand Kaptan .... +90 242 514 0101
Istanbul .... Bosphorus Pasha .... +90 216 422 0003
Kalkan .... Hotel Villa Mahal .... +90 242 844 3268
Kas .... Club Savile .... +90 242 836 1393
Kas .... Savile Residence .... +90 242 836 2300

PREFERRED PARTNERS

Preferred partners are those organisations specifically chosen and exclusively recommended by Johansens for the quality and excellence of their products and services for the mutual benefit of Johansens members, readers and independent travellers.

AT&T Global Services

Classic Malts of Scotland

Diners Club International

Dunhill Tobacco

Ercol Furniture Ltd

Hildon Ltd

J&H Marsh & McLennan

Knight Frank International

Honda UK Ltd

Moët Hennessy

NPI

Pacific Direct

HIGHLAND.
An almost feminine charm and character all of its own. Light and aromatic, the Gentle Spirit is rich in body with a soft heather honey finish.

ISLE OF SKYE.
Assertive but not heavy. Fully flavoured with a pungent, peaty ruggedness. It explodes on the palate and lingers on. Well balanced. A sweetish seaweedy aroma.

SPEYSIDE.
Finely balanced with a dry, rather delicate aroma, good firm body and a smoky finish. A pleasantly austere malt of great distinction with a character all its own.

WEST HIGHLAND.
Oban is the West Highland malt. A singular, rich and complex malt with the merest suggestion of peat in the aroma, slightly smoky with a long smooth finish.

ISLE OF ISLAY.
Seaweed, peat, smoke and earth are all elements of the assertive Islay character. Pungent, an intensely dry 16 year old malt with a firm robust body and powerful aroma.

LOWLAND.
Typically soft, restrained and with a touch of sweetness. An exceptionally pale smooth malt which, experts agree, reaches perfection at 10 years maturity.

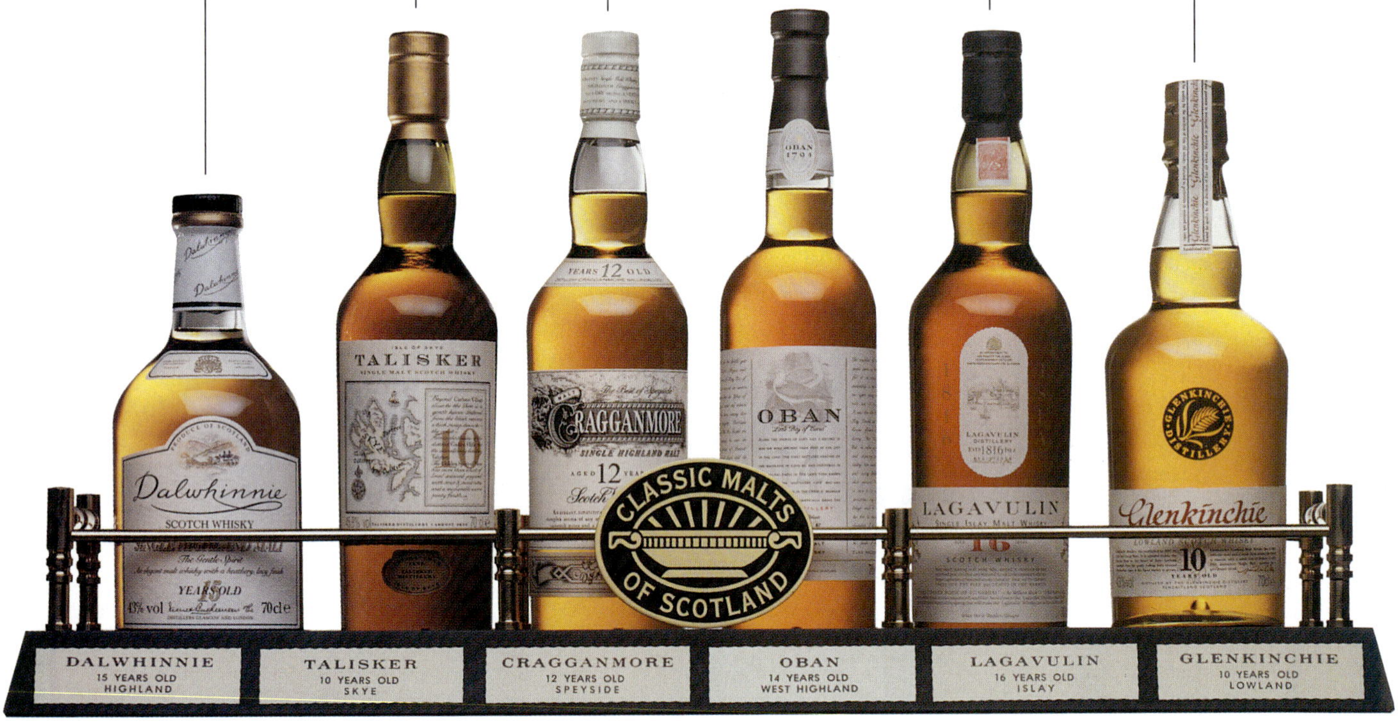

DALWHINNIE
15 YEARS OLD
HIGHLAND

TALISKER
10 YEARS OLD
SKYE

CRAGGANMORE
12 YEARS OLD
SPEYSIDE

OBAN
14 YEARS OLD
WEST HIGHLAND

LAGAVULIN
16 YEARS OLD
ISLAY

GLENKINCHIE
10 YEARS OLD
LOWLAND

Les grands crus de Scotland.

In the great wine-growing regions, there are certain growths from a single estate that are inevitably superior.

For the Scots, there are the single malts. Subtle variations in water, weather, peat and the distilling process itself lend each single malt its singular character. The Classic Malts are the finest examples of the main malt producing regions. To savour them, one by one, is a rare journey of discovery.

SIX OF SCOTLAND'S FINEST MALT WHISKIES

You'll also find that when your customers taste The Classic Malts, their appreciation will almost certainly increase your sales of malt whisky – in itself a discovery worth making.

To find out more, contact our Customer Services team on 0345 444 111, or contact your local wholesaler.

ORDER FORM

Call our 24hr credit card hotline FREEPHONE 0800 269 397

Simply indicate which title(s) you require by putting the quantity in the boxes provided. Choose your preferred method of payment and return this coupon (NO STAMP REQUIRED) to: Johansens, FREEPOST (CB264), 43 Millharbour, London E14 9BR. Your FREE gifts will automatically be dispatched with your order. Fax orders welcome on 0171 537 3594

PRINTED GUIDES

	Title	Price	Qty	Total £
A	Hotels – Great Britain & Ireland 1999	£19.95		
B	Country Houses and Small Hotels – Great Britain & Ireland 1999	£10.95		
C	Traditional Inns, Hotels and Restaurants – Great Britain & Ireland 1999	£10.95		
D	Hotels – Europe & The Mediterranean 1999	£14.95		
E	Hotels – North America, Bermuda, Caribbean 1999	£9.95		
F	Historic Houses Castles & Gardens 1999 *published & mailed to you in March '99*	£4.99		
G	Museums & Galleries 1999 *published & mailed to you in April '99*	£8.95		
H	Business Meeting Venues 1999 *published & mailed to you in March '99*	£20.00		
I	Japanese Edition 1999	£9.95		
J	Privilege Card 1999 *You get one free card with you order, please mention here the number of additional cards you require*	£20.00		

TOTAL 1

SPECIAL OFFERS

	Offer	Qty	Total £
SAVE £7.85	3 Johansens guides A+B+C .. ~~£41.85~~ .. £34		
	In a presentation box set add £5		
SAVE £12.80	4 Johansens guides A+B+C+D .... ~~£56.80~~ .. £44		
	In a presentation box set add £5		
SAVE £14.75	5 Johansens guides A+B+C+D+E .... ~~£66.75~~ .. £52		
	In a presentation box set add £5		
	+Johansens Suit Cover		FREE
	+P&P		FREE
SAVE £10.90	2 Johansens CD-ROMS K+L ~~£49.90~~ .. £39		
SAVE £10	Business Meeting Pack H+M..... ~~£40~~ .. £30		

TOTAL 3

CD-ROMs

	Title	Price	Qty	Total £
K	The Guide 1999 – Great Britain & Ireland *published and mailed to you in Nov 98*	£29.95		
L	The Guide 1999 – Europe & North America *published and mailed to you in Nov 98*	£19.95		
M	Business Meeting Venues 1999 *published and mailed to you in April '99*	£20.00		

TOTAL 2

Postage & Packing

UK: £4.50 or £2.50 for single orders and CD-ROMs
Ouside UK: Add £5 or £3 for single orders and CD-ROMs.

TOTAL 4

One Privilege Card — FREE
10% discount, room upgrade when available, VIP service at participating establishments

TOTAL 1+2+3+4

Name **(Mr/Mrs/Miss)**

Address

Postcode

☐ **I enclose a cheque for £** ______ **payable to Johansens**
☐ **I enclose my order on company letterheading, please invoice (UK only)**
☐ **Please debit my credit/charge card account (please tick).**
☐ **MasterCard** ☐ **Diners** ☐ **Amex** ☐ **Visa** ☐ **Switch** (Issue Number)

Card No

Signature **Exp date**

Prices Valid Until 31 August 1999
Please allow 21 days for delivery

Occasionally we may allow other reputable organisations to write to you with offers which may be of interest. If you prefer not to hear from them, tick this box. ☐

J17

ORDER FORM

Call our 24hr credit card hotline FREEPHONE 0800 269 397

Simply indicate which title(s) you require by putting the quantity in the boxes provided. Choose your preferred method of payment and return this coupon (NO STAMP REQUIRED) to: Johansens, FREEPOST (CB264), 43 Millharbour, London E14 9BR. Your FREE gifts will automatically be dispatched with your order. Fax orders welcome on 0171 537 3594

PRINTED GUIDES

	Title	Price	Qty	Total £
A	Hotels – Great Britain & Ireland 1999	£19.95		
B	Country Houses and Small Hotels – Great Britain & Ireland 1999	£10.95		
C	Traditional Inns, Hotels and Restaurants – Great Britain & Ireland 1999	£10.95		
D	Hotels – Europe & The Mediterranean 1999	£14.95		
E	Hotels – North America, Bermuda, Caribbean 1999	£9.95		
F	Historic Houses Castles & Gardens 1999 *published & mailed to you in March '99*	£4.99		
G	Museums & Galleries 1999 *published & mailed to you in April '99*	£8.95		
H	Business Meeting Venues 1999 *published & mailed to you in March '99*	£20.00		
I	Japanese Edition 1999	£9.95		
J	Privilege Card 1999 *You get one free card with you order, please mention here the number of additional cards you require*	£20.00		

TOTAL 1

SPECIAL OFFERS

	Offer	Qty	Total £
SAVE £7.85	3 Johansens guides A+B+C .. ~~£41.85~~ .. £34		
	In a presentation box set add £5		
SAVE £12.80	4 Johansens guides A+B+C+D .... ~~£56.80~~ .. £44		
	In a presentation box set add £5		
SAVE £14.75	5 Johansens guides A+B+C+D+E .... ~~£66.75~~ .. £52		
	In a presentation box set add £5		
	+Johansens Suit Cover		FREE
	+P&P		FREE
SAVE £10.90	2 Johansens CD-ROMS K+L ~~£49.90~~ .. £39		
SAVE £10	Business Meeting Pack H+M..... ~~£40~~ .. £30		

TOTAL 3

CD-ROMs

	Title	Price	Qty	Total £
K	The Guide 1999 – Great Britain & Ireland *published and mailed to you in Nov 98*	£29.95		
L	The Guide 1999 – Europe & North America *published and mailed to you in Nov 98*	£19.95		
M	Business Meeting Venues 1999 *published and mailed to you in April '99*	£20.00		

TOTAL 2

Postage & Packing

UK: £4.50 or £2.50 for single orders and CD-ROMs
Ouside UK: Add £5 or £3 for single orders and CD-ROMs.

TOTAL 4

One Privilege Card — FREE
10% discount, room upgrade when available, VIP service at participating establishments

TOTAL 1+2+3+4

Name **(Mr/Mrs/Miss)**

Address

Postcode

☐ **I enclose a cheque for £** ______ **payable to Johansens**
☐ **I enclose my order on company letterheading, please invoice (UK only)**
☐ **Please debit my credit/charge card account (please tick).**
☐ **MasterCard** ☐ **Diners** ☐ **Amex** ☐ **Visa** ☐ **Switch** (Issue Number)

Card No

Signature **Exp date**

Prices Valid Until 31 August 1999
Please allow 21 days for delivery

Occasionally we may allow other reputable organisations to write to you with offers which may be of interest. If you prefer not to hear from them, tick this box. ☐

J17

Guest Survey Report

Your own Johansens 'inspection' gives reliability to our guides and assists in the selection of Award Nominations

Name/location of hotel: ______________________ Page No: __________

Date of visit: ______________________

Name & address of guest: ______________________

______________________ Postcode: __________

Please tick one box in each category below:	Excellent	Good	Disappointing	Poor
Bedrooms				
Public Rooms				
Restaurant/Cuisine				
Service				
Welcome/Friendliness				
Value For Money				

PLEASE return your Guest Survey Report form!

Occasionally we may allow other reputable organisations to write with offers which may be of interest.
If you prefer not to hear from them, tick this box ☐

To: Johansens, FREEPOST (CB264), 43 Millharbour, London E14 9BR

Guest Survey Report

Your own Johansens 'inspection' gives reliability to our guides and assists in the selection of Award Nominations

Name/location of hotel: ______________________ Page No: __________

Date of visit: ______________________

Name & address of guest: ______________________

______________________ Postcode: __________

Please tick one box in each category below:	Excellent	Good	Disappointing	Poor
Bedrooms				
Public Rooms				
Restaurant/Cuisine				
Service				
Welcome/Friendliness				
Value For Money				

PLEASE return your Guest Survey Report form!

Occasionally we may allow other reputable organisations to write with offers which may be of interest.
If you prefer not to hear from them, tick this box ☐

To: Johansens, FREEPOST (CB264), 43 Millharbour, London E14 9BR

ORDER FORM

Call our 24hr credit card hotline FREEPHONE 0800 269 397

Simply indicate which title(s) you require by putting the quantity in the boxes provided. Choose your preferred method of payment and return this coupon (NO STAMP REQUIRED) to: Johansens, FREEPOST (CB264), 43 Millharbour, London E14 9BR. Your FREE gifts will automatically be dispatched with your order. Fax orders welcome on 0171 537 3594

PRINTED GUIDES

	Qty	Total £
A Hotels – Great Britain & Ireland 1999 .... £19.95		
B Country Houses and Small Hotels – Great Britain & Ireland 1999 .... £10.95		
C Traditional Inns, Hotels and Restaurants – Great Britain & Ireland 1999 .... £10.95		
D Hotels – Europe & The Mediterranean 1999 .... £14.95		
E Hotels – North America, Bermuda, Caribbean 1999 .... £9.95		
F Historic Houses Castles & Gardens 1999 *published & mailed to you in March '99* £4.99		
G Museums & Galleries 1999 *published & mailed to you in April '99* £8.95		
H Business Meeting Venues 1999 *published & mailed to you in March '99* £20.00		
I Japanese Edition 1999 .... £9.95		
J Privilege Card 1999 .... £20.00 *You get one free card with you order, please mention here the number of additional cards you require*		
TOTAL 1		

SPECIAL OFFERS

	Qty	Total £
SAVE £7.85 — 3 Johansens guides A+B+C .. ~~£41.85~~ .. £34		
In a presentation box set add £5		
SAVE £12.80 — 4 Johansens guides A+B+C+D .... ~~£56.80~~ .. £44		
In a presentation box set add £5		
SAVE £14.75 — 5 Johansens guides A+B+C+D+E .... ~~£66.75~~ .. £52		
In a presentation box set add £5		
+Johansens Suit Cover		FREE
+P&P		FREE
SAVE £10.90 — 2 Johansens CD-ROMS K+L ~~£49.90~~ .. £39		
SAVE £10 — Business Meeting Pack H+M..... ~~£40~~ .. £30		
TOTAL 3		

CD-ROMs

	Qty	Total £
K The Guide 1999 – Great Britain & Ireland *published and mailed to you in Nov 98* £29.95		
L The Guide 1999 – Europe & North America *published and mailed to you in Nov 98* .. £19.95		
M Business Meeting Venues 1999 *published and mailed to you in April '99* £20.00		
TOTAL 2		

Postage & Packing

UK: £4.50 or £2.50 for single orders and CD-ROMs
Ouside UK: Add £5 or £3 for single orders and CD-ROMs.

TOTAL 4 ______

One Privilege Card — **FREE**
10% discount, room upgrade when available, VIP service at participating establishments

TOTAL 1+2+3+4 ______

Name (Mr/Mrs/Miss) ______

Address ______

Postcode ______

Prices Valid Until 31 August 1999
Please allow 21 days for delivery

Occasionally we may allow other reputable organisations to write to you with offers which may be of interest. If you prefer not to hear from them, tick this box. ☐

☐ **I enclose a cheque for £** ______ **payable to Johansens**
☐ **I enclose my order on company letterheading, please invoice (UK only)**
☐ **Please debit my credit/charge card account (please tick).**
☐ **MasterCard** ☐ **Diners** ☐ **Amex** ☐ **Visa** ☐ **Switch** (Issue Number) ______

Card No ______

Signature ______ **Exp date** ______

J17

ORDER FORM

Call our 24hr credit card hotline FREEPHONE 0800 269 397

Simply indicate which title(s) you require by putting the quantity in the boxes provided. Choose your preferred method of payment and return this coupon (NO STAMP REQUIRED) to: Johansens, FREEPOST (CB264), 43 Millharbour, London E14 9BR. Your FREE gifts will automatically be dispatched with your order. Fax orders welcome on 0171 537 3594

PRINTED GUIDES

	Qty	Total £
A Hotels – Great Britain & Ireland 1999 .... £19.95		
B Country Houses and Small Hotels – Great Britain & Ireland 1999 .... £10.95		
C Traditional Inns, Hotels and Restaurants – Great Britain & Ireland 1999 .... £10.95		
D Hotels – Europe & The Mediterranean 1999 .... £14.95		
E Hotels – North America, Bermuda, Caribbean 1999 .... £9.95		
F Historic Houses Castles & Gardens 1999 *published & mailed to you in March '99* £4.99		
G Museums & Galleries 1999 *published & mailed to you in April '99* £8.95		
H Business Meeting Venues 1999 *published & mailed to you in March '99* £20.00		
I Japanese Edition 1999 .... £9.95		
J Privilege Card 1999 .... £20.00 *You get one free card with you order, please mention here the number of additional cards you require*		
TOTAL 1		

SPECIAL OFFERS

	Qty	Total £
SAVE £7.85 — 3 Johansens guides A+B+C .. ~~£41.85~~ .. £34		
In a presentation box set add £5		
SAVE £12.80 — 4 Johansens guides A+B+C+D .... ~~£56.80~~ .. £44		
In a presentation box set add £5		
SAVE £14.75 — 5 Johansens guides A+B+C+D+E .... ~~£66.75~~ .. £52		
In a presentation box set add £5		
+Johansens Suit Cover		FREE
+P&P		FREE
SAVE £10.90 — 2 Johansens CD-ROMS K+L ~~£49.90~~ .. £39		
SAVE £10 — Business Meeting Pack H+M..... ~~£40~~ .. £30		
TOTAL 3		

CD-ROMs

	Qty	Total £
K The Guide 1999 – Great Britain & Ireland *published and mailed to you in Nov 98* £29.95		
L The Guide 1999 – Europe & North America *published and mailed to you in Nov 98* .. £19.95		
M Business Meeting Venues 1999 *published and mailed to you in April '99* £20.00		
TOTAL 2		

Postage & Packing

UK: £4.50 or £2.50 for single orders and CD-ROMs
Ouside UK: Add £5 or £3 for single orders and CD-ROMs.

TOTAL 4 ______

One Privilege Card — **FREE**
10% discount, room upgrade when available, VIP service at participating establishments

TOTAL 1+2+3+4 ______

Name (Mr/Mrs/Miss) ______

Address ______

Postcode ______

Prices Valid Until 31 August 1999
Please allow 21 days for delivery

Occasionally we may allow other reputable organisations to write to you with offers which may be of interest. If you prefer not to hear from them, tick this box. ☐

☐ **I enclose a cheque for £** ______ **payable to Johansens**
☐ **I enclose my order on company letterheading, please invoice (UK only)**
☐ **Please debit my credit/charge card account (please tick).**
☐ **MasterCard** ☐ **Diners** ☐ **Amex** ☐ **Visa** ☐ **Switch** (Issue Number) ______

Card No ______

Signature ______ **Exp date** ______

J17

Guest Survey Report

Your own Johansens 'inspection' gives reliability to our guides and assists in the selection of Award Nominations

Name/location of hotel: ____________________ Page No: ________

Date of visit: ____________________

Name & address of guest: ____________________

____________________ Postcode: ________

Please tick one box in each category below:	Excellent	Good	Disappointing	Poor
Bedrooms				
Public Rooms				
Restaurant/Cuisine				
Service				
Welcome/Friendliness				
Value For Money				

PLEASE return your Guest Survey Report form!

Occasionally we may allow other reputable organisations to write with offers which may be of interest.
If you prefer not to hear from them, tick this box ☐

To: Johansens, FREEPOST (CB264), 43 Millharbour, London E14 9BR

Guest Survey Report

Your own Johansens 'inspection' gives reliability to our guides and assists in the selection of Award Nominations

Name/location of hotel: ____________________ Page No: ________

Date of visit: ____________________

Name & address of guest: ____________________

____________________ Postcode: ________

Please tick one box in each category below:	Excellent	Good	Disappointing	Poor
Bedrooms				
Public Rooms				
Restaurant/Cuisine				
Service				
Welcome/Friendliness				
Value For Money				

PLEASE return your Guest Survey Report form!

Occasionally we may allow other reputable organisations to write with offers which may be of interest.
If you prefer not to hear from them, tick this box ☐

To: Johansens, FREEPOST (CB264), 43 Millharbour, London E14 9BR